CRITICAL PERSPECTIVES ON RURAL CHANGE

Volume 5

REGULATING AGRICULTURE

REGULATING AGRICULTURE

Edited by
PHILIP LOWE,
TERRY MARSDEN
AND
SARAH WHATMORE

Routledge
Taylor & Francis Group
LONDON AND NEW YORK

First published in 1994 by David Fulton Publishers Ltd.

This edition first published in 2023
by Routledge
4 Park Square, Milton Park, Abingdon, Oxon OX14 4RN

and by Routledge
605 Third Avenue, New York, NY 10158

Routledge is an imprint of the Taylor & Francis Group, an informa business

British Library Cataloguing in Publication Data
A catalogue record for this book is available from the British Library

ISBN: 978-1-032-49781-5 (Set)
ISBN: 978-1-032-49706-8 (Volume 5) (hbk)
ISBN: 978-1-032-49761-7 (Volume 5) (pbk)
ISBN: 978-1-003-39526-3 (Volume 5) (ebk)

DOI: 10.4324/9781003395263

Publisher's Note
The publisher has gone to great lengths to ensure the quality of this reprint but points out that some imperfections in the original copies may be apparent.

Disclaimer
The publisher has made every effort to trace copyright holders and would welcome correspondence from those they have been unable to trace.

CRITICAL PERSPECTIVES
ON
RURAL CHANGE SERIES

REGULATING AGRICULTURE

EDITED BY

PHILIP LOWE
TERRY MARSDEN
SARAH WHATMORE

David Fulton Publishers
London

David Fulton Publishers Ltd
2 Barbon Close, London WC1N 3JX

First published in Great Britain by
David Fulton Publishers, 1994

Note: The right of Philip Lowe, Terry Marsden and Sarah Whatmore to be identified as the editors of this work has been asserted by them in accordance with the Copyright, Designs and Patents Act 1988.

British Library Cataloguing in Publication Data

A catalogue record for this book is available from the British Library

ISBN 1-85346-202-0

Typeset by Franklin Graphics, Formby
Printed in Great Britain by
Biddles Ltd., Guildford

Contents

Contributors

Paul Cloke	Department of Geography University of Bristol UK
Tracey Clunies-Ross	Agricultural Researcher *The Ecologist* UK
Graham Cox	School of Social Studies University of Bath UK
Andrew Flynn	School of Geography and Earth Resources University of Hull UK
Elizabeth Hawkins	Scottish Homes Inverness UK
Gizelle Hendriks	European Studies Division University of Kent Canterbury UK
Flemming Just	Agricultural and Co-operative Research Unit University of South Jutland Esbjerg DENMARK

Richard Le Heron	Department of Geography University of Auckland New Zealand
Philip Lowe	Centre for Rural Economy University of Newcastle upon Tyne UK
Philip McMichael	Department of Rural Sociology Cornell University USA
Terry Marsden	School of Geography and Earth Resources University of Hull UK
Neil Ward	Centre for Rural Economy University of Newcastle upon Tyne UK
Sarah Whatmore	Department of Geography University of Bristol UK
Ping Zong	Department of Economics Futan University Shanghai China

CHAPTER 1

Changing Regulatory Orders: The Analysis of the Economic Governance of Agriculture

Philip Lowe, Terry Marsden and Sarah Whatmore

Ensuring the security of food supplies is a basic social objective, and the organisation of agriculture is a key function of most modern states. The period since the early 1980s marks a major turning point for the state organisation of agriculture. The institutional structures established between the 1930s and 1950s which shaped the enormous expansion of agriculture in the post-war period are being replaced by new forms of regulation. Across the industrialised world, there has been a dismantling of state controlled or sponsored structures for the planning of agriculture, a move towards more market-based forms of regulation, and a reconstruction of agriculture–trade–industry relations on an international basis transcending and eroding the integrity of national and regional systems.

In considering such momentous changes from a very wide comparative perspective, it is important to adopt a broad conception of regulation free of specific ideological connotations. The 1980s was a decade when right-wing politicians in a number of countries pursued deregulation as a political project. This had different components in different contexts, including the weakening or repeal of various restrictions on firms, the exploration of the use of financial and fiscal measures to pursue public policy goals rather than bureaucratic controls, the liberalisation of trade, the privatisation of state industries, the introduction of certain competitive market principles into the running of the welfare state, and curbs on government expenditure. The common aspiration to roll back the state was informed by a pejorative view of regulation as that of state interference in the operation of otherwise undistorted markets. But the notion of a free market, outwith or otherwise prior to the state, is an ideological abstraction. Historically it has been states that have created the conditions under which trade or commerce could occur. And at a minimum, states remain the guarantors of property rights, freedom of contract and the soundness of money upon which the operation of any market depends.

Inevitably, the intervention of governments during the 1980s, ostensibly to reduce state interference in the economy, was itself beset with contradictions, often leading to apparently perverse outcomes. A classic example was the efforts to contain the costs of the European Community's Common Agricultural Policy (CAP) which, through such measures as dairy quotas and set-aside, brought about a much more highly regulated farm sector – a trend continued with the MacSharry reforms which were meant to accommodate the CAP to a more liberalised trading regime for food products under the General Agreement on Tariffs and Trade (GATT) (Swinbank, 1993). Likewise, the passage of the North American Free Trade Act in 1993, which ostensibly sought to extend wide-ranging US–Canadian tariff reductions to trade with Mexico, was accompanied by a whole host of exemptions, safeguards and sideline measures to protect key US food commodity interests (Hufbauer and Schott, 1993). Deregulation has thus often been accompanied by re-regulation, including the emergence or legitimation of forms that blur the distinction between the public and private sectors (Cloke and Le Heron; Flynn, Marsden and Ward, this volume). To analyse and compare such developments, we need to conceptualise regulation in a broad sense, as economic governance, that does not set up a false antithesis between the state and the market.

The papers presented here not only draw upon a variety of national contexts but also represent two separate traditions of analysis of economic governance. The first is a political economy tradition, known as regulation theory, whose application to agriculture has been elaborated in part around the notion of food regimes, globalised agriculture and technological control. The second is a sociological tradition of the study of institutions and interest groups whose application to agriculture has focused on the phenomenon of agrarian corporatism and the challenges it increasingly faces particularly from the rise of the politics of collective consumption. The following sections critically review these two bodies of thought and examine what each has to offer in understanding the contemporary reorganisation of agricultural production.

The political economy tradition: regulation theory

The major avenue of intellectual inquiry regarding the contemporary restructuring of capitalist societies is regulation theory. This seeks to identify the macroeconomic and institutional underpinnings of long cycles of growth in the world economy (Aglietta, 1979). The term used by political economists to characterise such a cycle is regime of accumulation, which Lipietz (1985: 13) defines as 'a systematic mode of dividing and reallocating the social product, which achieves over a period a certain match between the transformation of the conditions of production and final consumption'. The institutional and support systems which achieve this outcome are termed the mode of regulation. Modes of regulation, above all, are means of institutionalising struggles between competing interests, containing them within bounds that reproduce and legitimate the desired balance between production and consumption within a particular regime of accumulation (Lipietz, 1987; Jessop, 1990).

Two long surges of growth have been identified in the development of world capitalism: the first, a regime of extensive accumulation, from the 1870s to the 1910s; and the second, a regime of intensive accumulation, from the 1940s to the 1970s. The respective characterisations are based on the predominant accumulation tendencies and their associated regulatory modes (Aglietta, 1979). The extensive regime expanded mainly by absorbing new areas and activities into capitalist relations of production and was associated with a liberal phase of regulation. Accumulation in the intensive regime depended on increases in the productivity of labour through the introduction and extension of mass-production techniques.

The systematic deployment of this Fordist model of industrial development, it is argued, depended on the mass consumption that went with it, realised through the growth of disposable incomes and increasingly global markets. In addition, a critical set of norms and policies that maintained a congruent relationship between the growth of production and of consumption helped to sustain and legitimate the high level of economic growth. These consisted of such monopolistic forms of regulation as Keynesian economic management, the welfare state and collective bargaining. The international diffusion of the model and the growth of global markets also depended on liberal trading conditions and the role of the dollar as the international reserve currency.

Just as the turbulence of the inter-war years marked the demise of the extensive regime and the transition to the intensive regime, so, from the perspective of regulation theory, the present is also diagnosed as a period of significant change and crisis. Since the mid 1970s, indeed, advanced capitalist economies have become less stable, with the post-war growth model beset by so-called control problems (Roobeek, 1986), including rising wages, a decline in productivity growth, over-capacity and over-production, and environmental pollution. The development of new products, markets and production 'spaces' became essential and necessitated new forms of social capital and infrastructure, and modifications to labour conditions, if productivity and profitability were to be reinvigorated. At a political level, the response was advocacy of a free-market ideology of 'deregulation' and the extension of markets, combined with state intervention to reduce the corporatist power of industrial labour (Gordon, 1980; Boccara, 1985).

There is general agreement that one long cycle of growth (or regime of accumulation) and its institutional and social support systems (mode of regulation) have waned. Although new structural tendencies have emerged, some theorists consider that these have not become sufficiently consolidated to establish clearly the character of the successor period. Others discern the emergence of a new era based around 'flexible specialisation' in industrial production, dependent upon the increasing availability of generic and highly adaptable technologies, and the proliferation of market fragmentation and customised demand. It is variously characterised as an era of 'disorganised capitalism' or 'post-Fordism' (Piore and Sabel, 1984; Lash and Urry, 1987; Gertler, 1988; Gertler and Schoenberger, 1992; Hirst and Zeitlin, 1991). Its governing principles are seen to be non-standardised demand for goods and services, and vertically disintegrated production, based upon the decentralisation of tasks and responsibilities to loosely interconnected units. Inevitably, the centralised monopolistic structures and standardised universal forms that characterised mass production and mass consumption are regarded as increasingly obsolete features of a past system.

The political economy of agriculture has sought to explore the parallels and interconnections between the development of agriculture in the advanced economies and these wider processes of industrial restructuring. In doing so it has not only addressed the changing organisation and relations of agriculture but has also introduced new research questions into agrarian sociology. As Friedland succinctly puts it:

> the connotations of 'farming' – in particular, rurality and community, but also other categories that are limited to . . . national societies – are giving way to vertically and horizontally integrated production, processing and distribution of generic inputs for mass marketable foodstuffs. (1991: 3–4)

Agricultural development is thus seen as integral to a food system whose organisation cannot be separated from the development and transformation of national economies within the global capitalist economy. In consequence, the focus of attention has shifted from farming as such to encompass the social, economic and technological interrelations right across the food chain. The approach has its origins in the United States and France with studies of specific commodity chains as production filieres, typically of highly industralised agricultural commodities like salad crops (Friedland *et al.*, 1981) and broiler chickens (Blanc and Lacombe, 1990). More recently, it has been taken up in the analysis of agri-food complexes, a term coined by Friedmann (1982) to describe the industrial processes and relations of production and consumption of particular foods.

Some of the key facets of the post-war industrialisation of agriculture uncovered by such research include the following:

- the integration of farmers into circuits of consumption as consumers of mass-produced inputs such as fertilisers and tractors (Page and Walker, 1991);
- the growing dependency of farmers on sophisticated technological inputs and technical advice (Lowe *et al.*, 1990);
- the response of agriculture to the development of mass-consumption policies centred on basic food and feed grains and livestock products (Kenney *et al.*, 1989; 1991);
- change and standardisation in patterns of consumption, including increase in demand for meat as a consequence of rising living standards and reduced costs in rearing livestock on grain and soya, and the displacement of perishable, locally produced commodities by a range of durable food products (Friedmann, 1991; Kenney *et al.*, 1991; Marsden and Little, 1990);
- a partial shift in the orientation of agriculture from the provider of food commodities to that of a supplier meeting the demands for raw materials laid down by the food and other industries (Goodman *et al.*, 1987);
- regional specialisation in agriculture encouraged by the growth in durable foods and the development of transnational commodity and processing companies (FitzSimmons, 1986; Friedmann, 1991; Lawrence, 1990; Bowler, 1992);
- concentration in the corporate structure of the food system (Ward, 1990);
- the expanded role of banking capital and credit relations in determining agricultural investment (Le Heron, 1991; Marsden and Whatmore, 1992).

There remains, though, a basic divide in interpretations of the integration of agriculture into Fordist circuits of capital and commodity, between those who argue that it has been achieved through *accommodating* the distinctiveness of the agricultural labour process and those who argue that it has been achieved by *eliminating* that distinctiveness. Kenney and his colleagues adopt the latter position in typifying the post-war development of Midwestern agriculture as Fordist, arguing that:

> Regulation theory underscores the key factors important for an

> understanding of agricultural transformation: the ways in which the farmer is integrated into wider circuits of production and consumption; the effects of external economic processes . . . on the agricultural system; and the role of the state in [shaping] farmers' political responses. (1989: 136)

Le Heron, supporting such a position, disparages the continued currency of the 'myth that agriculture differs significantly from other activities' (1993: 189). Goodman and Redclift, however, maintain that:

> the attempt to equate agriculture and industry is misguided . . . Agriculture's contribution to Fordist consumption and accumulation is based on the failure to apply Fordist principles to the rural labour process. State intervention and its specific characteristics can be traced directly to this failure of industrial capital to regiment and rationalise productive capacity. (1991: 100–1)

According to this line of argument, the full penetration and development of capitalism in agriculture has been constrained by the individual ownership of land and the refractory nature of the biological and ecological processes which agricultural production harnesses and which still require the individual attention of the farmer. Against these limitations of organic nature and land, agricultural production has remained vertically disintegrated and the industrial innovation that has occurred has been fragmented. Capital has been forced to pursue partial appropriations of the rural labour process which are then re-incorporated in agriculture as valorised inputs or produced means of production, i.e. as bought-in fertilisers, pesticides, seed, feed and machinery. Thus capital has progressively but discontinuously and indirectly appropriated activities and value once regarded as essential to farming, leaving behind distinctively non-industrial labour processes.

From this perspective, state intervention has been necessary to overcome both the intrinsic instabilities in agriculture and the tendencies towards low returns and overproduction arising from the competition between such a multitude of small producers. The expansion and technological transformation of the sector have therefore been inextricably tied to state policies and agencies in the form of research institutions and extension services, and technological subsidies and farm price supports (Busch *et al.*, 1989). Crucially, also, the state mediates the relationship between farmers and the oligopolistic firms that dominate both farm-input provision and the purchase of farm outputs.

Accepting the perspective that agriculture is distinctive as an economic sector does help explain both the ubiquity and the resilience of state support for the sector. From this position, moreover, one can begin to see how divergence between state management of the agricultural sector and corporate control of the food system may be a major source of tension and instability.

Chapter 6 by Cloke and Le Heron examines the relevance of regulation theory to understanding agricultural change in the specific case of New Zealand - the only advanced economy to have pursued a comprehensive policy of agricultural deregulation. Previously, agriculture had been heavily regulated and subsidised as part of a more general stance by the state of support for capital and labour in export-oriented production activities. The apparently drastic step to remove most state subsidies for agriculture was taken in the mid 1980s because the costs involved had become unacceptably high and through fears for the competitiveness of New Zealand agriculture given the country's unique dependence on farm exports. Cloke and Le Heron discern signs now of more flexible accumulation conditions and a new regulatory environment favourable to international commodity interests and the larger agribusiness organisations. But this lacks the coherence of the earlier mode of regulation, suggesting a phase of 'continuing flux rather than the emergence of any particular order' (Cloke and Le Heron, this volume).

Food regimes

While debate will continue over the significance of the particularities of agriculture and therefore of the appropriateness of terms such as Fordism or post-Fordism applied to agricultural organisation, there is no disagreement over the centrality of the regulation of food production and consumption to any regime of accumulation. The concept of the international food regime has been put forward to express the pivotal role of the food system in the periodic expansion and transformation of the global capitalist economy (Friedmann and McMichael, 1989; Marsden *et al.*, 1993). Two such food regimes have been identified in contemporary history: the most recent one, which spanned the post-war period, was dominated by the USA; this replaced an earlier one, dominated by the UK, which had lasted from the 1870s to the 1910s.

In the earlier food regime, the role of agriculture was as a source of cheap 'wage goods' during a period in which the real price of food remained a primary determinant of the cost of the reproduction of labour. Extensive development of agriculture was encouraged by the major European nations largely through the vast extension of the frontiers of agricultural production and trade through colonialism and the imposition of free trade. In this way, international commodity markets were established as the focus of accumulation and rural areas, at home and overseas, became tied into them.

A crucial role was played by settler agricultures, particularly cattle and wheat production in North America, Argentina and Australia. Their productive advantages in supplying cheap food for the expanding European proletariat helped to establish a new set of international trading patterns beside the established colonial trade in tropical food products. Certain settler societies eventually yielded alternative models of economic and political development which contributed to the demise of Europe's colonial dominion. In striving to construct their own national economies, these states had to work within an international framework established by the colonial powers, while simultaneously seeking to regulate the effects of closer integration into the world market and to promote their own economic development. The result was the extensive progress of twin movements: for political and commercial liberalism on the one hand and economic nationalism on the other. Crucial to this process of nation-state building was the establishment of national commercial agricultural sectors.

The first food regime was thrown into crisis in the inter-war years. Productivity gains outstripped market capacity leading to a collapse of commodity prices which induced most industrialised nations to introduce measures to counteract instability in domestic agricultural markets.

A second food regime emerged after 1945 as part of the post-war global economic order established under US leadership and based on the US model of the relationship between industrial and agrarian development (Goodman and Redclift, 1991). Like other settler societies, the USA had been integrated into the global economy through export-oriented agrarian development that then provided the basis for the development of domestic industries (McMichael, 1984). The reciprocal relationship between agrarian and industrial development projected a national model of accumulation with 'articulated' sectors, well expressed in the early development of industrialised forms of agriculture, dependent upon mechanical and chemical inputs.

The New Deal, with its programmes of protection, price stabilisation, farm-income support and investment incentives, provided the initial context for the regeneration of US agriculture and its technological transformation (Gilbert and Howe, 1991). The technological base for this capital- and energy-intensive model of agro-industrial accumulation depended on a flow of genetic innovations, beginning with the hybridisation of corn in the 1930s. The convergence of mechanical and agrochemical developments on plant genetics gave rise to complementary, integrated technological 'packages' in major crop sectors (Goodman *et al.*, 1987). An evolving structure of price supports and production incentives together with public support for agricultural research and extension established the foundations for sustained growth of output and productivity.

The more intensive development of agriculture was encouraged as part of a shift towards a mass-consumption economy. With wages linked to productivity gains via collective bargaining, the industrial labour force was no longer regarded just as a cost to capital but also as an expanding market for manufactured consumer goods and food products. In this context active government support for domestic agriculture was oriented towards ensuring relatively cheap, abundant and secure food supplies. That support and the associated standardisation in patterns of food consumption facilitated the expansion of domestic agriculture, and its industrialisation also became a focus of accumulation.

In a context of grave food shortages, a concerted effort was made to expand world food trade in the immediate post-war period. The USA took the lead, as the largest food exporter and as part of its expanding economic hegemony, although the UK, as the largest food importer and the former orchestrator of global food markets, also played a significant role. Together, the two countries effectively blocked ambitious proposals brought forward by the first director-general of the Food and Agriculture Organisation (FAO) for a World Food Board to plan and regulate global food supplies (Peterson, 1990). They ensured that the integration of food trade would occur through market liberalisation and the agencies of investment, trade and aid, all of which favoured the USA with its economic power and ability to use the dollar's role as an aid mechanism. Subsequently, under the Marshall Plan, a framework was established for the reinvigoration of Western European agriculture as well as industry, which depended on the stimulus of the market as well as the political backing of the state, and which saw the widespread adoption of the intensive model of agro-industrial accumulation.

The food regime perspective has proved very influential. Some caution is needed in its use, however, as it suffers from the strengths and weaknesses of similar notions derived from neo-Marxist theories of political economy and international relations. Although specific regimes are inductively derived and refer to particular historical periods, the general notion of an international food regime is a theoretical construct rather than an empirical category. It is useful, therefore, as a heuristic framework, in ordering broad geographical and historical experiences and in directing research effort to critical periods and agents of transformation. On the other hand, it should be used sparingly as an explanation, otherwise there is a risk of imposing a categorical accumulationist logic that diminishes the significance of social agency, regional diversity and contingency, and that thereby fails to grasp the differential integration of agriculture into the global economy (Munton, 1992). Starting instead from the fact of differential integration, we can see that the food regime perspective illuminates certain facets but not others. In focusing primarily on global economic processes and distribution, it has most relevance to the analysis of international trade, the agencies and rules that regulate and orchestrate it and the regions and productive relations most closely involved in it.[1] However, in order to understand how such specific international regimes are contingently constructed, it is necessary to put aside the preoccupation with economic factors and acknowledge the independent significance of political power in shaping not only national regulatory systems but also international relations, including the world economic system.

McMichael, in a key contribution (this volume), interprets the protracted negotiations over international agricultural trade within GATT as marking a historic transition to a new food regime, consequent upon the decline in US hegemony. He documents a shift in US agricultural and trade policy from its insistence in 1955 that agricultural trade be excluded from GATT codes, to its campaign from the mid 1980s to deploy GATT against national restrictions on agricultural imports. In the post-war period policy was directed at protecting domestic agriculture. The accumulation opportunities both in the USA and elsewhere, as other countries followed suit in pursuing intensive development of their national agricultural sectors, were realised largely by transnational corporations. They have been the agencies for the development of world agricultural trade and have flourished as that trade has expanded. This in turn, along with the deteriorating US trade balance, helped catalyse the shift in US agricultural policy in the 1970s from domestic supply management and the stability of family farming, to demand management and export earnings. The export strategy sought trade liberalisation which suited both the interests of multi-national corporations and large exported-oriented producers anxious to cut production costs. The greatest challenge to this agro-export policy came from EC and Japanese protectionism and McMichael interprets the US stance in the GATT negotiations as an attempt to overcome this through pursuit of a free-trade regime.

Ultimately, he argues, it may not be US producers who benefit but the multinational corporations who have helped effect a new international agricultural division of labour through their global sourcing capacities. This division of labour is based on the export of low-value temperate cereals and oilseeds from the North and export of high-value fruit, vegetables and meat from the South. By subordinating producing regions to global production and consumption relations organised by transnational food companies, it threatens the integrity and autonomy of national agricultural sectors. The eventual outcome of a GATT-based free-trade order, McMichael concludes, would be the further reorganisation of world agriculture within the parameters of global, rather than national, forms of regulation under a corporate hegemony.

Globalisation: response and counter-response

There is agreement amongst various analysts that the breakdown in the post-war food regime has come about because the global integration of food systems during the past decade or so has undermined the national basis for their regulation leading to a disjuncture between accumulation and regulation (Le Heron, 1993; Buttel, 1989; Goodman, 1991; Tubiana, 1989; Friedmann and McMichael, 1989). It is important, however, to clarify what is meant by global integration.

Unfortunately, like much of the literature on globalisation, that concerned with the restructuring of the agro-food complex frequently conflates *global* processes (i.e. socio-economic processes articulated on a world scale) with *general* processes (i.e. socio-economic processes which are universal) (Whatmore, 1994).[2] As with our earlier criticism of international regimes, we would argue that it is important to avoid the latter interpretation, otherwise it risks a failure to understand globalisation as a dynamic, uneven and contested process (Pred and Watts, 1992). Recognised instead as a label for the world-wide construction of an integrated network of agencies, institutions and values, our attention is shifted to the social interactions and meanings through which globalisation is substantively and symbolically constituted or resisted (Lash and Urry, 1994).

What, in these terms, constitutes the globalisation of food systems. The literature refers to a number of elements:

- the growing prominence of multinational corporations in food production;
- changes in the ownership, control and financing of multinationals that loosen their links with particular national bases;
- the growing complexity, flexibility and geographical spread of the sourcing strategies of multinationals;
- the linking together of far-flung geographical areas in extended production and distribution filieres;
- advances in biological and chemical technologies that open up a multitude of new substitution possibilities and erode the dependence of food production on specific geographical areas;
- the internationalisation of consumer preferences and tastes promoted through an increasingly transnational mass media;
- the movement from national to transnational forms of regulation of food production and trade, as in the Common Agricultural Policy of the European Community and the inclusion of agricultural trade in NAFTA and GATT.

These undoubtedly represent powerful trends, but they are not ineluctable. Flynn, Marsden and Ward (this volume) present an interesting counter example where corporate concentration, food-system restructuring, the internationalisation of food supply and a politically dominant neo-liberal ideology have helped to consolidate nationally based forms of regulation. Their specific case is the UK food system. The most important feature of its contemporary restructuring, they argue, is the empowerment of the food retailing sector in relation to farmers, input suppliers and food manufacturers. This arises in part from the oligopolistic position of major supermarket chains, five of which control over 60 per cent of total grocery sales. While this allows them to dominate food supply, it also helps them to resist the penetration of the UK market by foreign companies. Equally, the high profitability of UK retailing compared with continental Europe has not stimulated UK firms to expand on the continent. Instead, their national concentration at the end of the food chain gives a strong coherence to the UK food system.

It might be argued that this is a unique case, and indeed the dominance of nationally based retailers is a distinctive structural feature of the UK food system. But other countries in Western Europe have even more firmly established national or regional food systems, maintained through the cultural conservatism of food tastes and practices, the regionalised nature of much food processing and distribution, and regional, national and EC regulations that entrench the position of certain producer groups and processors (Arnold and Villain, 1990; Flynn *et al.*, 1991; Van der Ploeg, 1990; INAO, 1985; Perrier-Cornet, 1990; Bertaux and Bertaux-Wiame, 1981).

In more general terms, the analysis of Flynn, Marsden and Ward illustrates the importance of consumption concerns in the national regulation of the food system. Traditionally such concerns related to food security, nutrition and public health. With food in surfeit and malnutrition no longer a major issue in most Western countries, there has been no diminution in public concern over food consumption issues, simply a broadening of the focus of concern, associated with a shift to a more discerning and capricious consumer. Increasingly food is no longer regarded as basic nutrition, but as an aspect of diverse lifestyles or of health-conscious living. Still governments are seen as the guarantors of the integrity and wholesomeness of food, and the issues they must now address include food quality, consumer protection and dietary balance. The growing salience of such issues ensures that states are unlikely to relinquish their oversight, not only of the quality and range of food supplies to their populations, but also of the conditions under which they are processed and sold. Here there are parallels with the argument about the special status of agriculture. Indeed both ends of the food chain – the growing of food and its consumption – have an organic dependence which partly insulates them from capitalist development and elicits direct state regulation.

Technological control

An important means of regulating the food system is through the promotion and control of technological change. From a political-economy perspective, current restructuring of the food system is based on a change in the provenance of new agro-food technologies. Periodic regimes of accumulation and the intervening crises are interpreted from a Schumpeterian perspective as the expression of Kondratieff long waves. Hence, the movement of capitalism out of crisis into a sustained growth phase is seen to rest on the appearance of a new techno-economic paradigm which, to yield its full growth potential, requires a fundamental transformation of the socio-institutional framework.

There is broad agreement that, in the agro-food sector, it is biotechnology that offers this radical potential, although control and information technologies based on microelectronics are often identified as the favoured candidates in other sectors (Blackburn *et al.*, 1986). Biotechnology's potential is seen to lie in the multitude of new substitution possibilities it opens up which promise to break down traditional food-sector and industrial boundaries. Goodman and Wilkinson, for example, suggest that 'biotechnologies now threaten to implode the long-standing organisation of the food system around specialised commodity chains by their ability to transfer genes across species barriers and adapt agricultural products for non-traditional markets' (1990: 134). Transnational chemical and pharmaceutical firms now dominate biotechnology research and increasingly are involved in producing intermediate and final products for the food industry. Concomitantly, leading food processors are diversifying into non-food outlets for agricultural produce. These developments, Goodman and Wilkinson (1990) argue, foreshadow the growth of a generic bio-industry whose ability to interchange different kinds of primary inputs will render it independent of agriculture and the primary processing sector.

There is, however, a marked tendency in the political-economy literature on technological change towards reification which, by detaching it from social processes, leads to a sense of technological determinism. However, particular technological developments are actively promoted and adopted by specific interests and agents. Here a shift in the institutional locus of control over agro-food R&D activities seems particularly significant: away from the public sector which dominated traditional research on agricultural commodities; and towards the corporate and venture capital which are at the forefront of research applying biotechnologies to the agro-food system (Munton *et al.*, 1990; Buttel, 1990; Hawkins, this volume).

There is also a presumption that most farmers are forced to adopt new agricultural technologies or otherwise face being marginalised. Farmers are seen to have little control over the process of technological change or its consequences, other than the rate at which they choose to take up the technologies available. However, empirical studies of farmers reveal a range of responses to technological pressures (Munton and Marsden, 1991), including many who are keen to innovate, who play an active role adapting and not simply adopting new products and processes. Moreover, some of the new types of technology - such as information technology and biotechnology - through their intrinsic adaptability may actually enhance the scope for choice and inflexion at the farm level.

Hawkins (this volume) emphasises the social relations surrounding applied research and the transmission of its results and products to farmers. For farmers, as with agribusiness companies, technological change may not only be a means of increasing returns but also of reducing the risks and uncertainties they face. But for the companies, such a strategy may also include devolving some of these risks on to their farmer-customers through the inculcation of technological dependency. The ability of farmers to retain their autonomy depends very much on the social organisation of production. To illustrate, Hawkins contrasts the experience of English dairy and potato producers.

In the dairy sector, until very recently, a single producer cooperative - the Milk Marketing Board - has had a monopoly over the supply of milk. With the MMB standing between the farmers and the processors and retailers, technologies are seen to stem from upstream rather than downstream sources, and research is largely publicly funded and oriented mainly to production control and techniques. As new breeding techniques have become available, such as embryo transfer, typically they have been taken up by the MMB and incorporated into its farm services. In consequence, dairy farmers enjoy considerable autonomy and discretion over technological change.

Potato producers face different market relations. Downstream 'quality' markets are controlled by a small number of retailers and processors who have exacting and distinct specifications for the supply, variety and quality of the potatoes they require. In the past, when most potatoes were grown for the 'bulk' wholesale market, research was mainly publicly funded and aimed at improving the efficiency of production. Current research by the industry itself concentrates on the standards demanded by various end-use markets. Recent developments in genetic engineering have revolutionised the process of creating new varieties which can now be tailored to specific user requirements. Increasingly, too, buyers stipulate and monitor cultivation and harvesting practices. Growers are thus increasingly dependent on specialist advice linked to downstream markets. A final twist to their encirclement was the privatisation of the breeding institute that supplied potato seeds and its acquisition by a multinational involved in the processing and pre-packaging business.

With the benefit of such research we can begin to see how unsatisfactory the notion of the technological treadmill is to characterise the general dynamic of agricultural change. The treadmill theory is appealing to political economists because it portrays farmers as being subsumed to a capitalist logic. According to the theory, output prices are forced down as production is boosted by the diffusion of the new technology, so that all farmers are eventually forced to adopt in order to remain in business (Cochrane, 1958). However, not only has agricultural policy tended to weaken the link between output and prices, but also the theory addresses only the development of the agricultural output market and not of the new technical input markets. As Allanson and his colleagues comment:

> It is at least arguable that post-war mechanical and chemical technologies became more rather than less attractive to farmers over the diffusion process as the expansion of the markets for these technologies led to a fall in (relative) user costs due to the realisation of dynamic increasing returns. (Allanson *et al.*, 1994: 20)

The sense of technological change becoming ever more facilitated and routinised along a certain direction is captured in the term technological paradigm which Freeman defines as 'a new set of guiding principles which become the managerial and engineering "common sense" for each major phase of development' (1984: 449). Such a paradigm is put in place and maintained through the establishment of networks that link together R&D institutions, manufacturers, suppliers, advisers and producers. The arrangement forged to promote past technological developments thereby set the preconditions for successor products and practices, which if compatible flow with ever greater ease along the established networks (Dosi, 1982; Hughes, 1987).

Clunies-Ross and Cox (this volume) examine the productivist paradigm of post-war agriculture and its underpinnings, from the perspective of the small minority of agriculturalists and enthusiasts who have persistently rejected its emphasis on the intensification of production based on a reliance upon chemical inputs. However, their own advocacy of organic farming was not so much rejected as ignored in official policy, research and advisory circles. The position began to change in the 1980s, mainly because of mounting problems for the productivist paradigm, including structural surpluses, the impact of modern agriculture on the environment, and concerns over food quality and health. Clunies-Ross and Cox reveal a technological paradigm to be a self-reinforcing complex of beliefs and practices, and deduce that the emergence of a sense of crisis for the dominant paradigm is a necessary condition for serious consideration to be given to alternatives.

The effective promotion of alternative technological paradigms requires in turn the establishment of new networks. It was when other bodies with influence and respectability outside the organic movement began to act as if organic farming was a realistic option that elements of the movement began to gain real influence. A key role was played in the UK context by certain supermarket chains agreeing to stock organic produce. Some official recognition also came with the inclusion of representatives of the organic movement in UK deliberations begun in response to a European Commission initiative to establish formal standards for organic produce. This particular case, with its alignment between an unconventional group of producers and green consumerism as expressed by the retail sector and food market regulators, underlines the shifting balance of power within the agro-food system which sets the broad context for technological change.

The sociological tradition: institutional analysis

The management of the agricultural sector by the state is a feature of most industrialised countries. In the socialist countries this involved, until recently, the direct control of most agricultural production through nationalised and collectivised farms which were subject to centralised planning and state control of systems of supply and distribution. In the liberal capitalist countries, state management has been mainly indirect through production subsidies and various forms of market intervention, but has also often involved some state or para-state control of agricultural research, extension and marketing. In general, in both East and West, there has been a move recently towards more market-based forms of regulation and a dismantling of some state-controlled or sponsored structures for the planning of agriculture.

In the former socialist countries, this has involved drastic moves to re-privatise farming, following on the rejection of state socialism. Besides the assertion of an individualistic ideology of private ownership there is also widespread suspicion of any forms of collectivism born of bitter experience of the Stalinist use of nominally co-operative structures as instruments of dispossession and authoritarian control. This presents a serious obstacle to the creation of a 'mixed economy' of agricultural regulation to replace the centralised planning and state control of supply and distribution. Inevitably, the initial consequence has been a pronounced fall in output. It remains to be seen whether or not this is a short-term problem, and whether domestic consumption or the drive for agricultural exports (to earn hard currency) will bear the brunt of the shortfall. What is more certain is that in the years to come the pattern and volume of agricultural exports and imports of the former socialist countries is likely to have as profound an impact on the balance of world food trade as they did in the 1970s.

This is particularly the case with China, where, unlike Eastern Europe and the Soviet Union, the Communist Party remains in power, but where also, since 1978 and following the death of Chairman Mao, the state has been seeking to liberalise the management of the economy. This has included systematic efforts to relax centralised state control of agricultural production and to rely more on price incentives to regulate production (Zong, this volume). Initially economic reforms helped make up a backlog in agricultural technology development, resulting in grain production being increased by an impressive 50 per cent between 1976 and 1984. But grain output stagnated through the mid and late 1980s, as the government experienced growing difficulties implementing its reforms. At the centre of these difficulties are the contradictions between planned state procurement and nascent market-based systems of food supply, now operating side by side.

The increase in prices that has followed has led to an escalation in state expenditures because the government has been unwilling to pass price rises on to urban consumers out of fear of the social unrest which might ensue. At the same time, with the relaxation of a highly disciplined system, there has been growing reluctance amongst farmers to fulfil their state production quotas. But the performance of the agrarian sector remains crucial as China seeks to emulate the rapid industrialisation of its East Asian neighbours, all of whom have experienced significant declines in grain production since the late 1960s as workers and land have been pulled out of agriculture (Redclift, 1990). It is unlikely that China can escape similar consequences especially since the government's abolition of the household registration system, introduced in the 1950s to keep the peasantry on the land by denying them access to urban jobs, housing and grain rations. Zong (this volume) concludes that there is little alternative for China but to press ahead with market reforms and to import additional grain, to overcome shortfalls in supply and to moderate domestic price rises. The emergence of China and other East Asian countries as major players in international food markets is likely to have as significant consequences for the geography and scale of food trade flows as any of the contemporary developments highlighted by food-regime theorists.

Whereas socialist countries in the post-war period pursued state management of the agricultural sector through the direct (and enforced) imposition of state ownership and control, liberal-democratic states had to forge more complex and delicate means of managing their agricultural sectors. All such states had to resolve the dilemma of how to intervene extensively but indirectly in a sector where the means of production were not only in private ownership but in the ownership of small producers. Not only did this necessitate extensive state bureaucracies but it also gave a key role to intermediate organisations to manage the complex two-way flow of information between producers and the state to ensure the responsive formulation and sensitive implementation of agricultural policy.

Agrarian corporatism

Arguably, it is this basic structural requirement which injects into the relationship between states and leading interest organisations in the agricultural sector qualities of co-operation and reciprocal dependence which have been extensively noted. In many countries, dominant agricultural organisations are treated as partners with state agencies in the corporatist regulation of the agricultural sector. The term corporatism is used by some authors to characterise whole political systems, but here it is employed in a more restricted but analytically useful sense to refer to a distinctive style of interest intermediation:

> It implies interventionist action of an indirect nature whereby the state operates in conjunction with organisations which are based on the division of labour in society. It is crucially distinguished, therefore, by the salience of producer groups, and their role in regulating their own constituencies reaching bargained agreements with state agencies. (Cox *et al.*, 1990a: 191)

Crucially, the structural requirement that underpins agrarian corporatism – namely, that the design and implementation of agricultural policy must engage the independent actions of a myriad of farmers working under diverse conditions – follows from the prior commitment of governments to interventionist agricultural supports in societal contexts in which liberal and private property ideologies ensure that, in Grant's words, 'The state penetrates beyond the farm gate, but it does so through the acceptable channels of financial and technical advice' (1983). This, of course, begs the questions of why such policies are pursued; how political support for them was engendered and is maintained; and what might be the consequences for state/interest organisation relationships if that support were to weaken.

In considering such questions we find not only striking parallels and commonalities between countries, reflecting the similar practical and technical problems with which states have had to grapple, but also differences rooted in the specificities of political structure and economic context, even though phases in the development of national agricultural organisation show marked synchronicity. Most of the agricultural unions and co-operatives that are now central to the management and representation of the farming sector had their origins in the late nineteenth and early twentieth centuries. They arose as farming groups combined, first in response to the extensive modernisation and monetarisation of rural areas and then in reaction to the overproduction brought about by the growth in farm trade (Gueslin, 1990).

When, in the crisis years of the 1930s and 1940s, states began to develop active agricultural policies, farm unions and co-operatives were usually deeply implicated. One can distinguish here broadly between liberal-democratic states (for example, in northern Europe and North America) which typically recognised farm unions as negotiating partners, and built upon the self-regulatory function of co-operatives to establish indirect control of the farming sector (Just *et al.*, 1984); and what were then authoritarian states (for example, in southern Europe and Latin America) which typically suppressed farm unions, especially those identified with the Left, and forcefully incorporated the rump of the co-operative movement within state-sponsored (fascist) agricultural corporations (Moyano, 1984). These distinct pathways have left quite different legacies of interest-group structure: for example, the large, influential and technocratic agricultural organisations of northern Europe; and the more fragmented, localistic and ideologically divided agricultural organisations of southern Europe (Just, 1990). There are also different patterns of interest intermediation. For example, in the de-ideologised contexts of northern Europe the typical relationship is a clientelistic one of mutual dependence between an administrative agency and representative interest groups. But in societies dominated by particular political factions, close fraternalistic ties with a political party rather than representativeness may be the key to gaining access and legitimacy, and this seems to have been the characteristic feature of farming unions in Italy (Albanese and Capo, 1992), Greece (Goussios and Zacopoulou, 1992) and Northern Ireland (Greer, 1994).

Such differences, which are obscured by the indiscriminate use of the term corporatism, have implications for both the political influence of national farm organisations and for the economic management of the sector. Michel Petit and colleagues (1987), for example, argue that the degree of influence is determined by four factors: cohesion within professional farm organisations; the functional relationship between the professional organisations and agricultural ministries; the importance that individual governments attribute to agriculture; and the relative political power within government of the agriculture minister. By and large, the farm organisations of northern Europe score high on the first two factors - i.e. professional cohesion and functional relationship with agriculture ministries - whereas those of southern Europe score low. This is not only reflected in their relative influence in national politics but also underpins the northern bias in the European Community's Common Agricultural Policy.

The economic management of agriculture also depends upon the scale and functional specialisation of the co-operative movement. Not only do co-operatives act as something of a buffer between farmers and the market, limiting the penetration of external capital, but they also facilitate strong ties between agricultural production and the purchasing/sale/processing levels thus establishing a vertical integration anchored in the primary sector. Here again, historical differences, as well as the extent of geographical specialisation, produce different national patterns: for example, the large-scale dairy and bacon co-operatives which play often a dominant role in the management of their respective sectors in countries such as Denmark, the Netherlands and Belgium; compared with the much more localised but often socially entrenched co-operative structures of France, Spain, Greece and Italy (Just, 1990; Hervieu and Lagrave, 1992).

Such arrangements enjoy official sanction of varying degrees, in legal privileges, in technical and financial support from the state, and in the delegation of authority. Therefore, in seeking to understand the different forms of the state–agriculture partnership, it is important to address not only interest-group structures but also the rationale for state intervention.

Just (this volume) gives a detailed account of the development of agricultural corporatism in the Scandinavian countries, where state intervention in the inter-war and post-war years could indeed build on existing co-operative organisations. He brings out an important structural factor, in distinguishing between states in which export-oriented agriculture is a key feature of the national economy and states in which agriculture is mainly oriented to the domestic market. In the former case, he argues, state–agriculture relations will be concerned more with questions of international competitiveness and the regulation of quality and standards; and in the latter case, with protecting farmers' incomes and safeguarding rural development. The regulation of the domestic market towards these ends, moreover, will be more interventionist because the goals will be more differentiated and precise, and because they aim specifically to curb the operations of the market. Just demonstrates this factor at work in differentiating the experience of Denmark (with an export-oriented agriculture) from that of Norway and Sweden. But he also brings out crucial differences in the historical and political context whereby agricultural organisations, largely due to differences in party structures, have enjoyed much easier access to the political system in Norway and Denmark than in Sweden. The combination of structural and cultural factors allows him to explain Denmark's tradition of export-oriented agriculture enjoying extensive state sponsorship but limited subsidies; Norway's heavily subsidised and protected agriculture; and Sweden's middle position, with farmers protected against world markets but not from internal competition.

The imperatives of state intervention vary not only between countries but also between farming sectors. Grant, for example, observes that 'There is no industry which is subject to as much government intervention short of ownership in the advanced industrial countries as the dairy industry' (1991: 4; see also OECD, 1983). Indeed, political scientists interested in the political management of advanced economies have devoted considerable attention to the dairy sector as typifying corporatist arrangements (Farago, 1985; Traxler, 1985; van Waarden, 1985; Cox *et al.*, 1990a, b; Grant, 1991). Cawson concludes that 'corporatism seems to be almost everywhere characteristic of this industry', and suggests that this is because the nature of the product determines the form of association and regulation to be found in the dairy industry:

> Milk is produced by a large number of small producers, but processed and marketed by collective arrangements whereby prices are established and insulated from immediate market pressures . . . the specific features of milk production (perishability and high transport costs) seem to promote even more strongly monopolistic forms of producer organisation than are found generally in agriculture, itself relatively highly corporatised. (1986: 110)

Public health is also a matter of particular concern in the regulation of milk production. Wine production shares some of the same characteristics (though with concerns about adulteration substituting those about public health), thus also accounting for the extensive state and co-operative regulation in this sector. But with grain production it would seem that it is the very transportability of the product, which on the one hand makes producers so dependent on distributors and on the other hand threatens the autonomy of regional and national markets, that has precipitated co-operative action and state intervention in this sector. Such factors, as well as others to do with food security, have provided the imperative behind the generally greater market regulation of these commodities than others such as meat, fruit and vegetables.

Of course, such commodity characteristics, however compelling, do not directly determine state action but are filtered through political and economic structures, and thus produce diverse responses. For example, the general existence of corporatism in the dairy industry has been challenged by Young (1990), who argues that although the American dairy industry was able to develop corporatist institutions in the 1930s, the capacity of the National Milk Producers Federation to enforce industry-wide norms was limited and was undermined by the emergence of the large regional co-operatives in the 1960s. Grant, moreover, argues that the most effective corporatist arrangements in the American dairy industry have been in those states where federal arrangements have not applied, such as California and Virginia (1991). North America, indeed, provides a wealth of evidence of territorially differentiated regulatory arrangements for the same commodity and within the same country, derived from regional differences in the histories of agrarian protest and political culture. Winson's (1993) comparative study of Nova Scotia and Ontario, for example, contrasts corporate–co-operative joint ventures in the one and producer-run marketing boards and processor organisations in the other, each with different links with state agencies and distinct market structures and dynamics of capital penetration.

Finally, it should be borne in mind that state regulation of, and support for, agricultural production is seldom justified solely in terms of sectoral imperatives and food supply. Typically, states also see the beneficial management of the farm economy as an indirect means of achieving other desirable, though not always clearly defined, objectives of public policy concerning rural areas, including the maintenance of rural populations and the management of the environment. An OECD review of dairy policy highlighted 'the awesome array of roles which the dairy sector is required to play in Member countries':

> It is not sufficient that the sector should provide a regular, assured and adequate supply of essential but perishable milk and milk-based foodstuffs . . . In almost all countries . . . it is expected to fulfil wider social and even strategic objectives, including the prevention of urban drift and rural depopulation, the maintenance of rural employment opportunities, and certain other regional and environmental considerations. (OECD, 1983: 71)

Indeed, for most states, agricultural policy lies at the intersection between sets of concerns to do with national food production and supply, and sets of concerns to do with spatial and territorial development. Agriculture's role in the formation of the rural environment and rural society implicates it not only in the state's sectoral management of the national economy but also in the spatial management of the national territory (Lowe and Bodiguel, 1990).

Such considerations not only determine domestic agricultural policy but also shape the positions of states on international food trade, as Hendriks (this volume) brings out in analysing Germany's role in the development of the European Community's Common Agricultural Policy and in the Uruguay round of negotations with GATT. For a hundred years protection of the agricultural population has been a constant, and largely unchallenged, feature of German politics. The turbulences which have successively engulfed German society over this period, far from dislodging that commitment, have if anything reinforced a sense that rural security is a necessary anchor of social and political stability.

The economic origins of the European Community are often crudely portrayed as an alliance between German manufacturing interests and French farming interests, each seeking to expand their markets in post-war Europe. However, once the principle of a common agricultural policy had been agreed, the German government doggedly shaped the development and implementation of the policy, to protect its own farmers. Germany's influence on the evolution of the CAP has been unequalled, due to a number of factors, including a strong national consensus behind the protection of farmers; the sustained dedication of successive German governments to the general development of the European Community; and their willingness to act as 'bankers' to the Community (the lion's share of Community funds, of course, going on agricultural support). In consequence, not only were German policy makers able to incorporate their model of a supported and protected agrarian economy within the CAP but also, in pursuit of income parity with the industrial sector, to overcome the resistance of other member states to setting Community-wide agricultural prices above those of most member states and well above world market levels.

Inevitably, therefore, the GATT negotiations posed particular dilemmas for Germany as the member state most committed to agricultural protection but also, as the second largest exporting country in the world, one with a vital interest in trade liberalisation. In the event, Germany's overriding national interest in a successful conclusion to the GATT round led it reluctantly to agree in 1991 to an overhaul of the CAP. This involved it tempering its traditional commitment to high, income-oriented price levels, in order to curb overproduction and to reduce external tariffs, but only in return for a package of long-term compensatory payments designed to maintain farm incomes.

The resultant (MacSharry) reforms of the CAP then formed the basis for the European Community's negotiating position on agriculture within GATT. In the Blair House accord the USA and the EC mutually agreed to exempt direct compensatory payments to farmers related to set-aside and other production limitation measures, as part of a compromise package which included modest measures to open up access to domestic agricultural markets and to cut back on subsidised food exports, plus a peace clause exempting domestic support measures for structural adjustment from the GATT disputes procedure for several years. That accord, subsequently amended to accommodate French objections, effectively sealed the agricultural part of the Uruguay round (Jenkins, 1993).

From this perspective, the final GATT agreement does not herald a new era (as food-regime theorists would claim) of agricultural deregulation, the multilateral liberalisation of world trade in farm produce and the subordination of the nation-state to transnational capital. On the contrary, it would seem to confirm the continued centrality of states in the regulation of agricultural production and the growing importance of regional blocs and bilateralism in the management of agricultural trade (Low, 1993).

Agrarian corporatism challenged: consumption politics and new types of regulation

From the perspective of agrarian corporatist analysis, a clear account emerges of the current crisis in agricultural regulation. At the root of the crisis are the difficulties occasioned by an expansion of national agricultural output under corporatist management at a rate that has outstripped the capacity of domestic markets (as well as the capacity of natural systems) to absorb the increase. In the past, incidental surpluses were disposed of through agricultural trade and food aid, which were essentially residues of national agricultural policies. This solution put off the need for changes in farm supports. The closed nature of agricultural policy communities, which typically exclude from decision-making organisations not directly involved in implementing policy, and the complex and interlocking interdependencies between state agencies and agricultural organisations mean that structures of agrarian corporatism are usually highly resistant to change and seldom generate reform from within. Major change tends to arise from external pressures particularly under conditions of crisis in which the management of the agricultural sector can no longer contain the problems it generates, thus politicising policy making.

Such conditions came about as exportable surpluses inexorably grew. Eventually in the 1980s the increasingly cut-throat competition as countries sought to off-load their growing agricultural surpluses on overseas markets severely depressed world commodity prices, thus wreaking economic havoc on traditional food-exporting countries and inflicting prohibitive budgetary costs on those countries with protected agricultures.

Thus agriculture's efforts to cope with its own structural overproduction spilled over into budgetary crises, and international trade conflicts (Goodman and Redclift, 1989). In such circumstances, states could no longer continue to regard agriculture's problems as matters purely internal to the sector. Policy communities which had been closed were prised open (Smith, 1990), and have had to contend with a range of non-agricultural interests, including collective consumption interests.

The politics of agricultural policy has long been dominated by the politics of production. The 1970s and 1980s, though, saw the emergence of a consumption-oriented politics led by consumer, recreational, amenity and environmental groups. These groups are diverse and pluralistic, oriented towards parliamentary lobbying and media campaigning rather than close links with the executive. Corporatism and the exclusive political access it gives to producer groups jars with democratic norms. Gradually, therefore, campaigning groups were able to challenge its legitimacy.

Whereas corporatist politics focused on production and the distribution of the fruits of production amongst those directly involved in it as owners, managers or workers, the politics of collective consumption is concerned with public, quasi-public and positional goods, such as the wholesomeness of food, a pleasant environment, the quality of the air we breathe and the vitality of rivers and streams. It is not concerned directly with the production process itself but with the outcomes or externalities of production, but from this perspective may actually challenge the acceptability of particular types of production. Decision-making systems oriented towards resolving questions of economic management and distribution largely through mechanisms of elite accommodation and bargaining, and policy adjustment at the margins often cannot cope with the challenges raised by these much more fundamental choices.

Politics of collective consumption has impinged upon the realm of agricultural production in the shape of environmental opposition, animal welfare concerns and food scares. Under such pressures, food producers find themselves subject to new types of regulation oriented to collective consumption and administered by non-agricultural authorities.

Conclusions

Undoubtedly, across the world, agriculture is being subjected to changes in regulatory structures. The political economy and sociological traditions offer parallel accounts: one emphasises long-term cycles of growth underpinned by breakthroughs and breakdowns in techno-economic paradigms; the other emphasises periods of political stability in sectoral economic management based on agrarian corporatism and the conditions which have brought that into crisis. It would be tempting to suggest that these accounts are complementary, with one addressing the international economics and the other the domestic politics of agricultural regulation.

Certainly the two traditions could enrich one another. At present, the political economy literature makes little if any reference to the comparative politics or sociology of agricultural regulation. Likewise, the literature on agrarian corporatism makes little reference to international trade cycles, technological developments or the political influence of transnational economic agents. These are critical blind spots which this volume seeks to address, in order to further our understanding of the key processes shaping agricultural regulation in these turbulent times.

Notes

1. Indeed, much of the scholarship has focused on specific concrete regimes such as NAFTA and GATT, using the term regime here in the way it is used by international-relations theorists to characterise a system of norms and rules legally specified among states to regulate national actions on a given issue.
2. We have already seen a similar conflation between international regimes conceived as concrete institutional arrangements (e.g. GATT) and as immanent processes (e.g. the second food regime).

References

Aglietta, M. (1979) *A Theory of Capitalist Regulation*. London: Verso.

Albanese, F. and Capo, E. (1992) 'Italie: L'empreinte des clivages politiques', pp. 161–83, Hervieu and Lagrave *op. cit.*

Allanson, P., Murdoch, J., Lowe, P. and Garrod, G. (1994) *The Rural Economy: An Evolutionary Perspective*. University of Newcastle upon Tyne: Centre for Rural Economy, Working Paper 1.

Arnold, R. and Villain, C. (1990) *New Directions for European Agricultural Policy*. Brussels: Centre for European Studies.

Bertaux, D. and Bertaux-Wiame, I. (1981) 'Artisanal bakery in France: how it lives and why it survives', pp. 121–54, F. Bechofer and B. Elliot (eds) *The Petite Bourgeoisie*. London: Macmillan.

Blackburn, P., Coombs, R. and Green, K. (1986) *Technology, Economic Growth and the Labour Process*. London: Macmillan.

Blanc, M. and Lacombe, P. (1990) 'Rural economics in France', pp. 144–64, Lowe and Bodiguel *op. cit*.

Boccara, P. (1985) *Intervenir dans les Gestions avec de Nouveaux Critères*. Paris: Messidor/Editions Sociales.

Bowler, I. R. (ed.) (1992) *The Geography of Agriculture in Developed Market Economies*. London: Longman.

Busch, L., Bonnano, A. and Lacy, W. (1989) 'Science, technology and the restructuring of agriculture', *Sociologia Ruralis*, 29: 118–30.

Busch, L. and Lacy, W. B. (1983) *Science, Agriculture and the Politics of Research*. Boulder, Colorado: Westview Press.

Buttel, F. H. (1989) 'The US farm crisis and the restructuring of American agriculture: domestic and international dimensions', pp. 46–83, Goodman and Redclift *op. cit*.

Buttel, F. H. (1990) 'Biotechnology and agricultural development in the Third World', pp. 163–80 of H. Bernstein, B. Crow, M. Mackintosh and C. Martin (eds) *The Food Question*. London: Earthscan Publications.

Cawson, A. (1986) *Corporatism and Political Theory*. Oxford: Basil Blackwell.

Cochrane, W. (1958) *Farm Prices: Myth and Reality*. Minnesota: University of Minnesota Press.

Cox, G., Lowe, P. and Winter, M. (1990a) 'Agricultural regulation and the politics of milk production', pp. 169–98, C. Crouch and R. Dore (eds) *Corporatism and Accountability*. Oxford: Clarendon Press.

Cox, G., Lowe, P. and Winter, M. (1990b) 'The political management of the dairy sector in England and Wales', pp. 82–111, T. Marsden and J. Little *op. cit*.

Dosi, G. (1982) 'Technological paradigms and technological trajectories', *Research Policy*, 11: 147–62.

Farago, P. (1985) 'Regulating milk markets: corporist arrangements in the Swiss dairy industry', pp. 168–81, Streeck and Schmitter *op. cit*.

FitzSimmons, M. (1986) 'The new industrial agriculture: the regional differentiation of speciality crop production', *Economic Geography*, 62: 334–53.

Flynn, A., Marsden, T. and Ward, N. (1991) 'Managing food? A critical perspective on the British experience', pp. 159–83, INRA *Changement Technique et Restructuration de l'Industrie Agro-alimentaire en Europe*. Grenoble: INRA.

Freeman, C. (1984) *Long Waves in the World Economy*. London: Frances Pinter.

Friedland, W. (1991) 'Shaping the new political economy of advanced capitalist agriculture', pp. 1–36, Friedland *et al. op. cit*.

Friedland, W. H., Barton, A. E. and Thomas, R. J. (1981) *Manufacturing Green Gold: Capital, Labor, and Technology in the Lettuce Industry*. New York: Cambridge University Press.

Friedland, W. H., Busch, L., Buttel, F. H. and Rudy, A. P. (eds) (1991) *Towards a New Political Economy of Agriculture*. Boulder, Colorado: Westview Press.

Friedmann, H. (1982) 'The political economy of food', *American Journal of Sociology*, 88: 248–86.

Friedmann, H. (1991) 'Changes in the international division of labour: agri-food complexes and export agriculture', pp. 65–93, Friedland *et al. op. cit.*

Friedmann, H. and McMichael, P. (1989) 'Agriculture and the state system: the rise and decline of national agricultures, 1870 to the present', *Sociologia Ruralis*, 29: 93–117.

Gertler, M. (1988) 'The limits of flexibility: comments on the post-Fordist visions of production and its geography', *Institute of British Geographers, Transactions*, 13: 419–32.

Gertler, M. and Schoenberger, E. (1992) 'Industrial restructuring and continental trade blocs: the European Community and North America', *Environment and Planning A*, 24: 2–11.

Gilbert, J. and Howe, C. (1991) 'Beyond state versus society: theories of the state and New Deal agricultural policies', *American Sociological Review*, 56: 204–20.

Goodman, D. (1991) 'Some recent tendencies in the industrial reorganisation of the agri-food system', pp. 37–64, Friedland *et al. op. cit.*

Goodman, D. and Redclift, M. (eds) (1989) *The International Farm Crisis*. London: Macmillan.

Goodman, D. and Redclift, M. (1991) *Refashioning Nature*. London: Routledge.

Goodman, D., Sorj, B. and Wilkinson, J. (1987) *From Farming to Biotechnology*. Oxford: Blackwell.

Goodman, D. and Wilkinson, J. (1990) 'Patterns of research and innovation in the modern agro-food system', pp. 127–46 of Lowe *et al. op. cit.*

Gordon, D. M. (1980) 'Stages of accumulation and long economic cycles', pp. 9–45, T. Hopkins and I. Wallerstein (eds) *Processes of the World-System*. Beverly Hills: Sage.

Goussios, D. and Zacopoulou, E. (1992) 'Grèce: Un syndicalisme sous le patronage du politique', pp. 115–39, Hervieu and Lagrave *op. cit.*

Grant, W. (1983) 'The National Farmers' Union: the classic case of incorporation?', in D. Marsh (ed.) *Pressure Politics*. London: Junction Books.

Grant, W. (ed.) (1987) *Business Interests, Organisational Development and Private Interest Government: An International Comparative Study of the Food Processing Industry*. Berlin: de Gruyter.

Grant, W. (1991) *The Dairy Industry: An International Comparison*. Aldershot: Dartmouth.

Greer, A. (1994) *Policy Networks and State-Farmer Relations in Northern Ireland*. Unpublished paper, School of Politics, University of the West of England, Bristol.

Gueslin, A. (1990) 'Introduction', pp. 11–23, Just *op. cit.*

Hervieu, B. and Lagrave, R. M. (eds) (1992) *Les Syndicats Agricoles en Europe*. Paris: L'Harmattan.

Hirst, P. and Zeitlin, J. (1991) 'Flexible specialisation versus post-Fordism: theory, evidence and policy implications', *Economy and Society*, 20: 1–56.

Hufbauer, G. C. and Schott, J. J. (1993) *NAFTA: An Assessment*. London: Longman.

Hughes, T. (1987) 'The evolution of large technological systems', pp. 51–82, W. Bijker, T. Hughes and T. Pinch (eds) *The Social Construction of Technological Systems*. London: MIT Press.

INAO (1985) *A Success Story for France: L'Appellation d'Origine Contrôlée*. Paris: INAO.

Jenkins, R. (1993) *Capping GATT and Gatting CAP*. London: SAFE Alliance.

Jessop, B. (1990) 'Regulation theories in retrospect and prospect', *Economy and Society*, 19: 153–216.

Just, F. (ed.) (1990) *Co-operatives and Farmers Unions in Western Europe*. Esbjerg: South Jutland University Press.

Just, F. *et al.* (1984) *Samspillet mellem staten, land-brugsorganisationerne og landbrugskooperationen*. Esbjerg: South Jutland University Press.

Kenney, M., Lobao, L. M., Curry, J. and Goe, W. R. (1989) 'Midwestern agriculture in US Fordism. From the New Deal to economic restructuring', *Sociologia Ruralis*, 29: 131–48.

Kenney, M., Lobao, L. M., Curry, J. and Goe, W. R. (1991) 'Agriculture in US Fordism: the integration of the productive consumer', pp. 173–88, Friedland *et al. op. cit.*

Lash, S. and Urry, J. (1987) *The End of Organised Capitalism*. Cambridge: Polity Press.

Lash, S. and Urry, J. (1994) *Economies of Signs and Spaces*. London: Sage.

Lawrence, G. (1990) 'Agricultural restructuring and rural social change in Australia', pp. 101–28, Marsden *et al. op. cit.*

Le Heron, R. (1991) 'New Zealand agriculture and changes in the agriculture-finance relation during the 1980's', *Environment and Planning A*, 23: 1653–70.

Le Heron, R. (1993) *Globalised Agriculture*. Oxford: Pergamon Press.

Lipietz, A. (1985) 'The world crisis: the globalization of the general crisis of Fordism', *IDS Bulletin*, 16: 6–20.

Lipietz, A. (1987) *Mirages and Miracles*. London: New Left Books.

Low, P. (1993) *Trading Free: The GATT and US Trade Policy*. New York: The Twentieth Century Fund Press.

Lowe, P. and Bodiguel, M. (eds) (1990) *Rural Studies in Britain and France*. London: Belhaven.

Lowe, P., Marsden, T. K. and Whatmore, S. (eds) (1990) *Technological Change and the Rural Environment*. London: David Fulton.

McMichael, P. (1984) *Settlers and the Agrarian Question: Foundations of Capitalism in Colonial Australia*. New York: Cambridge University Press.

Marsden, T. K. and Little, J. (eds) (1990) *Political, Social and Economic Perspectives on the International Food System*. Aldershot: Avebury.

Marsden, T. K., Lowe, P. and Whatmore, S. (eds) (1990) *Rural Restructuring: Global Processes and their Responses*. London: David Fulton.

Marsden, T. K., Lowe, P. and Whatmore, S. (eds) (1992) *Labour and Locality: Uneven Development in the Labour Process*. London: David Fulton.

Marsden, T. K., Murdoch, J., Lowe, P., Munton, R. and Flynn, A. (1993) *Constructing the Countryside*. London: UCL Press.

Marsden, T. K. and Whatmore, S. (1992) 'Finance capital and food system restructuring: global dynamics and their national incorporation', in P. McMichael (ed.) *Food Systems and Agrarian Change in the Late Twentieth Century*. Ithaca, NY: Cornell University Press.

Moyano, E. (1984) *Corporatismo y Agricultura*. Instituto de Estudios Agrarios, Pesqueros y Alimentarios, MAPA, Madrid.

Moyer, H.W. and Josling, T.E. (1990) *Agricultural Policy Reform: Politics and Process in the EC and USA*. Hemel Hempstead: Harvester Wheatsheaf.

Munton, R. (1992) 'The uneven development of capitalist agriculture', pp. 25–48, K. Hoggart (ed.) *Agricultural Change, Environment and Economy*. London: Mansell.

Munton, R. and Marsden, T. (1991) 'Dualism or diversity in family farming', *Geoforum*, 22: 105–17.

Munton, R., Marsden, T. and Whatmore, S. (1990) 'Technological change in a period of agricultural adjustment', pp. 104–26, Lowe *et al. op. cit.*

OECD (1983) *Positive Adjustment Policies in the Dairy Sector*. Paris: Organisation for Economic Cooperation and Development.

Page, B. and Walker, R. (1991) 'From settlement to Fordism: the agro-industrial revolution in the American midwest', *Economic Geography*, 67: 281–315.

Perrier-Cornet, P. (1990) 'Les filières régionales de qualité dans l'agroalimentaire: étude comparative dans le secteur laitièr en Franche-Comté, Emilie Romagne, Auvergne', *Economie Rurale*, 195: 27–33.

Peterson, M. (1990) 'Paradigmatic shift in agriculture: global effects and the Swedish response', Marsden *et al. op. cit.*

Petit, M., de Benedictis, M., Britton, D., de Groot, M., Henrichsmeyer, W. and Lechi, F. (1987) *Agricultural Policy Formation in the European Community: The Birth of Milk Quotas and CAP Reform*. Amsterdam: Elsevier.

Piore, M. and Sabel, C.F. (1984) *The Second Industrial Divide*. New York: Basic Books.

Pred, A. and Watts, M. (1992) *Reworking Modernity*. Rutgers: Rutgers University Press.

Redclift, M. (1990) 'The role of agricultural technology in sustainable development', pp. 81–103, Lowe *et al. op. cit.*

Roobeek, A.J.M. (1986) 'The crisis in Fordism and the rise of a new technological system', *Research Memorandum no. 8602*, Amsterdam: Department of Economics, University of Amsterdam.

Smith, M. (1990) *The Politics of Agricultural Support in Britain*. Aldershot: Dartmouth.

Streeck, W. and Schmitter, P.C. (eds) (1985) *Private Interest Government*. London: Sage.

Swinbank, A. (1993) 'CAP Reform 1992', *Journal of Common Market Studies*, 31: 359–72.

Traxler, F. (1985) 'Prerequisites, problem-solving capacity and limits or neo-corporatist regulation: a case study of private interest governance and economic performance in Austria', pp. 150–67, Streeck and Schmitter *op. cit.*

Tubiana, L. (1989) 'World trade in agricultural products: from global regulation to market fragmentation', pp. 46–83, Goodman and Redclift *op. cit.*

Van der Ploeg, J.D. (1990) *Labour Markets and Agricultural Production*. Boulder Colorado: Westview Press.

Waarden, F. van (1985) 'Varieties of collective self-regulation of business: the example of the Dutch dairy industry', pp. 197–220, Streeck and Schmitter *op. cit.*

Ward, N. (1990) 'A preliminary analysis of the UK food chain', *Food Policy*, 13: 439–41.

Whatmore, S. (1994) 'Global agro-food complexes and the refashioning of rural Europe' in A. Amin and N. Thrift (eds) *Globalisation and Changing Economic Prospects: Examples from Europe*. Oxford: Oxford University Press.
Winson, A. (1993) *The Intimate Commodity: Food and the Development of the Agro-Industrial Complex in Canada*. Toronto: Garamond Press.
Young, B. (1990) 'Does the American dairy industry fit the meso-corporatist model?', *Political Studies*, 38: 72–82.

CHAPTER 2

Agriculture and Corporatism in Scandinavia

Flemming Just

In the 1960s the very close interplay between agricultural organisations and state authorities and the success of agriculture in getting subsidies were seen as outcomes of pressure-group politics. But from the mid 1970s the concept of corporatism in political science offered a broader explanation seeing the interplay as part of a general system of interest mediation in which the influence of organisations is understood not to be limited to the input-side of policy-making.

This chapter defines corporatism in relation to the pluralist pressure-group tradition. The empirical-analytical part will show the different developments of agricultural corporatism in the three Scandinavian countries, Denmark, Norway and Sweden. Key points to arise are that corporatist structures must be analysed in their historical and political context and not just as structural features, and that theories of corporatism need some important nuances.

This will allow us to answer questions on the purpose and provenance of agricultural regulations. Did the agricultural organisations 'capture' the policy-making process, or did the state use the collaboration of organisations to pursue higher goals and to calm disappointed farmers? And last but not least: did the agricultural organisations, the administration and the politicians form an iron triangle as postulated, or is it more appropriate to speak about loose networks? (Jordan, 1981).

The debate on corporatism

From the beginning of the 1970s to the mid 1980s political scientists devoted considerable attention to the relations between the state and interest organisations. The intention was to create a new state theory in conscious opposition to the dominant pluralistic perception. It was obvious that pluralism's claim of a multiplicity of voluntary interest groups competing with each other on equal terms could not match reality in post-war Western Europe. Indeed, the proponents of a neo-corporatist approach observed that competition was effectively limited to a small number of peak organisations, where membership could not be regarded as entirely voluntary (Schmitter, 1974).

Another pluralistic presupposition was that the state was passive or reactive in relation to interest organisations. Adherents of corporatist theories here found clear evidence instead that the modern state played an active role in the establishing of interests by excluding or including them in consultative processes. And where pluralists claimed a sharp division between state and society, corporatists maintained that the public–private distinction was becoming blurred (O'Sullivan, 1988).

Many definitions have been formulated of corporatism.[1] The dominant one, championed by Philippe Schmitter, is that corporatism is a form of interest representation or interest intermediation as he prefers to describe it.[2]

A broader perception regards corporatism as first and foremost a form of policy-making with a high degree of collaboration between the state and centralised groups in forming and implementing public policy (Lehmbruch, 1979).

A still broader view sees corporatism as an independent economic system contrasted to capitalism and socialism, an 'economic system in which the state directs and controls predominantly privately owned business' (Pahl and Winkler, 1976: 7). Marxist political scientists have viewed corporatism as a tool for managing conflicts and exercising control over trade unions (Panitch, 1979).

However, political scientists have not been able to develop a macro-theory from which to characterize societies as corporatist or not. Empirical evidence shows that no West European society as a whole functions on a corporatist basis. The vast majority of policies made by states are not shaped by the same interests most or all of the time. A particular method of policy-making in one issue area may be corporatist in style, but the political form of the state overall may still be pluralistic (Cox, 1988).

In consequence adherents of corporatism have focused on the sector level, and theoretical aspirations have been lowered to develop a middle-range theory. So, from the mid 1980s the concept of meso-corporatism was introduced (Cawson, 1985; Grant, 1985). Meso-corporatism exists

> if public policy has sectoral, rather than system-wide concerns, and if it involves state agencies negotiating policies with organisations which have achieved monopoly representation of a specific sectoral interest, and if such policies are implemented through those interest organisations. (Cawson, 1986: 73)

This concept certainly seems more applicable to the analysis of agricultural policy than that of macro-corporatism.

But tailoring theory to reality has also meant a dilution and has laid meso-corporatism open to criticism from pluralists. Close observation of the interplay between the state and interest organisations reveals that, even on a sectoral level, it is not possible to characterize all the relations and actions as corporatist. In some cases organisations are deeply involved in bargaining and implementation, while in other, often politicised, cases, they act more like pressure groups. One of the results has been a revival of pluralist thinking on pressure groups (Cox and O'Sullivan, 1988). Opposition to corporatist thinking has been there all the time (Heisler, 1979; Jordan, 1981, 1984; Almond, 1983), but now it is possible for the two schools to communicate because of some convergence.

But still there is a lot of work to do if we are to develop a (combined) consistent and overarching theory of state/interest organisation relations which at the same time takes into account structural and functional features as well as the important individual and historical elements.

Community, market and the state

In the absence of such a theory, can we begin by specifying the sort of space in society that corporatist arrangements occupy. The basic precondition is the existence of an associational system or interest organisations. Conventionally, social scientists ascribe social order to the three central institutions of the community, the market and the state embodying respectively the principles of spontaneous solidarity, dispersed competition and hierarchical control. Streeck and Schmitter (1985) argue for a fourth distinctive, institutional basis of social order, namely the association with its guiding principle of organisational concertation. They claim that this fourth corner-stone 'is more than a transient and expedient amalgam of the three others' (p. 2).

The contrary position is argued here: that associative action is precisely an amalgam of the three others (see Figure 2.1). It is not a distinctive order, but arises from the interdependencies between community, market and state and only under the conditions of advanced capitalism.[3] Originally most associations were established in order to tackle challenges emerging where community met market. Such self-help associations as co-operative societies are examples, and local farmers' unions are others.

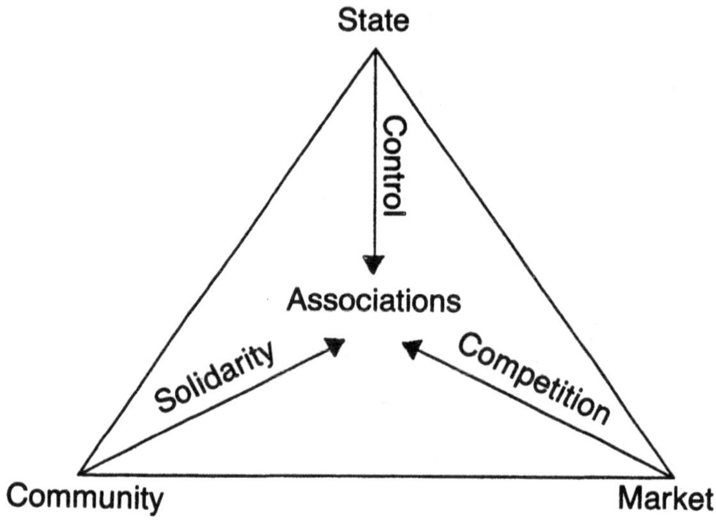

Figure 2.1 The connection between the basic institutions of society and associations

Problems related to reproduction are to be found on the community–state axis, for instance kindergardens and sick-benefit associations, which initially were run by private and voluntary associations.

The examples mentioned are all from the first period of the modern liberal state (i.e. the last third of the 19th century), and all associations originated from civil society. With the increase in international competition and the growing complexity of society, both market and state expanded at the expense of community. In the words of Habermas: the system world was colonising the life world.

The associations both responded to and were an integral part of this transformation. Local associations formed national federations in order to match the demands of market and state, and these organisations soon joined together to build peak organisations in order to have a more monolithic representation of a whole sector in relation to the state, other organisations and foreign interests. In many countries such national peak organisations were established for farmers, workers, employers, and industrial firms around the turn of the century.[4]

A similar move away from civil society has been seen in the reproductive sphere where, with the gradual establishment of the welfare state from the 1930s, the state and local authorities took over more and more of the tasks previously performed by voluntary associations.

With this model in mind it is possible to distinguish the roles agricultural organisations have played in the political economy of different countries over the years. In an open, export-oriented economy the agricultural organisations will be found close to the state–market axis, where questions of maintaining international competitiveness and the regulation of quality and standards will be to the fore (de Vroom, 1987). In an economy oriented to the home market, it is assumed that the main efforts of agricultural organisations will be found more along the state–civil society axis and be preoccupied with regulation of the domestic market in order to secure farmers' income and rural development. It is assumed that regulation of the latter kind will have a more interventionist character, because the goals will be more differentiated and precise, and because they aim specifically to curb the market.

Thus the overall structure of the economy and politics frames state/interest organisation relations. In the United States the very pluralistic character of politics and competing farmers' organisations identified with rival political ideologies, mean weak relations with the Department of Agriculture. In contrast, farmers' interests in Western Europe are more uniform and monolithically organised and enjoy much closer collaboration with agricultural ministries. Even in France with several rival farming groups, the FNSEA has monopolised most of the formal and informal contact with the government (Ball and Millard, 1986).

But this structural feature must be combined with a functional one. Here the decisive factor, overlooked by most corporatist and pluralist writers, is the *content and context of regulation*. The content and context decide how much energy organisations, governments and civil servants will devote to a given case, and how much authority a government will delegate to an interest organisation.

This implies two things. First of all, state/interest organisation relations are not a static structure but a dynamic process. This means that an issue previously the subject of bargaining between only agricultural organisations and the Ministry may at a highly politicised time be opened up to other interests or be taken out of that forum altogether.[5]

A second, often overlooked implication is that the state has the power to delegate and to withdraw authority. The latter may be difficult because of tradition, the political situation or the strength of the organisation concerned, but that does not change the fact that the delegation of authority is not once and for all, and can be rescinded.

Although we thus combine structural and functional factors the nature of state/interest organisation relations is not thereby specified. Similar structures and functions may at another time and in another country give totally different relations, due to cultural factors shaped by historical traditions and the role of individuals. Both are more important than usually assumed in political science. Agricultural policy will of course depend on the attitude of the government, but more importantly on the authority of the minister. Usually a minister will have considerable scope to do what he finds right, and the same is the case with an organisational leader. On paper an organisation may be equipped with strong structural powers; in practice they will be of little value without strong leadership.

In the following sections some of these assumptions will be explored by looking at how the interplay between agriculture and the state has developed in the last 100 years in the three Scandinavian countries: Denmark, with an export-oriented agriculture enjoying limited subsidies; Norway, with a heavily subsidised and protected agriculture; and Sweden in a middle position, with farmers protected against world market but not internal competition and with a rather interventionist state.[6]

1880–1930: organisational interventionism

The breakthrough of capitalism in the 19th century was based on three pillars - private property, the free market and the autonomy of civil society (for example parliaments and popular movements). But fundamental problems of liberal capitalism could not be solved without interference from the state, which through various reforms secured the survival of the pillars, although in a slightly moderated form.

Regulation of work and habitation and help for the poor and the sick were necessary in order to secure tranquility on the labour market. But commerce itself also had to be regulated. Laws on trade, closing times, companies, veterinary and hygienic conditions and so on, all had the objective of curbing unrestrained trading, safeguarding consumers against sub-standard products, protecting competitors from unfair competition, and securing stockholders and creditors against fraud, as well as helping national industries to compete in world trade.

All these regulations demanded specialist knowledge which central administrations did not possess; nor, in the prevailing spirit of liberalism, was there a political desire to build up such expertise in most countries. Instead, special expertise was established on a voluntary basis in the many interest organisations formed in the period 1890–1914. At this time organisational structures were laid down, as separate organisations struggled for position in relation to the state and competing organisations. For instance, the Federation of Danish Co-operative Bacon Factories established in 1897 had several clashes with the Farmers' Unions about authority over pig breeding, testing stations and state funds (Just, 1987). Indeed, because of the tremendous importance of both pig and butter exports, the organisations for co-operative bacon factories and dairies in Denmark had a much more independent influence in relation to state and farmers' unions than co-operative organisations in most other countries (Just, 1990).

One of the ways to further the interests of members was through bargaining with the state. But it is worth stressing that this way of solving problems was not always the first chosen. In most cases an interest organisation would try first to resolve matters on its own in order to protect its independence. The Danish Lur mark, for instance, was introduced in 1900 by the dairy organisations, so that British consumers could have confidence in the Danish origin of the products. Within a few years almost all dairies had joined the Danish Butter Mark Association. But in order to encompass 100 per cent and to have an official stamp, the butter organisations asked the Minister of Agriculture to codify the arrangement, which it did in 1906. All administration, however, was delegated to the association (Bjørn, 1982: 147ff).

Because of deregulation and a liberalistic current in the 1920s, World War I with its many regulations has often been considered a parenthesis. But the war taught several lessons. Governments learnt that they could achieve better industrial control with a diminished administrative load, if the different top organisations undertook responsibility on behalf of a whole sector. The organisations on their side learnt that they had to strengthen their administrative and political capacity in order to be able to deal with the state and other interests. In Denmark the Agricultural Council was established in 1919 by the Farmers' Unions and the co-operative organisations in order to match the Industrial Council and the commercial organisations, and in order to speak with one voice in negotiations with the state. Another tendency was internal centralisation with more influence given to peak and branch organisations at the expense of member associations and member firms. Such a centralisation was necessary during the war, but did not cease after the armistice (Just, 1986: 108).

Looking at the macro level, the role of agricultural organisations is almost the same in all the countries, oriented to three basic goals, namely preservation of family farming and traditional rural life; equality of farm incomes in relation to other sectors; and provision of services (Micheletti, 1990: 16). But in practice the means were very different in every country depending on the structure of the economy, the nature of the polity, and the ability of organisations to take advantage of their position.

This was fully illustrated in the period from 1890 to 1930 when the modern state and interest organisations were established. In Germany and Belgium and other countries with agricultures oriented to the home market, most state/interest organisation relations were concerned with protection, in an effort to preserve family farming and incomes. In exporting countries like

Denmark and the Netherlands most endeavours were concerned with international competitiveness. It was essential to fulfil quality demands from the export markets, so in the end most initiatives in state/interest organisation relations can be traced back to a desire to introduce adequate hygienic and veterinary standards. Quite often the agricultural organisations were opposed to such regulations, but leaving much of the regulation and administration to the organisations themselves made it that much more palatable to member firms. This close collaboration between state and organisations contributed to form a sort of joint 'system view', for instance about the necessity of high standards, although it would mean an immediate cost for members. In this sense it is possible to speak about a developing interest intermediation from the 1920s.

1930–47: slough of despond?

The two decades from 1930 to 1950 are often seen as overcast by the spectres of depression, war and difficult recovery. But from an organisational perspective, was the period – in the words of Bunyan – simply a Slough of Despond or was it the beginning of the road to eternal salvation for interest organisations?

Denmark

In many countries the 1930s are seen as marking a departure in the relations between state and interest organisations. But in the case of Danish agriculture most of the changes rested on well-established traditions. Here the regulations of the 1930s had many elements of continuity, in the way administrative problems were tackled and in the way solutions were the outcome of known balances of political power. But the elements of discontinuity are easier to recognise, because the interplay expanded so much both in degree and quality.

If we are to speak about corporatism, it requires relations of exchange between state and organisations and both parties must be in possession of unique powers, in which the other is interested. Before the 1930s there was no political will to give governments and their administrations authority to intervene and regulate agriculture. But from that time, this authority was given and delegated to the agricultural organisations, which in turn guaranteed to exercise an administration encompassing all farmers and securing the state a minimum of criticism and administration.

The real difference in relation to earlier experiences is not the quantity of regulation, but the different role of the state. Danish agriculture has traditionally been very liberal, because of the great dependence on imports of feedstuffs and fertilizers and its ability to export two-thirds of its production. Where most countries during the crisis of the 1880s and 1890s protected their agriculture, a majority of Danish farmers and politicians chose to let market forces rule. This was only possible because of the open British market which imported 70 per cent of the surplus production.

When the world crisis hit Danish agriculture in late 1930, the sector once again reacted in classical market terms by expanding production and attempting to regulate a proportion of the exports on a voluntary organisational basis. However, extended protectionism such as quotas and differentiated levels of duty on the second most important market, Germany (20–25 per cent of the exports), made voluntary regulation inadequate. At the same time strong pro-Commonwealth feelings in the UK threatened the Danish access.

In November 1932, the UK insisted on a 'voluntary' and immediate reduction of Danish bacon exports of 30 per cent. This demand, together with great problems with butter exports, reluctantly led to an abandonment of resistance to state intervention, and a Bacon Board and a Butter Export Board were established under the Ministry of Agriculture. In 1933 similar export boards were formed for most other agricultural products in order to regulate exports and, through export fees, level out prices to the producers (Just, 1992). In 1933 pig production was strongly regulated by assigning every farmer a fixed number of pigs to be produced (pig cards), probably the first example in the world of a marketing quota system for an agricultural product (Tracy, 1989: 210).

In 1950 the state export boards were abolished as part of the general political desire to liberalise commerce. But where the agricultural organisations and their supporting political parties in 1932 only accepted state intervention with considerable reluctance, they were after the war opposed to a liberalisation of the export trade. The reasons why agriculture learnt to value state intervention were several.

First of all the agricultural organisations discovered that state boards could be useful tools to pursue organisational goals without losing independence. The boards were totally dominated by the agricultural and co-operative organisations with very few seats for the private export sector. Usually civil servants did not participate, the Ministry just took cognizance of the boards' transactions; and giving seats to external representatives such as from worker and consumer organisations was not even considered.

Furthermore, the agricultural organisations held sway over the authorities given in the Agricultural Export Act of 1932 which empowered the Minister to establish export boards, as the legislation specified that the Minister could not take any initiative without recommendation from the Agricultural Council.

Another important factor was that the administration of the boards was situated either at the co-operative organisations if they controlled most of the product concerned (butter, cheese and bacon), or else at the Agricultural Council (cattle, horses, eggs, potatoes). The organisations soon realised what possibilities this gave for increasing their own influence on the export trade at the expense of the traditional private export sector.

Last but not least agriculture learnt to value state intervention because the export boards had the right to collect fees on exports. Gradually the organisations were allowed to use the export pools for any purposes that served the common interests of agriculture. One of those interests was to subsidise the secretariats in the organisations (Just, 1992).

In the very close interplay between agriculture and the Ministry of Agriculture, the organisations played a decisive role. But they did not have a monopolised representational system. The influence was divided between four organisations, the Farmers' and the Smallholders' Unions and the strong co-operative organisations. Together they formed the Agricultural Council. All of them were recognised by the state as acceptable representatives of agriculture, whereas the agrarian protest movement, LS, that for a couple of years in the 1930s was the largest union, never was accepted by the Social Democratic government.

Thus, a monopolised structure and many members are not a prerequisite for establishing a corporatist system: traditional procedures and a coincidence of values between political and organisational leaders are more important.

Sweden

In Sweden agriculture was not organised to the same extent as in Denmark. When crisis hit the Swedish farmers and especially the dairy farmers they did not have a strong co-operative organisation to regulate supplies and prices. Thus, the farmers' union SAL (Sveriges Allmänna Lantbrukssällskap) asked the Social-Liberal Minister of Agriculture to propose an act providing it with a monopoly to regulate the market. Furthermore the co-operative dairies should be supported through a right to collect fees even from non-members, and internal competition between dairies should be abolished by the establishing of a national dairy organisation (Rothstein, 1992: 112). The Milk Regulating Act was carried through in 1932 and must be characterised as the initial step towards a very close collaboration between the state and organisations in Sweden.[7]

In 1933 this collaborative policy was cemented in the great Crisis Agreement between the new Social Democratic government and the non-socialist parties. This agreement implied a strengthening of farmers' and workers' organisations by giving them resources to monopolise the supply of respectively agricultural products and the work force (Micheletti, 1990: 62f).

It also gave them influence over the implementation and administration of state policies. The 'cost' for the organisations was acceptance of state intervention (Rothstein, 1987).

The result was a remarkable growth in organisational memberships. The proportion of organised industrial workers rose from 63 per cent in 1930 to 83 per cent ten years later. Inside agriculture the development was more profound. A national recruitment drive was first initiated around 1930. At that time the producer co-operatives had 160,000 members and state policies helped them to expand to 721,000 members only ten years later. The RLF, that later became the leading farmers' union, was established in 1929 and its membership rose from 19,000 to 76,000 in 1940 (Therborn, 1988: 60).

The Swedish political parties and governments played a very active role in the formation of powerful organisations in agriculture in the early 1930s. The co-operative movement, in particular, was favoured as it was considered a way to cushion falling prices by abolishing competition between farmers. The benefits for the state was a legitimate farmer-dominated organ able to control markets and participate in state regulations. The experience of the First World War showed that a solely bureaucratic regulation was not flexible enough and failed to gain legitimacy among both consumers and producers (Heckscher, 1946: 231ff). Thus, large-scale organising functioned both as an appropriate remedy for implementation and as an instrument to discipline farmers and their organisations to follow the line in national agricultural policy.

Norway

The world crisis also forced Norwegian farmers to organise themselves more effectively. As in Sweden the milk sector became the driving force in the organising process and in closer collaboration with the state. More than 40 per cent of farmers' incomes derived from milk sale, and as one-third of the population lived by farming it had very broad consequences when prices fell dramatically at the end of the 1920s because of overproduction and sharp competition between local dairies.

In 1929 Norges Bondelag (the Norwegian Farmers' Union) took the initiative to form regional, co-operative milk centres and above them a national association in order to regulate supplies and abolish competition. The farmers joined in great numbers, but still many free riders did not participate, and financing losses on the export of milk products was not solved. So the Social-Liberal government, which identified closely with the farming community, carried through a Trade Act in June 1930 with the support of all political parties. The purpose of the Act was, through co-operative organisations, to establish central sale structures for milk, butter, cheese and meat. The Labour Party in particular regarded co-operatives as a means to develop social equity and looked to the measure to strengthen co-operative organising vis-à-vis private traders (Omholt, 1984: 91).

The implementation of the Trade Act was followed by a Trade Board with the right to collect fees. It solely consisted of agricultural and co-operative organisations and with only one reprsentative from the businessmen's association. The Ministry of Agriculture did not want to be represented. With almost all other interests excluded from regulation of the market, the agricultural organisations were given extensive possibilities of self-government. The co-operative organisations especially became more powerful and several sub-sectors, for instance milk processing, were totally dominated by co-operatives thanks to government policies.

There were several reasons why the state left regulation and implementation to agriculture itself. Most politicians believed that the regulations were a temporary expedient. But more important was the political culture. The farming community was dominated by strong liberalistic sentiments and opposition towards state regulations. This outlook was shared by the liberal parties that had been in government most of the time since 1884, and which had close connections to the Smallholders' and Farmers' Unions (Vatn, 1984, 1990).

1947–80: from expediency to permanency

Thus while farmers were in deep financial crisis in the interwar years, their unions and co-operative organisations achieved an unprecedented position of political and administrative influence. Many of the schemes and interventions established in the 1930s were seen as temporary responses to a passing crisis. The political consciousness of agricultural interventionism as a more permanent state of affairs came after the Second World War, when politicians and organisational leaders realised that the most stable feature of agricultural markets was instability. Technological development combined with the treadmill effect made it evident that problems of surplus production would prevail again as soon as the immediate post-war demands were satisfied (Cochrane, 1979).

No country dared to choose a market solution to solve the problems. The social and political consequences of letting market forces sweep over the countryside were one of the reasons behind continuing and growing interventionism. The long cycle of production also made it difficult to adjust to strict market conditions without pronounced fluctuations. Another reason was that the war-time experience had taught governments the need to pay for self-sufficiency. Last but not least was a changed attitude among politicians, civil servants, experts and organisational leaders towards regulation in general. Supporters of both Keynesianism and a planned economy demanded a more active state involvement in the economy and more policy strings to play upon and with much greater refinement.

So, the scene was set for continued agricultural interventionism in the post-war period, although the rationality and objectives were broadened. But this did not automatically imply strong involvement and influence for agricultural organisations. On the contrary, the broadening of the scope of policies and the much higher regulatory ambitions among politicians and administrators might have implied a 'colonising' of agricultural politics by state and non-farming interests. Why then did the agricultural organisations succeed in gaining so much influence in all developed countries after 1945, although agriculture's share of the population and national product was dramatically falling?

First of all, the agricultural organisations had proven in the 1930s that they were able to administer comprehensive schemes, and in this respect the post-war regulations built upon this experience. Secondly, the agricultural organisations had themselves become significant political forces, partly thanks to the organising processes which many states had helped them to pursue in the 1930s. The precise position and power of the agricultural organisations of course depended on the role of the farming community in the particular society.

Agriculture in Scandinavia in the post-war period

1947 was an epoch-making year in many countries for the relations between agriculture and state. In Norway and Sweden relatively precise income goals were then determined which established the direction for policy for the following decades. The two countries were governed by strong Social Democratic parties with declared aims of income equalisation. In Denmark a Social Democratic government also took power in 1947, but neither then nor later did it pursue such a policy.

Denmark

The Social Democratic Party had put out a new programme in 1945 about 'Future Denmark' that toyed with the notion of a planned economy, partly in order to head off support for the Communist Party. But two years later they gave up this stance in favour of a truly Keynesian programme that gained support from most parties. As regards agriculture the Social Democrats never formulated an overarching commitment to fixed income goals. Investment and production plans were made, but only because of the requirements put forward by the USA in the Marshall Plan. The agricultural organisations were very watchful lest the government should meddle more than was strictly necessary, and after the Recovery Programme ceased in 1952 no government made production plans.

The Social Democratic Party was dependent on support from the Social Liberal Party and while the former had some support from smallholders, the latter had very close relations with that group. So the parcelling out of land into small holdings continued until the early 1960s and the administration of land policies was totally dominated by the Farmers' and Smallholders' Unions.

Nor was there a break in the support for export policies. Because of lack of energy and natural resources and an industrial sector that still in the 1950s was strongly home-market oriented and small, Denmark needed agricultural exports to earn foreign currency. Not until 1962 did industry assume the role of the leading exporting sector.

The development of trade relations from the late 1950s strongly disadvantaged Danish agriculture. The formation of the EEC meant exclusion from the important continental European market, and EFTA explicitly exempted agriculture from its free trade arrangements. The Farmers' Union and the Liberal Party were ready to join the Common Market from the outset, but the other parties and the Smallholders' Union would not give up the traditional British market and connections to the Nordic countries. But from now it was considerations of industrial competitiveness and Denmark's position in a broader European economic and political context which would determine the matter (Just, forthcoming).

As compensation for falling world 'market' prices and relative incomes, Danish governments were willing to subsidise agriculture through home-market schemes, tax reliefs, direct subsidies, support to young farmers etc. By the end of the 1960s this amounted to one-third of the total income in agriculture. Negotiations between government and agriculture took place every second year immediately after the conclusion of collective bargaining on the labour market. Estimates of the consequence of these agreements formed the basis for the amount of compensation to farmers.

The policy-making process was self-contained as no other interests were represented. This gave the organisations considerable influence over the amount and division of subsidies. Furthermore, all implementation was delegated to the agricultural organisations: for instance, under the home-market schemes the organisations for dairies and bacon factories were allowed to impose a levy on consumer prices.

From 1973 this system was fundamentally changed by membership of the European Community. Most of the subsidies were removed and the Ministry of Agriculture was enlarged and gained a more independent position in relation to the agricultural organisations. The influence of agriculture was further weakened by the fact that many decisions now were taken in Brussels.

However, the real loss of influence did not correspond to the formal loss. Levels of financial support, for example, did not decline although they now came through different channels, and very close collaboration between civil servants in the Ministry of Agriculture and officials of the agricultural organisations meant that the needs of the sector exercised much influence over Danish attitudes in Brussels.

Until EC membership the Smallholders' Union had made much capital of its independence of other organisations. But EC structures forced the different organisations to work closer together in order to express as strongly as possible a common Danish point of view and so from 1976 the smallholders rejoined the Agricultural Council that it had left in 1939.

Norway and Sweden

Despite several similarities between Norway and Sweden, for example, in terms of agriculture's share of population and exports, there were also fundamental differences. In Norway broad political consensus emerged about more precise income goals for agriculture which culminated in 1975 with binding commitments. This consensus came about as part of the national collaboration of the immediate post-war years. But its more permanent existence was primarily determined by the relations between the Social Democratic Party and the smallholders (Feiring, 1972; Steen, 1985). Ideology also played a role as the Norwegian Social Democratic Party was strongly influenced by ideas of a planned economy and incomes equality. It was also important that one-quarter of the MPs were farmers, and several of the leaders in the Farmers' Union and the co-operative organisations held seats for the non-socialistic Farmers' Party (later the Centre Party).

In Sweden the farmers did not have the same possibilities to be heard politically. In 1965 only 1 per cent of the votes of the Social Democratic Party came from farmers, whereas in Norway they counted for 10 per cent. Nor could the Swedish farmers expect undivided support from the Liberal Party: in the 1950s and 1960s the Swedish Centre Party reoriented itself towards white collar workers and away from farmers, and the proportion of MPs with agricultural connections was only about 12 per cent (Steen, 1985: 59).

This situation had obvious consequences for the form of political organisation. In Norway negotiations on agricultural prices were extremely distinct. The Farmers' Union and the Smallholders' Union were given an exclusive right to negotiate with the Ministry of Finance and the government. The Storting (the parliament) and the other parties just functioned as a rubber stamp and did not change anything when agreements were reached. The whole implementation and administration were left to the co-operative organisations which in this way were equipped with a monopoly in several sectors and acted as semi-state agencies.

In Sweden the political organisation was much more corporative. Negotiations took place, and still do, in special committees with representatives from farmers, workers and consumers. In this way interest organisations were played off against each other, while the state kept its role as 'neutral store-keeper'. Incomes equalisation was the central objective at the outset, but increasing criticism from the Social Democrats and the labour movement meant more weight to consumer prices. So subsidies were given in exchange for efficiency in farming through structural rationalisation. Only farms of more than 10 ha should be considered as potentially rational units. As for the implementation and administration of the price regulations, these were delegated to regional state bodies.

The differences between the two countries were also reflected in parliamentary debates. In Norway most of the agreements ended in unanimity in the Storting. None of them did in Sweden. None the less, the farmers have been much more inclined to demonstrate in Norway. It was easier to mobilise when your counterpart was the state instead of consumer organisations. The broad support for the farming community in Norway also made it more likely that the outcome of an action would be in favour of the farmers. This was not the case in Sweden. The lack of political influence was one factor. Another one was that the Swedish co-operative organisations participated as the dominant negotiators for the farmers, and they had no interest in disrupting supplies.

Steen concludes that if the farmers' votes are important to other parties besides the farmer party, especially to the Social Democrats, then compromises in agricultural policy-making are expected to favour farmers (p. 48). This analysis may well be right for food-importing countries, where agricultural policy also is a question of incomes distribution along the civil society-state line. But with an important exporting agricultural sector, as in Denmark, the situation is different.

Capture?

The conspicuous strength of agricultural organisations has opened up discussion on the capture of the policy-making process by agriculture. The point of departure is a thesis on asymmetry with the costs of state support spread and the benefits concentrated (Wilson, 1983). It is easy to find examples of that in Norway and Denmark, where the combination of an indirect way of distribution of the costs and a non-pluralistic representational structure has favoured the farmers.

For many years the farm organisations have not been checked by other interest organisations and have therefore been able to exercise maximum pressure on the state. Capture, therefore, is the right term. However, when we look at the motives and logic behind the integration of farmers' organisations it must be remembered that it also served some of the interests of governments, political parties and central administrations.

The crisis in the 1930s was of course an initiating factor, but it does not explain why regulation took the form it did, of using the offices of peak interest organisations. The most important reasons were administrative, as a top civil servant has explained:

> Besides the wish to involve expertise in the work, the reasons have always been the same, namely that it was an impossible task at any moment for an overburdened state administration to establish new offices and find qualified leaders, and that the state felt insulated against criticism of administration when it was done by the trades themselves. (Just, 1992: 481)

The involvement of expert knowledge and possibilities for a more flexible administration were also the central reasons mentioned by the agricultural organisations. But the role of creating harmony and avoiding criticism, as mentioned by the civil servant, must not be under-estimated.

There was also a political rationale behind the wish to use interest organisations as administrators. A non-socialist opposition will always be wary lest a Social Democratic government try to expand the influence of the state, and the integration of strong trade organisations is regarded as one of the best means to hinder such a growth of state administration. Quite often the organisations concerned consciously see themselves playing that role.

A Social Democratic government, on the other hand, may also take advantage of close co-operation with interest organisations. An agreement with one of the trades is difficult for the opposition to criticise, and the government will be shielded against criticism from the producers.

Meso-corporatism and corporate pluralism

Is it then appropriate to describe the relations between agriculture and state in Scandinavia in the period 1930–80 as corporatist? It is possible to find some of the traits Schmitter and others highlighted when starting the debate on corporatism. States have not just been passive in relation to competing interest organisations. They have taken an active part in establishing corporatist arrangements within agriculture and helped to include or exclude interests from the political process. It has been important for governments, parties and administrations to believe in the negotiating organisations as responsible partners and have confidence in their willingness to generate support from all members to fulfil agreements. Therefore it is vital that any organisation so involved should have a similar understanding of problems and solutions. In contrast, an oppositional group, such as the above-mentioned Danish agrarian protest movement, LS, did not have support from an accepted political party to carry its demands, and thus to be incorporated.

This investigation has focused on agriculture. The most important feature has been the very strong demarcation of agricultural politics. This might be thought to accord with Cawson's concept of meso-corporatism, wherein public policy has sectoral rather than system-wide concerns, involves state agencies negotiating policies with interest organisations, and such policies are implemented through these organisations (Cawson, 1986).

However, Cawson's definition is not sufficiently nuanced. First of all it leaves the impression that all the politics in a sector will involve close interplay between state and organisations. That impression is not true. Moreover, governments often make proposals that are routinely submitted to affected organisations, and after receiving the answers they and the political parties make their own decisions, perhaps in accordance with the organisations' wishes, perhaps not – that depends on the case.

In some cases we will only find loose networks in the policy-making processes between organisations, the relevant ministry and the government, while in others we will find iron triangles (Jordan, 1981): such as if policy is concerned with internal sectoral matters, for instance land policy, if agriculture plays a very important economic role as in Denmark, and if the political structures give organisations easy access as in Norway and Denmark.[8]

So, in conclusion, although we may find many meso-corporatist traits in the relations between agriculture and the state in the Scandinavia countries as well as in most other Western countries, sectoral policy and politics overall are better characterised as corporate pluralism (see Heisler, 1979 and Jordan, 1984). This was the situation in the period 1930–80, and the intrusion since then of other politics on the traditionally distinct agricultural field, as well as deregulatory tendencies certainly make the pluralistic elements in the meso-corporatist game more obvious.

Notes

1. The definition most often referred to is Schmitter's from 1974, but as it is rather simplifying (Wilson, 1983) and has been given up by Schmitter himself (1982), Alan Cawson's more nuanced definition (1986) is to be preferred:

   > Corporatism is a specific socio-political process in which a limited number of monopolistic organizations representing fundamental interests engage in bargaining with state agencies over public policy outputs. In exchange for favourable policies, the leaders of the interest organizations agree to undertake the implementation of policy through determining the co-operation of their members.

2. In his 1979 article Philippe Schmitter rejected the use of the concept 'interest

representation', as it could give the impression that the objective of the organisations was just to reflect or faithfully transmit the demands and preferences of their members. The concept of 'interest intermediation' indicates broader objectives, for instance teaching their members what their interests should be or acquiring private governmental functions of resource allocation and social control (p. 93).

3. Bager (1992) in his major work on developmental processes in co-operative organisations operates with the same triangular division of social order, whereas Pestoff (1992) proclaims to follow Streeck and Schmitter.
4. Some examples of the formation of national peak organisations and their early role in policy-making in Scandinavia are treated in Heckscher (1946) and Back (1967) in the case of Sweden, and in Just (1986) in the case of Denmark.
5. Cawson (1986: 37) differentiates between corporate groups and preference groups, the latter existing in a mutually competitive political environment. He thereby overlooks that an organisation usually operating as a corporate group in many other cases may function as a preference group depending on the issue and political climate.
6. It must be emphasised that when speaking of agriculture I mean peak national organisations. In the nature of the case local unions and co-operatives are occupied with local questions along the market–civil society line. King (1985) and the comprehensive Study of the Distribution of Power in Norway speaks about local corporatism in cases where big firms or local organisations are negotiating with local authorities (Hernes and Selvik, 1981), and Cawson (1985) mentions micro-corporatism. I will not neglect the importance of this, but the aim here is to look at the general distribution of authority between state and national organisations.
7. Usually the collectivism and corporatism that afterwards became such a feature of Swedish society are connected with the Social Democratic Party. But in fact the Social Democrats were opposed to the Milk Regulating Act. They found it harmed the consumers and thought it a very dangerous course to extend the authority of private organisations to non-members.
8. Steen (1985) concludes that the different positions of agriculture in relation to the state can be explained by the roles the Social Democratic parties played in agricultural policy-making. In this way he finds that the power of the farm unions is more a reflection of structural opportunities and restraints created by the Social Democrats than a result of the strength of the farmers' interest organisation (p. 61f). Steen here seems to overlook that the strength of Social Democratic parties is a result of basic social and economic conditions in society, and thereby also a result of the strength of the farming community.

References

Almond, G. A. (1983) 'Corporatism, pluralism and professional memory', *World Politics*, 35, 245–60.

Back, P.-E. (1967) *Sammenslutningarnas roll i politikken 1870–1910* (The role of associations in politics 1870–1910). Umeå.

Bager, T. (1992) *Andelsorganisering. En analyse af danske andelsorganisationers udviklingsprocesser* (Co-operative organising). Esbjerg: South Jutland University Press. With an English summary.

Ball, A.R. and Millard, F. (1986) *Pressure Politics in Industrial Societies. A Comparative Introduction*. New Jersey: Humanities Press International.

Berger, S.D. (ed.) (1981) *Organizing Interests in Western Europe. Pluralism, Corporatism, and the Transformation of Politics*. Cambridge: Cambridge University Press.

Bjørn, C. (1982) 'Dansk Mejeribrug 1882–1914' (Danish Dairies 1882–1914) in C. Bjørn (ed.) *Dansk Mejeribrug 1882–2000*. Odense, 11–188.

Blackwell Encyclopedia of Political Thought (1987) Oxford: Blackwell.

Cawson, A. (ed.) (1985) *Organized Interests and the State. Studies in Meso-corporatism*. London: Sage.

Cawson, A. (1986) *Corporatism and Political Theory*. Oxford: Blackwell.

Cochrane, W.W. (1979) *The Development of American Agriculture. A Historical Analysis*. Minneapolis: University of Minnesota Press.

Cox, A. (1988) 'Neo-corporatism versus the corporate state', in A. Cox and N. O'Sullivan (eds) *op. cit.*, 27–47.

Cox, A. and O'Sullivan, N. (eds) (1988) *The Corporate State. Corporatism and the State Tradition in Western Europe*. Cambridge: Edward Elgar.

Feiring, T. (1972) 'Jordbruksorganisasjonene etter krigen' (The agricultural organisations after the war) in *Etterkrigshistorie*, 3. Oslo, 20–32.

Grant, W. (ed.) (1985) *The Political Economy of Corporatism*. London: Macmillan.

Heckscher, G. (1946) 'Staten och organisationerna' (The state and the organisations). Stockholm.

Heisler, M. (1979) 'Corporate pluralism revisited: where is the theory', *Scandinavian Political Studies*, 2, 278–98.

Hernes, G. and Selvik, A. (1981) 'Local corporatism', in S. Berger *op. cit.*, 103–19.

Jordan, G. (1981) 'Iron triangles, woolly corporatism and elastic nets', *Journal of Public Policy*, 1, 95–123.

Jordan, G. (1984) 'Pluralistic corporatism and corporate pluralism', *Scandinavian Political Studies*, 7, 137–53.

Just, F. (1986) *Banen fri for fremtiden – eller kampen om andelsloven 1909–1917*. With a summary in English. Esbjerg: Sydjysk Universitetsforlag.

Just, F. (1987) 'Det begyndte i Horsens' (It started in Horsens. Danish Bacon Factories 1887–1987) 7–63, in E. Helmer Pedersen (ed.) *De første hundrede år. Danske Slagterier 1887–1987*. Published by the Organisation of Danish Bacon Factories.

Just, F. (1990) 'Butter, bacon and organisational power in Danish agriculture', 137–56, in F. Just (ed.) *Co-operatives and Farmers' Unions in Western Europe. Collaboration and Tensions*. Esbjerg: South Jutland University Press.

Just, F. (1992) *Landbruget, staten og eksporten 1930–1950* (Agriculture, the state and the export, 1930–1950). With an English summary. Diss. Esbjerg: Sydjysk Universitetsforlag.

Just, F. (forthcoming) 'Danish agriculture and the EC affiliation 1950–72', in B. Nüchel Thomsen (ed.) *Denmark and the European Integration 1950–1992*. Copenhagen.

Just, F. *et al.* (1984) *Samspillet mellem staten, landbrugsorganisationerne og landbrugs-kooperationen* (The interplay between the state and the agricultural and co-operative organisations). Esbjerg: Sydjysk Universitetsforlag.

Keeler, J. T. S. (1981) 'Corporatism and official union hegemony: the case of French agricultural syndicalism', in S. Berger *op. cit.*

King, R. (1985) 'Corporatism and the local economy', in W. Grant (ed.) *op. cit.*, 202–28.

Lehmbruch, G. (1979) 'Liberal corporatism and party government', in P. Schmitter and G. Lehmbruch *op. cit.*, 147–83.

Lehmbruch, G. and Schmitter, P. C. (eds) (1982) *Patterns of Corporatist Policy Making*. London: Sage.

Micheletti, M. (1990) *The Swedish Farmers' Movement and Government Agricultural Policy*. New York: Praeger.

Omholt, K. (1984) 'Samspillet mellom landbrukets organisasjoner og den norske stat fram til 1980' (The interplay between agriculture and the Norwegian state until 1980) in F. Just *et al. op. cit.*, 82–118.

O'Sullivan, N. (1988) 'The political theory of neo-corporatism', in A. Cox and N. O'Sullivan *op. cit.*, 3–26.

Pahl, R. E. and Winkler, J. T. (1976) 'Corporatism in Britain', in Pahl and Winkler (eds) *The Corporate State – Myth or Reality?* London.

Panitch, L. (1979) 'The development of corporatism in liberal democracies', in P. Schmitter and G. Lehmbruch *op. cit.*, 119–46.

Pestoff, V. A. (1992) 'Third sector and co-operative services. An alternative to privatization', *Journal of Consumer Policy*, 15, 21–45.

Rothstein, B. (1987) 'Corporatism and reformism: The social democratic institutionalization of class conflict', *Acta Sociologica*, 30(3/4).

Rothstein, B. (1992) Den korporative staten. Intresseorganisationer och statsförvaltning i svensk politik (The corporate state. Interest organisations and state administration in Swedish policy). Stockholm.

Schmitter, P. C. (1974) 'Still the century of corporatism?', *The Review of Politics*, 36, 85–131. Also in P. C. Schmitter and G. Lehmbruch *op. cit.*, 7–52.

Schmitter, P. C. (1979) 'Modes of interest intermediation and models of societal change in Western Europe', in P. C. Schmitter and G. Lehmbruch *op. cit.*, 63–94.

Schmitter, P. C. (1982) 'Reflections on where the theory of neo-corporatism has gone and where the praxis of neo-corporatism may be going', in G. Lehmbruch and P. C. Schmitter *op. cit.*

Schmitter, P. C. and Lehmbruch, G. (eds) (1979) *Trends Towards Corporatist Intermediation*. New York and London: Sage Publications.

Smith, M. J. (1989) 'The annual review: The emergence of a corporatist institution?', *Political Studies*, 37, 81–96.

Steen, A. (1985) 'The farmers, the state and the social democrats', *Scandinavian Political Studies*, 8(1–2), 45–63.

Streeck, W. and Schmitter, P. C. (1985) 'Community, market, state – and associations. The prospective contribution of interest governance to social order', in W. Streeck and P. C. Schmitter (eds) *Private Interest Government. Beyond Market and State*, 1–29. London: Sage publications.

Therborn, G. (1988) 'Den svenska socialdemokratin träder fram' (The emergence of the Swedish Social Democratic Party). *Arkiv för studier i arbetarrörelsens historia* (27–8) 3–71.

Tracy, M. (1989) *Government and Agriculture in Western Europe*, third edition. New York: Harvester Wheatsheaf.

Vatn, A. (1984) *Teknologi og politikk* (Technology and politics). Oslo: Landbruksforlaget.

Vatn, A. (1990) 'Melk og makt' (Milk and power) in E. Hovland *et al. Det som svarte sig best*. Oslo, 143–55.

de Vroom, B. (1987) 'The food industry and quality regulation', in W. Grant (ed.) *Business Interests, Organizational Development and Private Interest Government. An International Comparative Study of the Food Processing Industry*. Berlin: Walter de Gruyter.

Wilson, F. L. (1983) 'Interest groups and politics in Western Europe. The neo-corporatist approach', *Comparative Politics*, October, 105–23.

CHAPTER 3

Challenging the Productivist Paradigm: Organic Farming and the Politics of Agricultural Change

Tracey Clunies-Ross and Graham Cox

Introduction

An actor's move to the centre of the stage all too easily creates the illusion that the wait in the wings has been of only a brief duration. Nowhere would that illusion be more marked than in the case of organic farming. Now enjoying the glare of the spotlight it was, for a very substantial period, not even inside the theatre building. With not even the beginnings of a voice in the processes of agricultural policy-making, its status was that of a quirky fringe activity: marginalised to the point of almost total disregard.

Recent developments have, therefore, seemed particularly dramatic. The 1991 edition of *Farm Incomes in the United Kingdom* includes reference to responses from farms with a total of some 14,000 hectares of organic crops in 1989, with a further 4,100 hectares in the process of transition. In July 1992 an EC Regulation governing organic food production and processing came into force and, in the wake of the agreed CAP reforms, MAFF was developing plans to introduce payments for organic farmers under the agri-environment programme. In 1979, by comparison, Barry Wookey a prominent farmer in the process of converting his 660 ha. farm to an organic system had no success with his persistent attempts to interest the Ministry of Agriculture, Fisheries and Food (MAFF) in investigating the problems and possibilities associated with organic farming (Wookey, 1987: 147). In terms of scale of activity, forms of organisation and regulatory strategy the 1980s has been marked by very significant shifts.

This chapter, which seeks to account for those shifts, will argue that the changing status of the organic case can best be understood in terms of the progressive demise of the productivist paradigm which has dominated agricultural policy in the post-war period. Certainly the increase in the effectiveness with which organic ideas have been put has been marked: but the content of those ideas has changed little since the 1930s and 1940s when they were first articulated. It is the altered context of their presentation which has been critical to their present positive reception. So the account needs to focus as much upon the way in which domain assumptions have been called into question as upon any internal reconstitution of what can only loosely be called the organic movement. The process by which organic ideas have come to acquire credibility has, indeed, entailed a movement away from purist positions towards more pragmatic stances. None the less, the implications of organic ideas are so at odds with the presuppositions of conventional agriculture that relations between the two are bound to remain uneasy.

Towards a framework

Three conceptual elements are helpful in understanding the history of the organic farming case, drawn from the literatures on power, pressure groups and policy communities, and the sociology of science. It would be all too easy to present past disregard of the organic case and the virtually total denial of the resources which might have improved its knowledge base in conspiratorial terms. Such an emphasis would be misplaced however. Whilst instances of what Bachrach and Baratz (1970) termed non-decision-making have been evident, it is the more general mobilisation of bias within the system which has been of greater significance. Bias can, in Lukes's words, 'be mobilised, recreated and reinforced in ways that are neither consciously chosen nor the intended result of particular individuals choices' (1974: 21).

Lukes's conceptualisation of what he terms the third face of power, however, sets up an unfortunate opposition between agency and structure. Giddens (1979: 49–95) avoids this dichotomous approach while also moving away from the idea of power being rooted in individual or group action. For him action is a continuous process and, through what he terms the duality of structure, the most trivial of actions can be understood as reinforcing structure. The structure of a social system is produced and reproduced through the application of 'generative rules and resources'. Such underlying rules within a social system can be followed without actors necessarily being able to express them, although they may on occasion also be the subject of dispute. Resources, as structural properties of social systems are the 'bases' of power which are drawn upon as parties interact.

The struggle between advocates of organic methods and the agents of conventional agriculture did not take place in a vacuum. The conflict related to wider social issues: but for the most part these were kept stringently compartmentalised. As Giddens emphasises, unintended consequences of action feed back into the conditions of action. For this reason, among others, the outcomes of struggles cannot be predetermined solely by analysing the sides involved in the struggle. There is no 'game plan' which unfolds in a predictable way. Indeed, the means of action available to agents depend on conditions outside their control and that observation applies with particular force to the advocates of organic methods.

In the post-war period the overwhelming priorities were for yields in agriculture to be increased and prices to be brought down. These factors encouraged the development of a particular kind of agriculture so that in quite subtle ways the rules and resources of society militated against the organic option. Thus, although exercises of power have not been absent - for instance, advocates of organic methods have been denied the funds to pursue effective research - of far greater significance has been the overwhelming prominence of presuppositions which have, as it were, denied the organic option any space within which it could be articulated.

The agricultural policy community, in the post-war period, has been a conspicuously closed one. Indeed, the relationship between the ministry and the sector's peak organisations has been, by common consent, strongly corporatist in character (Cox *et al.*, 1986a). In contrast to a large and diverse constituency for rural conservation the agricultural policy community has until very recently had only three main participants: MAFF, the NFU and the CLA (Cox *et al.*, 1986b). A difficulty which compromised the presentation of the organic case during the past decade was the failure of its leading advocates to orient themselves clearly towards one or the other community - a failure that can be considered both a consequence of political inexperience and a cause of rejection. In the terminology provided by Giddens it could be said that the process of reflexive monitoring was taking place with a disabling understanding of the situation. The unintended consequences of such myopia in turn had a detrimental effect on the conditions of action available to the organic 'movement'. Its attempts to gain influence in both policy communities, either simultaneously or consecutively, prejudiced its chances of progress by making each community wary.

The recent sociology of science furnishes insights which can help us understand the nature of the difficulties that organic advocates faced until very recently. Thomas Kuhn's concept of a 'paradigm' is of clear relevance here (1970), encapsulating, as it does, the insight that scientists working in a given area will share an approach to their subject that leads them to interpret evidence in a particular way. The ordering of concepts and their attendant research exemplars is, for most of the time, a strong one; the more a new theory threatens the fundamentals of a prevailing world view the less likely it is to be readily accepted (Collins, 1985). Particularly in its pure form the organic case has fundamental implications not only for farming practice, but also for research, food processing, marketing and retailing as well as human health care. Serious consideration of its claims would have threatened to prise open the conceptual world of scientists and policy-makers associated with the conventional productivist paradigm.

The nature of the links between systems of belief and practice has been particularly strong in the case of both organic and conventional production. So, not only is it appropriate to apply the term paradigm to them, but it can also be justifiably suggested that they were characterised by – to use another of Kuhn's terms – an incommensurability which almost foreclosed any prospect of mutually enlightening communication. Indeed, they could be said to have existed in 'parallel worlds'. Collins, in discussing the relationship – or, rather, the absence of one – between physics and parapsychology draws attention to the institutional counterparts of the cognitive divide separating the two activities (Collins and Pinch, 1982). The communities relay their ideas through different journals and other media and rarely compete directly for funding. There is, as he graphically puts it, a fundamental division of 'life, literature and lucre'.

A similar divide has existed between conventional and organic ideas, but the parallel worlds have begun to interact. Although it is still the case that its products are overwhelmingly valued in negative terms – for the absence of chemical residues, for instance – the enhanced credibility enjoyed by the organic case is arguably as precise an indicator of the progressive demise of the productivist paradigm as might be found.

Presenting the organic case

Amongst the current leaders of the organic movement who have adopted a more pragmatic approach there has been a general tendency to present the challenge of their predecessors to conventional methods as weak and ineffective. Certainly it had virtually no impact on policy-makers, farmers or consumers: but the arguments presented were coherent and were articulated in many instances by people with impeccable scientific credentials. When the first generation of 'organic writers' set down their views in the 1930s and 1940s the use of pesticides was not an issue. The dominant theme was the 'humus versus chemicals' controversy and the wider implications for man and society of the abandonment of traditional farming practices. Most argued not only about the details of using artificial fertilisers, but, taking this as an example, about the breakdown of health and society.

Albert Howard has been cast in the role of 'founding father' of the British organic movement. He was a scientist who became disillusioned with the traditional approach to research and sought, instead, to break down barriers between laboratory workers and those actually working the land. His work in a new kind of research station which began in India in 1924 did not find favour with his fellow scientists, however, and after his retirement he increasingly concentrated his efforts on a popular audience. His *Agricultural Testament* published in 1940 and his *Soil and Health* which appeared in 1947 both warned of the consequences of soil destruction and called for agricultural reform.

Pivotal to any account also are the work and ideas of Lady Eve Balfour whose book *The Living Soil* was published in 1943. It sought to establish the scientific evidence for the superiority of organic over chemical methods and led to the formation of the Soil Association in 1946. In drawing extensively on the experiments of, among others, Howard, McCarrison and Rayner she argued that the health of the soil, good farming practice, and health in humans and animals were inextricably linked. Like Howard, McCarrison worked in India where he was Director of Nutrition Research. His experiments with rats showed the close links between diet and health and Howard's work too focused on disease resistance arguing, in relation to soil, that it could not be achieved by the use of artificial fertilisers but only by the application of scientifically manufactured humus composed of both vegetable and animal waste products. Rayner was a scientist working on Forestry Commission land at Wareham Forest who showed the complex way in which compost acted indirectly by stimulating the activity of soil fungi which, in turn, enhanced the root and shoot development and disease resistance of tree seedlings.

It was not so much the work that Balfour drew upon, however, that deviated from mainstream views but the conclusions to which she came. By collecting evidence from many different fields of inquiry she was able, whilst having the highest regard for scientific methods, to develop a powerful holistic approach linking the soil and its fertility to questions of animal and human health. In her book Balfour proposed that a test be undertaken to resolve the compost versus chemical debate. Indeed, she was already involved in setting up just such an experiment on 200 acres at Haughley in Essex. The Soil Association ran the experiment from 1947 until 1969 when a new generation with a majority on its Council decided to pursue applied work on organic techniques rather than continue with basic research.

The experiment was always strapped for cash and it is tempting to account for the failure to attract the support of grant-giving bodies by supposing that some of those involved were too emotionally committed to achieving particular results (Payne, 1971). Close inspection of the evidence suggests otherwise. The independent scientists and agricultural consultants involved with the project were eminent in their fields, and the experiment was never criticised by those outside the movement on grounds of experimental technique (Clunies-Ross, 1990: 157).

The persistent difficulties experienced are better understood in terms of developments within the conventional sphere. The legacy of the Second World War and the resulting 1947 Agriculture Act gave fresh impetus to the intensification process with its increased reliance on chemicals for fertiliser and crop protection. During the life of the experiment those advocating organic methods found themselves transformed from a group thinking that its preferred methods were likely to be proved superior to one whose claims were summarily dismissed, if not subjected to ridicule.

Whereas the earlier period had been characterised by genuine debate communication was now foreclosed. Significantly there are no written explanations by conventional agriculturalists indicating why the Haughley Experiment came to be seen as having no value. It would seem that no one felt any obligation to offer a justification for their disregard. Later studies of a similarly controlled kind both here and in other countries suggest that the work was neither irrelevant nor ill-conceived. The absence of serious debate was instead due to the overwhelming prominence of the presuppositions which dominated the conventional approach. The use of chemicals in agriculture was seen as both necessary and progressive by farmers, research scientists and policy-makers alike.

Even intense concern over the use of pesticides in the late 1950s and early 1960s did not prompt serious consideration of the organic case and, finding itself progressively more marginalised, the organic movement increasingly turned in upon itself. By the time the Haughley Experiment ended there was not even any great emphasis on publishing the data which had been generated. The advocates of organic methods and those adopting conventional techniques came to occupy utterly distinct worlds. Whereas the former identified problems of exhausted soils, deteriorating food quality and declining health and suggested naturally sustainable systems through the use of rotations and recycling of nutrients, the latter emphasised the need to increase production and, in order to accomplish that, ways had to be found of growing continuous food crops and controlling pests, weeds and diseases.

The gaping cognitive divide had its counterparts in equally stark distinctions in the matters of fund raising and literature. The Soil Association, the Henry Doubleday Research Association and the Bio-Dynamical Agricultural Association all produced their own journals and their efforts to attract funding saw them reliant on minimal sources utterly distinct from those which drove the productivist priorities of the conventional approach. Indeed, so straightened were the financial circumstances of the Soil Association that it was forced to sell the Haughley Experiment assets.

Those who formed and led the organic movement from the 1940s onwards included the famous, the rich, eminent scientists and agriculturalists, doctors and professors, all concerned about the relevance of their ideas for the reconstruction of society and other wide-ranging holistic concepts. By the

1970s the majority of them had retired or passed away and the new leaders and supporters of the movement were as different as the priorities they sought to establish. The shifts of position which have taken place within the organic movement in the more recent period can only be adequately understood in terms of the progressively more pronounced recognition of the anomalies which have come to characterise the conventional sphere and it is to a brief indication of these that we now turn.

Anomalies within the conventional sphere

A number of concerns have become prominent in the 1970s and 1980s and taken together they constitute the sort of accumulation of anomalies which, in the Kuhnian sense, creates the potential for paradigm change. The pesticide controversy of the 1960s stimulated concern about the environment and prompted the recognition that new scientific methods might have unintended and unwelcome consequences. Rachel Carson, whose book *Silent Spring* did so much to precipitate concern, refused to link her fears about pesticides with the organic movement's call for an end to the use of all agricultural chemicals and the issue did little directly to benefit the organic cause. But since the 1960s other issues have emerged to challenge the wisdom of conventional agricultural policy and together they have created an opening for the organic case.

The rapid rise in oil prices in 1973 and again in 1975 as a result of the actions of the Organisation of Petroleum Exporting Countries cartel generated a fear that dependence upon fossil fuels would have to be radically reduced. Although interest in alternative forms of energy production grew in the mid 1970s, there was little evidence within the agricultural sphere of any major reassessment of methods. But the period did witness rapid growth in the number of small organic farms and holdings and many of the new entrants were influenced by the energy crisis and were concerned to develop sustainable systems. The issue contributed to the emergence of a sense of unease which other controversies sharpened dramatically.

Most prominent among them was the increasing concern about the deleterious impact of modern farming methods on the diversity of the countryside. Clashes between the agricultural lobby and conservationists which had centred on particular cases during the 1970s preceded the emergence of a sustained critique of the whole system of agricultural support and its priorities. Galvanised by their experiences during the passage of the 1981 Wildlife and Countryside Act conservation groups began to act with a greater degree of coordination and effectiveness (Lowe *et al.*, 1986). As the decade progressed discussion of the problems posed for environmental conservation by the continuance of agricultural practices designed to maximise production with little regard for other concerns became a constant theme, focusing not only on questions such as soil erosion and the destruction of the countryside, but also on the great dependence upon chemical fertilisers, pesticides, hormones and antibiotics (Shoard, 1980; Body, 1982, 1987; Bowers and Cheshire, 1983; Pye-Smith and North, 1984; Goldsmith and Hildyard, 1986).

In the late 1980s moreover, concern about the impact of agriculture on the environment took on a further complexion as the issue of nitrate levels in water supplies became prominent. In 1989, after increased pressure from the European Community whose Directive banning nitrate levels higher than 50 milligrammes per litre had not been effectively acted upon, MAFF drew up proposals for Nitrate Sensitive Areas involving restriction on the use of artificial nitrogen fertilisers and other farming practices.

Issues relating to food quality re-emerged in the 1980s. This area had always been important for advocates of organic methods. But whereas Lady Eve Balfour had been concerned with the intrinsic quality of food in general the issues which have become prominent recently have centred on the connections between ill health and the balance of different types of foodstuff as well as on the chemical residues found in food as an accidental by-product of modern production methods. But concern has also arisen regarding the ways in which scientists are attempting to develop new products to boost production or enhance the keeping qualities of food. Two examples which have met with considerable consumer resistance are the genetically engineered hormone BST (Bovine Somatotrophin) and irradiation which can produce physical, chemical and biological changes in food.

General concern about methods of food production was further exacerbated by a number of problems which seemed to link animal and human health with particular clarity, including the prevalence of salmonella in egg production; fears about listeria in cheese and cook chill foods; and the emergence of Bovine Spongiform Encephalopathy, a disease apparently spread to cattle from sheep through commercially produced concentrated food rations containing parts of dead animals. Although the Ministry and commercial food producers sought to allay public fears, widespread concern about food contamination was reflected in increased demand for organic food.

Whereas the issues of food quality and safety have been highly prominent as particular problems have become apparent, the problem of surplus food production has been at the centre of critiques of the food production system throughout the 1980s. Previously, during the 1970s, there was a pre-occupation with the need to increase yields – both as part of a drive towards self-sufficiency and as a response to world food shortages. The introduction of milk quotas in April 1984 signalled a fundamental shift of policy priorities, and subsequent policy changes, such as set-aside and price reductions have further emphasised the need to reduce production. But despite the parallel desire to achieve a better balance between production and conservation aims, payments for reducing the intensity of production, as opposed to limiting the area under production, have been restricted to schemes such as Environmentally Sensitive Areas and Nitrate Sensitive Areas in parts of the country seen to be marginal or particularly vulnerable. Notwithstanding this apparent reluctance on the part of policy-makers to acknowledge that organic or less-intensive farming could achieve surplus reduction, the production of surpluses and associated costs, were clearly established as the main reasons for the recent round of CAP reforms.

Taken together these concerns about the use of pesticides and fossil fuels, food quality and health, anxiety about the impact of modern agricultural practices on the environment, and the moral and economic iniquity of persistent surplus production have contributed to a greatly enhanced context of presentation for organic ideas. Organic groups have increasingly found themselves in a situation where the effective presentation of their claims was at least possible. That qualification is important, because there is no sense in which the uptake of organic ideas was inevitable. Indeed, the examples of ESAs and set-aside indicate clearly enough that the process of giving serious consideration to organic options has been a relatively slow one.

There should be no surprise at that, because organic farming concepts challenge the assumptions and practices of the conventional system in a fundamental way. However, the anomalies which accumulated – particularly in recent years – did finally create a situation in which even farmers, farming organisations and policy-makers began searching for new solutions. The emergence of 'crisis' can, in that sense, be seen as a necessary condition for the serious consideration of the organic farming case. Much then depended on the effectiveness with which that case has been put.

Developments within the organic world

The processes of reorientation which increasingly characterised the world of conventional agriculture in the years between the late 1970s and the early 1990s had their counterparts within the organic sphere. Indeed, most of the changes which occurred within and between organic groups can be seen as related to a greater or lesser extent to the changing opportunities being presented to them. Almost wholly marginalised during the 1950s and 1960s as the precepts of the productivist paradigm acquired the status of absolute presuppositions they now found themselves confronting a realistic possibility of advancing their case. The question of how best to accomplish that inevitably brought to the fore issues which had been in the background at least since the formation of the Soil Association. The tensions between purist positions reflecting adherence to strict definitions and exclusive policies and more pragmatic stances which offered the possibility of drawing as many people as possible into the movement became marked.

The potential for such internal conflict was apparent in the study of organic farming conducted by Vine and Bateman in 1981. They identified six schools of thought underpinning interest in organic farming. This stark absence of any common ideology compromised, we would argue, the ability of the movement to respond in a clear way to the opportunities presented in the 1980s. Balfour had, herself, seen the problems over the Haughley Experiment in the 1960s as indicative of a division within the Soil Association between commitments to basic and more applied research. The increasing prominence of the latter emphasis indicated a recognition by many within the movement that the very existence of conventional farming could no longer be effectively challenged and that attention should instead be directed towards the possibilities for organic farmers to farm profitably within their own terms.

Balfour was inclined to see the conflicts as generational and it is, indeed, the case that during the 1970s a new group of enthusiasts sought to become involved with practical organic production and then to seek representation within existing groups. But such descriptive categories do little to increase our understanding of the shifts that took place. Differences in age prove to be less significant than differences in outlook. It is worth noting, however, that the leaders of the 1980s, in contrast to the earlier period, did not include professionals from other spheres taking an interest in organic matters; rather they were people who were above all committed practically to organic ideals.

Until 1975 three groups represented the organic movement in Britain; whereas the Soil Association was concerned with farming, the Henry Doubleday Research Association with gardening, the Bio-Dynamic Agricultural Association represented a separate tradition within the movement based on the teachings of the German philosopher, Rudolf Steiner. In 1975 Organic Farmers and Growers became the first of a number of new groups to emerge and although initially set up with the approval of the Soil Association it soon accentuated the purity/pragmatism division within the movement. Set up as a cooperative its aims were to encourage organic producers to grow commercial crops and market them effectively. David Stickland, its director, was also instrumental in founding the International Institute of Biological Husbandry (IIBH) and both organisations worked to rid organic farming of its 'muck and mystery' image by establishing a scientific basis for it.

By the early 1980s two more groups representing producer interests had been formed, the Organic Growers Association and British Organic Farmers, and they began to form a sub-group within the Soil Association, in opposition to Organic Farmers and Growers. Conflict emerged in 1983 and 1984 over the promotion by Organic Farmers and Growers of a second grade of produce. Whereas its existing first grade was very similar to the 'Soil Association Symbol' Grade, the new one was to be of a less rigorous standard intended to help farmers make the transition to organic production. The Soil Association objected to the term Biological in its title and in 1984 Stickland, who had put together a promotional package with the supermarket chain Fine Fare, announced that it would henceforth be known as Conservation Grade. Conflict persisted however. The approach of Organic Farmers and Growers which implied that chemical farming and organic farming could be integrated at the level of the farm, broke with the holistic stance of the organic movement. Such a stance sees organic farming as a positive package, with benefits for the soil, the environment and food quality, whereas the alternative is a more negative view of organic produce as 'free from artificial contaminants'. The introduction of new grades thus at once encapsulated issues of both ideology and control.

Formed before the British market developed Organic Farmers and Growers had concentrated on export markets while the Soil Association forged links with supermarket chains including Safeway and Sainsbury. Although until recently there has been little direct competition, rivalry over influence within the movement has always been marked. Attempts to produce a united front were short lived and antagonisms persisted during the negotiations over the United Kingdom Register of Organic Food Standards (UKROFS) which were much taken up with the problems posed by there being two sets of standards in Britain. A single set of standards might have been readily accepted by government, but the inability of the two sides to resolve their conflict opened the possibility of significant power to control developments passing out of the hands of the organic movement.

Conflicts within the Soil Association, meanwhile, attended the process of shaking off its old image and seeking to transform it into a more radical pressure group. The new members who had worked their way on to Council pushed through significant changes in image both for the organisation and for the Soil Association Quarterly Review. Whilst the holistic approach to organic production was never directly challenged, the presentation of arguments gave far greater emphasis to the need for practical developments. Attempts to reverse such changes through AGM resolutions became a constant feature of the Association's internal politics throughout the mid 1980s as it developed a much higher media and political profile.

Some members and regional groups also expressed their disquiet about the increasingly close links between the Soil Association and the two producer groups it had spawned, the Organic Growers Association and British Organic Farmers, lest the interests of producers be allowed to override the fundamental principles on which the Soil Association was founded. Issues related to the marketing of organic produce highlighted such concerns. Retailing through multiples entails significant compromises of the ideal of using decentralised systems for processing, distributing and marketing of products. It also involves considerable wastage in terms of produce which does not make the grade, and fails to tackle packaging and transport issues.

The concern to maintain purity and the drive to develop a more pragmatic approach are clearly, at one level, manifestations of the desire to retain power over developments within the movement. With their emphasis on production and marketing the producer side of the movement is encouraging organic farming to be seen as an agricultural production option whereas for many non-producers this is far too narrow a perspective. Such conflicts have, of course, had an impact on the effectiveness of the movement as a pressure group.

The lack of unity within the movement has been accompanied by the absence of a coherent strategy towards outside groups, towards lobbying and even towards MAFF itself. This has been despite the keen awareness by the new leadership of the need to engage in politics and of their own pressure group status. In practice conflicts between individuals, the committee style of decision-making and the large numbers of people involved in deciding on policy direction led to a movement with strong principles but few policies. The choice, which has always been there, of seeking alignments with groups within the environmental policy community or within the agricultural policy community has never been clearly confronted. Despite a minimal involvement in the environmental policy community of the 1970s, the Soil Association was still isolated in its beliefs during the early 1980s and its attempts to begin to put pressure on those in power and to act in concert with others were sporadic and unsustained.

In the 1980s three distinct phases can be discerned as the organic movement tried to ally itself first with the agricultural policy community, then with the environmental policy community, and then moved back towards the agricultural sphere again. The first of these phases was an almost inevitable consequence of the increasing dominance of organic groups by producers, who thought that growth of the organic sector could only be accomplished by persuading producers to convert to organic methods. Although the potential for cooperation with environmental groups was recognised, almost all discussion with environmental groups were viewed by the organic movement as opportunities to educate the environmental groups into seeing organic farming as in their best interests. Strongly critical of the 'cosmetic' emphasis of much conservation activity they were disinclined to accept that any of their own attitudes or practices might need to be modified.

Gradually, however, the situation began to change and in December 1987 the SA initiated a meeting with representatives of major conservation organisations to discuss common ground and examine ways in which they could work together. Further meetings the following year saw genuine dialogue result in modifications to the SA's conservation guidelines to avoid the possibility of farmers ploughing ancient or species-rich meadows in order to gain an easy entry into organic farming. A conference in September 1988 saw Jonathan Porritt from Friends of the Earth putting forward the idea of an organic alliance, a clear indication of changing relations between the organic and environmental movements.

Despite the appearance of cooperative activity, the strength of feeling about maintaining the integrity of the organic message, together with the lack of any tradition of cooperation within the movement, meant that there was little fundamental change. Although critical of the methods employed by conventional farmers, the organic movement also condemned the Royal Society for the Protection of Birds for supporting measures such as set-aside which might encourage the intensification of non set-aside land. Indeed, throughout the 1980s the organic movement remained almost uniquely isolated. Those with decision-making power within the movement had no experience of working for other pressure groups, those outside the movement rarely wrote articles for organic publications and those within the movement rarely published in other places. Neither did the movement have any significant success in attracting outside funding.

By the end of the 1980s there was a reorientation back towards the agricultural policy community, where the attainment of insider status seemed at last to be an achievable goal. During the 1990s good contacts were established with certain policy-makers within MAFF, and support for the organic option began to materialise. The formation of the SAFE (Sustainable Agriculture Food and Environment) alliance, which brought together small farmer groups, animal welfare organisations, environmentalists and Third World campaigners, as well as consumer and organic groups, provided a new framework within which the organic movement could operate. Although SAFE has yet to have a major lobbying and media impact it has proved significant for the organic movement by encouraging real cooperation between groups operating in very different policy communities.

Until the 1990s the organic movement did not find it easy to engage in effective pressure group activity. Indeed, whilst it is true that the subject has been accorded considerable attention by the media and has attracted the interest of the public and environmental and agricultural groups, it cannot be said that such attention has been the consequence of adept presentation of the organic case by the movement itself.

Great pressure is being placed on the agricultural policy community to look beyond its traditional boundaries to adapt and survive. But the impulse is more obviously occasioned by the build up of anomalies within the system than by any other factor. Developments within the conventional sphere have provided the organic movement with unprecedented scope for presenting its case, but that presentation has been neither as coherent nor as sustained as it might have been. Nevertheless, the parallel worlds have moved closer together and we now turn to consider the often subtle shifts that have constituted that uneven movement.

Processes of adjustment

The rules that constitute the conventional and organic worlds are in many respects incompatible, so the process of adjustment is never readily accomplished. Dominant leaders of the organic movement have thought its best interests would be served by taking an active part in the agricultural policy community. The desire to be taken seriously as a mainstream farming group has led to a drive for respectability and the rejection of any 'alternative' image. The tension between the need to achieve credibility while articulating a revolutionary standpoint has often been evident. Commercial success has often involved difficult compromises, not least in matters relating to marketing. Indeed, economic pressures have led many organic producers to come to accept aspects of the conventional system which had traditionally been eschewed.

MAFF, for its part, has been put under pressure to consider the role of organic farming. As early as 1985 the prospect of a draft EC directive on organic farming was being discussed. Political expediency and financial stringency have, in any case, dictated that lower input systems of agriculture can be taken seriously as the environmental critique of conventional systems has become more pressing. It is difficult, though, for the agricultural policy community to acknowledge a legitimate place for organic farming without conceding that there is anything inherently wrong with conventional practices and produce.

Given the premiums associated with organic produce there has been a tendency to categorise it as supplying a niche market: an option for the rich and those overly anxious about food quality issues. The impulse to accord organics only a marginal status is easily understood. Farmers and policy-makers are attracted to the organic option because of expanding markets and its positive image, but they have been reluctant wholeheartedly to embrace an option which is critical of existing agricultural practices and which might enhance the demands of environmentalists for greater controls over agriculture. Changes have, therefore, been both gradual and piecemeal.

Commercial success has, however, been critical. It is not easy to generalise about organic food since there are distinctions between different sectors. In Britain in the early 1980s a demand existed for organic cereals and fresh fruit and vegetables, but it was much less apparent for organic meat and dairy products. Early marketing initiatives concentrated on the former, therefore, and the need to have a wholesaler and distributor specialising in organic produce led to the formation of Organic Farm Foods in 1983. Its growth, the development of organic packhouses and the formation of a number of co-operatives together provided a marketing network which encouraged and enabled organic producers to become more professional while providing a reliable supply of organic food on which supermarkets and wholesalers could depend.

The involvement of multiple retailers has been vital to the progress of the movement. The market for fresh organic produce would have become saturated without it. The involvement, moreover, has made the multiples 'allies' and they have strengthened the negotiating position of organic groups by accepting that produce must be grown and processed within the standards laid down by the Soil Association.

Responding similarly to pressure of demand, organisations involved in education and training have become involved in the organic sector. Neither they nor the multiples can be considered, in network terms, to be as close to the centre of the 'web' as policy-makers and chemical companies, for instance, but their response to the demand from producers and students for practical training has done much to enhance the credibility of the organic case. Before the mid 1980s there were few ways of obtaining a formal training in organic methods and there was no government funding for students. But in 1984 Writtle Agricultural College in Essex began to take an interest and towards the end of 1986 Worcestershire College of Agriculture announced the establishment of a three-part block-release organic course. Even more significantly the Royal Agricultural College at Cirencester became involved in organic research, promising not only some answers to technical questions being asked, but constituting a breakthrough for the image of the organic movement in Britain.

Subsequent development further extended training possibilities and, significantly, agricultural and horticultural colleges, universities and the Agricultural Training Board (ATB) accepted the ascendancy of the Soil Association as a regulatory body for organic training. The position of British Organic Farmers and the Organic Growers Association within the agricultural community was similarly helped by the ATB's decision to link training with their regional groups. By retaining control over the direction of developments in organic training and the content, of course, the organic groups avoided the possibility of the development of parallel systems.

Closer to the centre of the 'web', the National Farmers' Union has inevitably been cautious. But their attitude showed a marked change during the 1980s as it became clear that organic farming had to be taken seriously as an agricultural option. In 1985 organic leaders had talks with NFU officials about organic standards and the need for research into conversion. But shortly after, the decision to ban the sale of unpasteurised milk was taken and they were disenchanted by the NFU's tacit support for the measure and no further attempts to negotiate were made. In 1986 relations between the organic and conventional lobbies became more strained as official investigations into the problem of nitrates in water began with the NFU deciding against any support for the idea of nitrogen rationing.

By the end of 1987, however, leaders of the NFU and CLA were actively supporting plans for less intensive farming and an amendment to the Farm Land and Rural Development Bill was sought which would pay farmers to convert to a range of options, including less intensive cereal or livestock farming and organic production. This typified the position taken by both the NFU and MAFF in the late 1980s. The place of organic farming in the future of agriculture was to be as a response to the need to reduce production. Cast in such a role it could be treated as a non-threatening option with the arguments about connections between farming methods, food quality and human health effectively marginalised. In 1989 the NFU President agreed to write a preface for a Handbook being prepared by British Organic Farmers and the Organic Farmers Association which was aimed at conventional farmers and which gained most of its publicity and credibility from that association and from its sponsorship by Barclays Bank. The price to be paid for increased influence in the agricultural policy community is, however, the persistent presentation of organic farming as an extensification option.

If the NFU's position was only cautiously developed, the response of MAFF and its Agricultural Development and Advisory Service (ADAS) was even more measured with token gestures as evident as serious consideration. A couple of small-scale monitoring projects conveyed the impression of 'being seen to be doing something'. Certainly, by comparison with other countries little practical work was carried out and the promotional and experimental resources directed towards ESAs, set-aside and farm diversification were massive by comparison. At the practical level within ADAS a significant change of attitude did take place, particularly after the mid 1980s. Conferences were organised with ADAS officers taking an active interest and, in 1988, the announcement of the appointment of an organic co-ordinator within ADAS indicated that the relationship between the organic and conventional worlds had become much closer.

The involvement of MAFF in practical projects, and the role of ADAS in general, is somewhat different from MAFF's role as policy-maker. Having assiduously promoted the intensification of agriculture the Ministry did not find it easy to embrace the organic option. Indeed, over the last decade it can be seen as having moved from a position where its own inaction militated against the uptake of organic farming to a position where it has conceded a minor role for the option. The change has been slow: articulated through a series of conflicts which have entailed moderate shifts of position. The struggle between the two sides has centred on views of what action it would be appropriate for MAFF to take given the demand of the organic movement that it actively encourage organic production.

The inaction in the early 1980s often took the form of MAFF asking for a list of priorities after discussions with leaders of the organic movement which, when produced, would elicit no response. In 1984 the movement's leaders participated in a number of media events, thus raising their profile as a pressure group. Then, in the July of that year, the House of Lords Select Committee on Agricultural and Environmental Research was severely critical of what it saw as an artificial and bureaucratic separation of agricultural and environmental policy-making. The organic movement welcomed the observation and were encouraged by an announcement later that year by the Minister of State for Agriculture that an investigation into the research needs of organic agriculture would be carried out. Again, priorities were set out but no action ensued.

Statements by the new Director General of ADAS and Chief Scientific Adviser to MAFF during 1985 encouraged the view that the battle for state funding was being won, but again the optimism proved short lived. By the end of the year bitterness at the lack of progress was evident in the *Soil Association Review* editorial and shortly afterwards the withdrawal of co-operation was called for since it was felt that the Ministry was pursuing only ad hoc pieces of research unlikely to benefit the movement. The desire to involve MAFF has, in any case, always been tempered by a concern that the movement would thereby become powerless to direct developments.

A 1986 report by two ADAS advisers drew attention to longstanding state support for research on organic agriculture in Germany and Holland. But no intention to act on the report's recommendations was indicated. However, following a government reshuffle one of the junior ministers announced that he had been asked to assume responsibility for organic matters in general. Discussion described as productive by organic leaders followed but no plans for any form of funding or for an organic experimental husbandry farm emerged. Instead attention became focused from 1986 onwards on the question of organic standards.

Where the organic movement had found itself in direct opposition to the Ministry on such issues as milk pasteurisation, appropriate methods of warble fly treatment and the use of organo-phosphorous compounds in sheep dips, it was unable to press successfully its point of view. MAFF's stance created major problems for many organic farmers and, as such, was indicative of an insensitivity which still typified the whole machinery of agricultural policy-making. Its enforcement of rules relating to these issues simply prevented farmers from conforming to organic standards. On the matter of those standards themselves though, the organic movement was to be accorded a significant degree of influence.

The EC's proposal for a directive which might provide a unified control system in all member countries clearly necessitated some response and MAFF established an internal Organic Working Party to make recommendations regarding MAFF funding and involvement in organic standards. Given the presence of the rival standards of the Organic Farmers and Growers it was not thought appropriate merely to endorse the Soil Association standard and in July 1987 the Minister announced that Food From Britain, the national marketing body, would be setting up a United Kingdom Register of Organic Food Standards (UKROFS).

The organic movement was circumspect, fearing an attempt at regulating the burgeoning organic industry whilst providing no resource commitment for the development of genuine organic production. Moreover, their relations with Food From Britain were not easy since the Soil Association had, in 1983, led a campaign against its use of the 'Naturally British' slogan. The fear that a lowest common denominator principle would be used to set standards was very real, but a positive potential was no less apparent since effective standards would give more weight to organic certification schemes and do much to eliminate fraudulent trading. Moreover, a strong official British standard would be a bulwark against any dilution of standards by the EC and might, in addition, presage a policy of making conversion grants available.

A survey of their members by British Organic Farmers and the Organic Growers Association revealed an overwhelming determination for co-operation with UKROFS to be allied with firm resolution regarding certain key points. Indeed, 82 per cent of respondents wanted the Soil Association to retain control over the administration and inspection of standards. A series of consultative and advisory committee meetings showed most UKROFS board members in favour of setting high standards. But some contentious issues including inspection and policing, certification, promotion, and education were being deferred. The potential for conflict was thus considerable, but as negotiations proceeded it seemed clear that organic leaders had established a position of some strength. The Soil Association faction had secured a significant victory and stringent organic standards had, at least, been placed on the agricultural policy-making agenda.

It would be wrong to make too much of this policy-making episode. The issue would have had to be confronted at some point so the setting up of UKROFS, unaccompanied as it was by any resource commitment, could not be considered a fundamental shift of position by MAFF. But taken together with other developments, proceeding with varying pace at different levels, a considerable difference between the early and late 1980s was clearly discernible. Early interest in organic methods within conventional agricultural circles was largely of a top–down nature, evidenced most obviously by the sort of interest taken by the Prince of Wales. By the later years of the decade considerable 'ground-level' support for organic farming had developed and changes within ADAS in particular were apparent.

A clear indication of the changed status of the organic movement came with the process of negotiation over the details of the scheme for Nitrate Sensitive Areas (NSAs), intended to protect vulnerable water sources from nitrate leaching. The original MAFF proposals contained elements which would have made it difficult for organic farmers to operate within NSAs because, for instance, of a prohibition on clover. In a written response to the initial proposals, in June 1989, organic groups outlined their objections. What was significant, however, was their being invited to private discussions with key MAFF officials and the fact that the revised proposals showed that many of the aspects which had caused them concern had been changed. Within the 1980s organic farming had not only achieved the status of being on the agenda of agricultural policy-making, but organic groups had, in addition, come to be considered a relevant part of the now rapidly changing policy community.

Conclusions: the structure of explanation

The developments which have been reviewed together indicate clearly enough that during the 1980s the image and perceived role of organic farming in British society changed considerably. The disregard and disdain of policy-makers and conventional farmers which had been predominant in the early years of the decade was transformed as it became more obviously apparent that demand for organic food was not just a 'passing fad'. All major supermarkets indicated a desire to stock organic food. Premium prices for organic vegetables and grain were well established and during 1989 and 1990 Unigate pioneered the sale of organic milk whilst Safeway and Sainsbury began to investigate the organic meat market. Although 60 per cent of organic food sold in the UK was being imported, the development of co-operatives, packhouses and a distribution system meant that marketing problems for new entrants to organic farming were less daunting than they had been even in the 1980s.

The Minister of Agriculture's announcement in January 1990 that he intended to use the EC extensification scheme to provide help for farmers wanting to convert to organic methods showed a resolution at policy-making level that had for most of the decade been conspicuous only by its absence. The willingness to give serious consideration to the organic option had become apparent already in the education and training sectors and interest from conventional farmers was such that by the end of the decade 30–40 new applications a month were being received for the Soil Association Symbol. Whereas at the beginning of the decade organic farming was not considered a serious agricultural option, its closing years saw many with influence in policy-making circles keen to develop a British organic agricultural sector.

In seeking to account for such an evident change we find that many of the more obvious factors cannot furnish an adequate explanation. There is little justification for characterising the efforts of the first generation of organic enthusiasts as insufficiently rigorous. Neither can it be plausibly claimed that the organic case has been more scientifically or logically presented in recent years. If anything the reverse is true. Nevertheless, an increasingly receptive climate has enabled organic groups to build a case without providing any strong or novel supporting evidence. The serious regard accorded organic farming cannot be accounted for in terms of an enhanced internal coherence or force of argument. Indeed, there is remarkably little experimental evidence to show that organic food is better for human health or its methods of production better for wildlife and the environment.

For a plausible account it is to the structural context that we must look. A period of relatively open debate in the 1930s about the future of agriculture gave way in the post-war period to an overwhelming commitment to intensification which entailed a reliance on chemical methods of production. By the 1950s and early 1960s the dominance of the conventional approach was reinforced by the vested interest of chemical companies and there was literally no space within which the organic case could be effectively articulated.

Warnings about the dangers associated with the over-use of pesticides did not, on their own, provoke any crisis of confidence in the priorities of conventional agriculture. When allied to concern over rising oil prices, surpluses, damage to the environment and wildlife habitats, food quality, and animal welfare, however, just such a crisis came to be acknowledged both within policy circles and more widely.

But if such developments can be said to have generated a potential, the extent to which that was realised by the advocates of organic farming must be accounted for in other ways. As we have emphasised the organic movement has been internally diverse and the process of advocacy has always been contested. It is important to recognise that factors outside the narrow sphere of conflict have contributed to the shifting patterns of alliances that provide the key to understanding the process of change.

Of critical importance have been the 'allies' (Hindess, 1982) whose involvement has progressively enhanced the credibility of the organic case. It was when other bodies with influence and respectability began to talk and act as if organic farming was a realistic option that elements of the movement began to gain real influence. Supermarkets and education and training institutions that translated 'grass-roots' interest into real support and the pressure that this, in turn, put on ADAS to develop its organic services proved vital. A gradually enhanced credibility has been achieved irrespective of the factual content of the arguments advanced, the number of farmers using organic methods or, indeed, the skill with which the organic movement's leaders have articulated the case. Once started the process of acceptance has reinforced itself.

That reinforcement has been most apparent in the gradual attainment of a modified insider status in matters of policy-making. As media and public interest began to develop in the early 1980s organic leaders sought to engage MAFF in public debate of a confrontational nature so as to expose its indifference. Such open confrontation declined, however, as the movement was drawn into discussions relating to the development of UKROFS. As Richardson and Jordan (1979) have suggested, confrontation and campaigns are often the language of the unsuccessful. The Soil Association, however, has continued to campaign publicly over issues such as pesticide-free food and additive-free meat while becoming involved at an early stage in discussions with MAFF and the NFU over the future of organic farming.

Where groups are seeking to effect fundamental change, insider status is often of dubious value. Acceptance of such a status must, after all, involve some balance between significant change within the policy community and modification of the ideas being advanced. Such modification has, as we have seen, occurred within the organic movement in relation, for instance, to marketing and packaging issues. Significant change within the policy community is less apparent however. The resources being used to encourage the organic option are still minimal compared to those being channelled into research and development for conventional agriculture. Indeed, at the precise time that organic production was about to be encouraged through the mechanism of grants, two of the producer organisations, British Organic Farmers and the Organic Growers Association, were in such financial difficulty that they were having to cut back on their scale of activities.

But at a time when crisis is everywhere acknowledged a preparedness to be pragmatic does not nullify the sense in which the key tenets of even a modified organic case constitute a fundamental challenge to the foundations of the existing agricultural system. It is in that sense that the organic movement's developing links with conservation organisations and consumer groups and its growing influence within the agricultural policy community indicate shifts of the latter's hitherto rigid boundaries. Assailed from all sides the productivist paradigm is now in retreat and, though it has been perceived for the most part in negative terms, the organic option has been a vehicle for the articulation of that discontent. It cannot be said to have precipitated crisis, but it has certainly been a beneficiary of the processes by which anomalies have accumulated. Indeed it can be said to have accentuated their impact. But although it is not yet clear whether it will transcend niche market status its new position within a transformed agricultural policy community is itself a clear indication of fundamental change.

References

Bachrach, P. and Baratz, M. (1970) *Power and Poverty: Theory and Practice*. Oxford and New York: Oxford University Press.

Balfour, E. B. (1943) *The Living Soil*. London: Faber and Faber.

Body, R. (1982) *Agriculture: The Triumph and the Shame*. London: Maurice Temple Smith.

Body, R. (1987) *Red or Green for Farmers*. Saffron Walden: Broad Leys Publishing.

Bowers, J. and Cheshire, P. (1983) *Agriculture, the Countryside and Land Use*. London: Methuen.

Clunies-Ross, T. (1990) *Agricultural Change and the Politics of Organic Farming*, PhD Thesis, University of Bath.

Collins, H. M. (1985) *Changing Order*. London: Sage.

Collins, H. M. and Pinch, T. (1982) *Frames of Meaning: The Social Construction of Extraordinary Science*. London: Routledge and Kegan Paul.

Cox, G., Lowe, P. and Winter, M. (1986a) 'Agriculture and conservation in Britain: A policy community under siege' in G. Cox, P. Lowe and M. Winter (eds) *Agriculture: People and Policies*. London: Allen and Unwin.

Cox, G., Lowe, P. and Winter, M. (1986b) 'From state direction to self regulation: the historical development of corporatism in British agriculture', *Policy and Politics*, 14(4), 475–90.

Hindess, B. (1982) 'Power, interests and the outcome of struggles', *Sociology*, 16.

Giddens, A. (1979) *Central Problems in Social Theory*. London: Macmillan.

Goldsmith, E. and Hildyard, N. (eds) (1986) *Green Britain or Industrial Wasteland*. Cambridge: Polity Press.

Kuhn, T. S. (1970) *The Structure of Scientific Revolutions*. Chicago: University of Chicago Press (2nd edition).

Lowe, P., Cox, G., MacEwen, M., O'Riordan, T. and Winter, M. (1986) *Countryside Conflicts: The Politics of Farming, Forestry and Conservation*. London: Temple Smith Gower.

Lukes, S. (1974) *Power: A Radical View*. London: Macmillan.

Payne, V. (1971) *A History of the Soil Association*. MSc Manchester University.

Pye-Smith, C. and North, R. (1984) *Working the Land*. London: Temple Smith.

Richardson, J. J. and Jordan, A. G. (1979) *Governing Under Pressure*. Oxford: Martin Robertson.

Shoard, M. (1980) *The Theft of the Countryside*. London: Maurice Temple Smith.

Vine, A. and Bateman, D. (1981) *Organic Farming Systems in England and Wales: Practice, Performance and Implications*. Aberystwyth: Department of Agricultural Economics, University College of Wales.

Wookey, B. (1987) *Rushall: The Story of an Organic Farm*. Oxford: Blackwell.

CHAPTER 4

Technological Change in the Regulation of Agriculture

Elizabeth Hawkins

The changing environment for technology and food production

Agriculture under advanced capitalism is a highly intensive and technical industry which for the most part is still conducted in small-scale, family-based units. Throughout the post-war era in Britain, state policies have sought to encourage the expansion of production and to provide farmers with a stable market environment in which to innovate and reproduce their businesses. But changing political, social and economic outlooks, coupled with high levels of indebtedness in the farm sector challenge this commitment to productivity. Thus, while state and commercial interests continue to encourage gains in efficiency, international competitiveness and the adoption of new technologies, the high economic and environmental costs are no longer seen as either acceptable, or necessary, by a predominantly urban population.

Almost all farm businesses are closely integrated into the agro-food sector, through the supply of feed, seed, fertilisers and pesticides and through the purchase of farm produce by food processors, wholesalers and retailers (e.g. Marsden *et al.*, 1986; Burns *et al.*, 1983). The upstream and downstream firms are large, often multi-national companies which have become more concentrated and vertically integrated (Ward, 1990). Such oligopolistic structures suggest that the farmer is in a disadvantaged position for trade. However, they also mean that declining agricultural fortunes do not only affect the farmer, but, together with increasingly stringent end user demands, create instability within the food chain as a whole. Within this context, technology can be seen as one of the key means of coping with market uncertainties, but with particular interests differentially placed to pursue their favoured technological solutions.

Technological change in the agricultural literature

The regular study of agricultural technology dates back to the period of rapid mechanisation in the 1950s (see the review contained in Beradi (1981) and the innovation theories of Wilkening (1958) and Rogers (1962)). Although the technological treadmill model of Cochrane (1958) began to link farm economics and farm policy, it was not until the late 1970s that studies began to address the origins of technologies and the effect they had on farm production relations. This was stimulated by growing dissatisfaction with some of the social and environmental consequences of technological change (Carson, 1965; Shoard, 1980). The assumption that technological advance was inherently beneficial originating from and driven by a scientific logic separate from social institutions, was challenged (Rose and Rose, 1976; Cicotti *et al.*,1976). In agricultural sociology this was expressed mainly within the extension literature and was highlighted by the lack of success in transferring and integrating new technologies to culturally different agricultural systems. As McInerney argued:

> technology is more than just resources, or knowledge, or methods of production, it embraces the whole system of technical, economic, institutional, social and political arrangements that characterise the way a society functions. Because technology change is a system adjustment therefore the full effects of a development project are always diffuse, usually complex, frequently unanticipated and sometimes perverse. (McInerney, 1984: 10)

With a broader view of farms embedded within food producing chains and notions of a socially derived technology, Friedland and his colleagues (1975, 1981) began to describe how agribusiness and state interests orchestrated the direction of technological change. Through case studies of the mechanical tomato harvester and refrigeration techniques for lettuces, they showed how the specific agronomy and labour conditions found in the production of a commodity shaped the type of technology produced. More recently, Goodman *et al.* (1987) and Kloppenburg (1988) have considered the application of biotechnology to agriculture and its origins within industrial capital and state policy.

As Kloppenburg (1988) argues scientific advancements are important, but do not, in themselves, explain why a technology is produced. The production of technology has goals and objectives which can be planned and manipulated and with consequences which can be regulated (Rose and Rose,

1976). In the case of hybrid seed breeding:

> the very production of scientific knowledge that culminated in hybridization was itself shaped and directed by social relations.... That is, the subordination of population improvements to the service of hybrid production is not a matter for scientific discretion, but of political economy. Hybrids are amenable to commodification; open pollinated varieties resist it. (Kloppenburg, 1988: 129)

In the productivist period of agriculture it appeared that the state, farmers and industry were all working towards similar goals which tended to reinforce research relations (Goodman *et al.*, 1987: 13). With present political and economic changes, it is more likely that separate requirements from different individual viewpoints will create conflict rather than consensus. Research priorities may ultimately depend as much on the bargaining power of individual sectional interests as on the logic of capital or science.

This chapter draws on empirical work to show how technology is shaped by the specific research interests and agents involved in its funding and direction. It further argues that if technological change is a social construct then the social organisation of production and particularly the transmission of technical advice become crucial to analysis.

Instability in food and technology production

Market instability is an important consideration in the way technology is used to regulate production. Supply industries rely on the continual updating of their products to hold market share. Likewise, ensuring a regular supply of a product that fits processing and consumer specifications reduces the uncertainty for processors and retailers. In agriculture, production processes are less than perfect for standardising products and their supply, and technology, including technical advice, plays a key role in allowing upstream and downstream industries to specify conditions of production. It is not surprising then that these same industries are directly and increasingly involved with the research networks that originate such technology.

During the 1980s, the main research body for the sector in the UK, the Agriculture and Food Research Council (AFRC), suffered severe budgetary cuts, resulting in loss of staff and the amalgamation and sale of several institutes. At the same time, agro-food sector companies who were expanding their R&D effort were encouraged to take financial responsibility for near-market research projects previously undertaken within public institutes (House of Lords, 1988). In consequence, there has been a marked shift in research priorities from agronomic practice to food quality and storage, the control of production and biotechnical techniques. Much basic research remains in the public domain but even here the AFRC, for example, has increased its research into plant genetics, microbiology and immunology at the expense of such traditional topics as crop production, ruminant lactation, silage and nutrition (AFRC, 1989). With the focus of research moving away from farm-based production, farmers may find their managerial control severely constrained by the resultant technologies.

The next two sections seek to illustrate how technological change acts as a mechanism in the regulation of British agriculture. Using two cases studies, of milk (pp. 86–90) and potato (pp. 90–94) production,[1] shows how different agents, markets and policies shape separate research networks and the technology they produce.

Although complaining about the cost and complexity, farmers continue to integrate new technologies, despite uncertain markets for both milk and potatoes. This is in part because their underlying faith in technology remains strong but also because it is not solely an individual decision, many farmers feeling obliged to 'keep up'. This argument is followed through the specific market and technological environment for milk and potato production, to consider to what extent and by what means technology is used to regulate farm-based production.

The use of technology in the regulation of milk production

The milk market

All milk produced by farmers in England is sold to the Milk Marketing Board (MMB), a statutory producer co-operative, with a monopoly over milk supply, which is set to become a voluntary co-operative in 1994. The milk is pooled and distributed by the MMB to dairy processing and retailing industries. Farmers receive a price, per litre of milk, fixed nationally, irrespective of distance to market or transport costs (Winter, 1984; Cox *et al.*, 1990; Flynn and Hawkins, 1990). Dairy farmers therefore have a powerful organisation, economically and politically for the marketing of milk, but with the disadvantage that, at present, with quotas on output and regulated prices, there is little that individual farmers can do directly to add value to the commodity.

Two options remain. One is to reduce costs and increase marginal returns on milk by substituting home-produced feed for bought concentrates, and family for hired labour (Cox *et al.*, 1990). The second is to increase stock value, cross-breeding dairy cattle to produce good beef calves for market, or increasing the pedigree of the herd to get better prices for dairy replacement calves.

The production of milk technology

Dairy research has traditionally received considerable public funding, arguably because of the political strength of dairy producers through the MMB (see Flynn and Hawkins, 1990) as much as for its contribution to agricultural production. In 1989 dairy research received approximately £10 million through AFRC institutes, but even dairying was not immune to cuts, losing nearly £1.7 million in the period 1986–89 (AFRC, 1987, 1989). But the direction of milk research has remained largely unaffected.

Large centralised research projects predominate aimed at production control and techniques. For example, robotic milking has been investigated initially in public and latterly in private–public collaborations (Matthews, 1982). The yield-increasing hormone bovine somatotropin was pioneered in Britain and then commercially developed in the USA (McBride *et al.*, 1988). Basic research tends to remain in the public domain, because of the high input of public funding and the low commercial incentive for private research. The common thrust of all the new technologies is to make the production process more stable and controlled whether it be in milk supply, quality of calf or expected demand for feedstuffs.

Case study 1: the production of embryo transfer technology

> Dairy cow reproduction relates to two aspects of the dairying enterprise, the ability to cross-breed producing beef calves for market and the desire to improve the dairy herd's pedigree. Both aspects increase the returns farmers can gain from the dairy herd, if not from milk per se. In the past these aims were fulfilled by artificial insemination (AI) which allowed the farmer access to good pedigree bulls from a wide range of breeds. Embryo transfer (ET) has improved this process further by allowing farmers access, not only to high quality sire progeny, but also to a high quality dame.[2] However, the complexity of the techniques involved take them out of the realm of traditional stockmanship and make farmers more dependent on external sources of advice.
>
> Embryo transfer was pioneered in the Cambridge AFRC Research Institute in 1951 with public funding, but commercial applications were developed mainly in American Land Grant Colleges. Use of embryos in the USA is almost 10 years ahead of Britain; back in 1981 it was a £20 million industry (Seidel, 1981), whereas it remained mainly a 'talking point' amongst British farmers until the late 1980s.
>
> In Britain the application of embryo transfer began with a private company already involved in artificial insemination sales. However, the take-up was quite limited. Recent commercialisation of British

embryo transfer is due to the multiple ovulation and embryo transfer (MOET) scheme developed again in a publicly funded AFRC institute. As MOET became more widely discussed in the farming press, producer and commercial interest grew. In 1989 the main private company with an embryo transfer service was acquired by the MMB and incorporated into its Farm Services.

The production of embryo transfer offspring technology such as cloning and twinning also has commercial relevance. In the USA the research has been taken on by private venture capital. But most of the British work remains publicly funded (by MMB and MAFF), or collaboratively operated with research institutes and colleges. It is not surprising that private interests have been less evident. The MMB, although with quite a low profile of research funding in basic areas, prioritises breeding research through collaborative programmes with the AFRC. Through its AI services, the MMB already has an organisation for the distribution of breeding technology and advice to the farmer. Private firms entering the market would have to compete with a nationally based, established breeding programme, to which farmers have easy access as milk producers.

Integration of milk technology

In the milk sector, with the MMB standing between farmers and the processors and retailers, technologies are seen to stem from upstream rather than downstream sources. Moreover, with no effective link between output and price, farmers are not obliged to adopt new technologies just to stay in business. However, as the case study of embryo transfer showed, technology itself is becoming increasingly complex, placing farmers in a position where they have to look more to external advisers for help, and it is this which, in recent years, has allowed agribusiness more influence over farm production in the dairy sector.

The following case study illustrates these features, describing the importance of technological advice in the corporate strategy of a cattle feed company.

Case study 2: a national feed manufacturer

Dairyfeed, a subsidiary of a multi-national, is one of the largest national feed manufacturers in Britain. Through its parent company Dairyfeed has access to extensive research facilities and experimental farms which are used to update feed nutrition practice continually.

Since quotas, Dairyfeed has suffered considerably both from declining concentrate markets and strained loyalty to it as a manufacturer and to its product lines. Farmers still need concentrate supplements but seem more prepared to shop around for them. In response the company established a network of regionally based specialists providing on-farm advice on feed, to act as permanent contact points for farmers. Almost half of Dairyfeed's customers use their costings service (28,000) to work out yields from different feed inputs. One of the feed specialists commented, 'they can get as much advice as they need'. He continued that most farmers knew their margins approximately but they could be computed on individual cows if farmers supplied the requisite information.

It is this technical contact that appeared to be the main strategy of the company in retaining customers' loyalty. As one specialist said the company 'offered a large package of management tools, like costings and forecasts, which is in advance of the competition'. 'So farmers are still with us' he continued, 'because of our specialism and managerial input.'

Indeed, perhaps more important than the costings is the management advice that is imparted with them. The costings are returned to the farmer monthly when a specialist visits the farm to discuss the results. As one farmer explained 'the adviser that comes to see us, we have a day with him every month and we go right through what we have done and take management decisions then. You know big decisions. I talk about them with the men (farm-workers), then when he comes we say we are thinking of doing this, this and this. We work it out as to whether we can or not.' Another farmer described a similar pattern: 'The rep comes here about once a month and takes all the figures and then brings the report back. Then usually we sit down and talk about it and decide what we are going to do, or what we want to do.'

Interviews with farmers revealed positive feelings towards the advice. While costings remain a free service, farmers use them as a helpful aid in managing the business and may come to rely on them. As one specialist described, 'Some get to the stage where they won't do anything without asking for advice first. It gets to ridiculous levels. "You tell me what to do" they say, "and I'll do it".' In this way the farmer, although remaining responsible for the farm and the risk entailed, shares management of the dairy herd. However, as such advice is not linked to the downstream market (which is monopolised by the MMB) farmers do not face the same pressures to accept it as the potato producers discussed.

The use of technology in the regulation of potato production

The potato market

For many years potato producers, like milk producers, have operated in a regulated market, but with crucial differences. The Potato Marketing Board, which is also a producer co-operative, indirectly affects the market in two ways: through a system of support buying which prevents the market price falling too low in years of surplus, and through a planting acreage quota system. But, unlike the MMB, the PMB does not market potatoes nor does it become involved in the many different forms of agreement entered into between growers and downstream industry.[3]

The fact that potato growers market their own produce means that they can increase returns either by cutting costs or by aiming at specific markets and getting a better price. In the past the majority of potatoes were sorted and graded on the back of the harvester, then packed and sold in sacks to a wholesale market. A change in consumer preference to prepacked potatoes sold in supermarkets and processed potato products has led to new markets for raw potatoes in the concentrated retail and processing sectors. These buyers desire a constant supply of a specific variety and quality of potato to enable factories and packing houses to run at full capacity, features rarely achieved in the traditional market. Thus, most retail merchants and processors enter into forward contracts or informal agreements with growers on the quantity, type and price of potatoes they will receive.

The production of potato research

Research in the potato industry reflects these structures. Most early research was publicly funded and directed into projects aimed at improving the efficiency of potato production. Later projects, with greater financial responsibility being taken by the potato industry, have been aimed at the standards required by various end-use markets. Recent research, for example, has addressed damage reduction on harvesting, improved automatic grading facilities and storage systems to prolong retail shelf life (PMB, 1986).

The following case study describes the production of potato seed technology which has been responsible for much of the change in marketing since the mid 1980s. It illustrates how technology is intricately interwoven with marketing and commodity production.

Case study 3: seed breeding

> Using conventional methods of seed breeding it is difficult to create new varieties. But sophisticated techniques of cell culture have revolutionised the process in two ways. First, a technique called

protoplast fusion can be used to induce new traits into the genetic make-up of potatoes, for example high dry matter content for processing, an improvement in skin appearance for the fresh retail market, or perhaps in the near future specific maturity dates to give a longer supply season. Second, micropropagation, a technique to grow scaled-down versions of potato tubers from shoot cultures, has enabled the rapid turnover of new varieties from trial to market (Ahloowalia, 1990). The result has been a flood of new varieties. As one marketing co-operative manager stated, 'It seems that hardly a day goes by without another new variety landing on the desk here. It's a question of keeping up with them all.'

Traditionally the potato breeding programmes were centred in publicly funded institutes, and this remains so for Ireland, the Netherlands and partially for Scotland where seed potatoes are a considerable export business. But in England the privatisation of the Plant Breeding Institute in 1987 has meant that breeding, as such, is in one set of private hands.

When the institute came on the market a number of multi-nationals in the potato trade expressed interest. The company which ultimately bought the institute was involved in processing and prepacking. This is significant because it means that they are 'uniquely placed to maintain both consumer trends and end-user requirements, thus ensuring that varieties are bred to fit the needs of both current and future markets' (PBI Report, 1989). In this there is no mention of the producer. Indeed, the situation is no longer one of public breeder working for the farmer, but of a multi-national corporation developing technologies at one end of the food chain and using market power at the other to integrate the technology into farm-based production.

The integration of potato technology

As the discussion on the market control of production shows, the quality and variety of potatoes are vital to buyers who therefore choose which growers to buy from, and stipulate harvesting and cultivation practice.

Production control is sometimes explicit in the marketing contract, for example the grower may be required to record the incidence and nature of all agrochemical applications and cultivative operations and to allow regular monitoring. But it is more usual for this control to be less formal, instigated through regular visits and advice from retail and processing company agronomists. The companies say they are 'working with' the grower. Crucially, the risks, say, of crop failure remain with the grower. The following case study shows how even informal agreements profoundly influence the ability of growers to enter markets and adopt new production practices.

Case study 4: prepacker merchants

Potpack is a nationally based prepacking marketing company. It is one branch of the food division of a large multi-national company; other branches in the same division include a crisp processor and retail supermarket chain. The company itself has seven prepacking shed branches and seed growing operations in Scotland. Supplies are gained from all over the country, and a proportion (5 per cent) is imported.

Only 20 per cent of the supplies at present are forward contracted. This is a relatively recent but expanding practice. In addition short contracts are drawn up during the summer from one week to the next. Prices for the short-term contracts are negotiated at the time of delivery, which means that Potpack is never paying above market prices. All deals are made directly with growers so that instructions can be passed on to them. As the manager of Potpack remarked 'It is company policy to deal directly with growers. When we are involved with customers saying we are going to produce something for them it is very important that we talk to the grower about that and tell him how we want it done.'

The way the deals operate and the potatoes are marketed involves a series of operations best explained using the manager's own description:

> Once we are ready to lift we agree the price with the grower. It might be days, weeks or months in advance, or even on the day. We go out for the first load produced to make sure the standard is right. That's company policy. We always inspect the first loads.... The price depends on a number of things, quality, the variety, number of bakers and skin finish. Some of them are marginal price changes, some are quite large.... The potatoes go down to quality control (QC). On the first load QC may do four to five samples to make sure the standard is consistent. QC then accepts it or says to the grower, look there is a problem you better come and have a look at it.... If it's a first load from a grower and we are quite confident that the field's OK, we will speak to him and explain. We will not fall out over one load of potatoes. The potatoes are then taken off, split graded and go into a chamber which is set at about 9 degrees for a tuber temperature of 10.... They go through the washers and on to grading tables. They are put into polythene bags which range from 1 kg to 1 lb packs, then loaded into lorries equipped with fridge units and dispatched.

To grow potatoes for the retail market is quite complicated and the requirements made of the grower exacting. It therefore requires considerable specialism in potato growing, a large acreage and a technically progressive grower. As the manager commented, 'We talk to them [growers] constantly, about any new methods that are coming out and encourage them. With the growers that want to work for us we don't have any problems, they are as keen as we are to have new methods.' He continued, 'It's easier for us to have growers who know what they are doing and are looking to try new things, better than having to badger them to put their house in order.'

But, as this statement shows, what is also important is the willingness of the grower to adapt to their standards. The manager continued 'Some of the not so forward-thinking ones expect us to find homes at top prices for sub-standard potatoes .... They don't try and put their problems right. The good growers say well I will go and have a look and come back to you. That's the sort of attitude we want.'

For such growers, the threat of losing a remunerative market outlet was stimulus enough to try to keep up with market demands which were both exacting and changing. Flexibility and technical expertise contributed to both the farmers' and the agribusiness notion of what being a 'professional grower' entailed. As one such grower commented 'I think we are becoming more professional and we can take the advice better. People are becoming more specialised. You see the smaller growers disappear and the bigger growers are more in tune with the market requirements.'

These examples show that a new working relationship is developing between buyers and growers. The marketing outlets are seen to have considerable control over the production of potatoes on farms through the stipulations they place on technology, growing conditions and on the variety, quality and quantity of potatoes accepted. Growers for these markets need objective and technical knowledge of production and a 'professional' business approach to deal with the legalities and economics of the specialised markets. Growers who remain out of such markets do not face such strict standards but neither do they receive the same returns. Unfortunately, with declining wholesale markets such growers may no longer have the choice.

Conclusion

This chapter has examined the crucial role of technology in the control of farm-based production. The two commodities used have very different market and research environments, but illustrate a number of similar constraints influencing the integration of technologies into commodity production. These fall into two categories, market constraints and technological constraints.

Agribusiness operates within highly unstable markets and although oligopolistic in structure this is not reflected in any safe cartel arrangements; competition and uncertainty, although acknowledged to be on a different scale from the pressures farmers face, are rife. Agribusiness has sought both to stabilise its own market by attracting numbers of loyal customers, and to ease factory production processes by standardising, in quality and quantity, farm produce. Technological change has allowed agribusiness to operate this control over production indirectly, thereby passing on some of the market risks to the farmer.

The second set of contraints is technological. As expressed in advisory form, these are more important for commodity producers. Advisory links have increased in number but have also become regular and broad in remit as a result of increasingly complex technologies and changing product markets. With such direct contacts in place, the chapter has suggested, it is easier to encourage farmers to buy new technologies, especially when advice is linked to downstream markets, as it is for many potato growers.

However, this may paint too negative a picture. Changing technologies also offer opportunities to farmers. New potato technology, for example, gives growers the chance of increasing returns and opening new market links; the extension of technical advice allows farmers on-site help with increasingly complex processes, whilst regular meetings with advisers may reduce a farmer's isolation. The ability of individual farmers to respond to the opportunities as well as constraints brought about by agribusiness is quite varied. Indeed, a criticism of the political economy literature has been its preoccupation with the concentrated oligopolistic structure of the food chain, which is unable to explain the diversity of production at farm level (Marsden *et al.*, 1989).

Hence, the relative integration of technology is neither solely the result of the farmer's 'rational decision-making' nor of the scarcity or surplus of labour (see Friedland *et al.*, 1981). It is best described as being intimately associated with marketing arrangements, and relationships with supply companies, through which the demands and pressures of uncertain markets can be transferred from agribusiness to the farm. This process is itself facilitated by the continued desire to innovate from sections, at least, of the farming community.

Acknowledgements

This research is based on a three-year project funded by an Economic and Social Research Council studentship award (and supervised jointly by Dr T.K. Marsden at South Bank Polytechnic and Prof. R.J.C. Munton at University College London).

Notes

1. Field work was carried out in Cheshire, northwest England in 1988. It consisted of two farm surveys (one of milk producers and one of potato producers), a second less-structured survey of a sample of these farms, a survey of agribusinesses relevant to milk and potato commodities, some at national, some regional but mainly at a local level, and a number of interviews with representatives of state agencies again concerned specifically with production of milk and potatoes.
2. The progeny tested dame donor is induced to produce multiple embryos which are transferred to a recipient herd cow where, if the transfer is successful, they develop in a normal pregnancy (Seidel, 1981). Recipient cows have to be managed to be at exactly the same day of the oestrus cycle when they receive the embryo. A major breakthrough in the process is that these embryos can now be stored 'in vitro' for a considerable length of time, allowing a recipient herd, often in different countries, to be managed ready to receive the embryos.
3. Downstream industry includes several elements: (i) processors of frozen chips, (ii) processors of potato crisps, (iii) prepackers of washed and peat-dressed potatoes into clear bags of varying sizes for the retail chains, and (iv) merchants who sell on to wholesale markets.

References

AFRC (1987) *Biotechnology in Agriculture*. London: AFRC.

AFRC (1987 and 1989) *Corporate Plans*. London: AFRC.

AFRC (1988) *Science, Agriculture and the Environment*. London: AFRC.

Ahloowalia, B. S. (1990) 'Seed potato: small is beautiful', *Science*, 247, 31–2.

Beradi, G. M. (1981) 'Socio-economic consequences of agricultural mechanisation in the United States: needed redirections for mechanisation research', *Rural Sociology*, 46 (3), pp. 483–504.

Beradi, G. M. and Geisler, C. C. (eds) (1984) *The Social Consequences and Challenges of New Agricultural Technologies*. Boulder, Colorado: Westview Press.

Burns, J. A., McInerney, J. D. and Swinbank, A. (1983) *The Food Industry: Economics and Policies*. London: Heinemann.

Carson, R. (1965) *Silent Spring*. London: Penguin.

Cicotti, G., Cini, M. and de Maria, M. (1976) 'The production of science in advanced capitalist society', in H. Rose and S. Rose *op. cit.*

Cochrane, W. W. (1958) *Farm Prices: Myth and Reality*. Minneapolis: University of Minnesota Press.

Cox, G., Lowe, P. and Winter, M. (1990) 'The political management of the dairy sector in England and Wales', in T. K. Marsden and J. K. Little (eds) *Political, Social and Economic Perspectives on the International Food System*. Aldershot: Avebury.

Fliegal, F. C. and van Es, J. C. (1983) 'The diffusion-adoption process in agriculture: changes in technology and changing paradigms', in G. F. Summers (ed.) *Technology and Social Change in Rural Areas*. Boulder, Colorado: Westview Press.

Flynn, A. and Hawkins, E. A. (1990) 'Agricultural co-operatives and the state: the case of the Milk and Potato Marketing Boards', in F. Just (ed.) *Co-operatives and*

Farmers' Unions in Western Europe: Collaboration and Tensions. Esbjerg, Denmark: South Jutland University Press.

Friedland, W. H. and Barton, A. (1975) *Destalking the Wild Tomato: A Case Study in Social Consequences in California Agricultural Research*. Department of Behavioural Sciences Research Monograph No 15. University of California: Davis.

Friedland, W. H., Barton, A. and Thompson, R. J. (1981) *Manufacturing Green Gold: Capital, Labour, and Technology in the Lettuce Industry*. Cambridge: Cambridge University Press.

Goodman, D., Sorj, B. and Wilkinson, J. (1987) *From Farming to Biotechnology: A Theory of Agro-Industrial Development*. Oxford: Basil Blackwell.

Hightower, J. (1973) *Hard Tomatoes, Hard Times*. Cambridge, MA: Schenkman.

House of Lords (1988) *Agricultural and Food Research*. Select Committee on Science and Technology 13-1. London: HMSO.

Jinks, J. L. (1985) 'It's in the pipeline', Unpublished paper presented at the 39th Oxford Farming Conference, Oxford.

Kloppenburg, J. (1988) *First the Seed*. Cambridge: Cambridge University Press.

Long, N. (ed.) (1989) *Encounters at the Interface: A Perspective on Social Discontinuities in Rural Development*. Department of Sociology, Agricultural University, Wageningen.

Long, N., van der Ploeg, J., Curtin, C. and Box, L. (1986) *The Commoditization Debate: Labour Process, Strategy and Social Network*. Working Paper of the Department of Sociology, Agricultural University, Wageningen.

Lowe, P., Marsden, T. and Whatmore, S. (eds) (1990) *Technological Change and the Rural Environment*. London: David Fulton.

MAFF (1987) *Dairy Facts and Figures*. London: HMSO.

Marion, B. W. and Willis, R. L. (1990) 'A prospective assessment of the impacts of Bovine Somatotrophin: a case study of Wisconsin', *American Journal of Agricultural Economics*, 72, 326-35.

Marsden, T. K. (1989) *Commoditisation of the Labour Process: Farm Households in British Agriculture*. Sociology of Agriculture Working Paper Series No. 2, University College, London.

Marsden, T. K., Munton, R. J. C., Whatmore, S. J. and Little, J. K. (1989) 'Strategies for coping in capitalist agriculture: an examination of the responses of farm families in British agriculture', *Geoforum*, 20, 1–14.

Marsden, T. K., Whatmore, S. J., Munton, R. J. C. and Little, J. K. (1986) 'The restructuring process and economic centrality in capitalist agriculture', *Journal of Rural Studies*, 2, 271–80.

Marsh, J. S. (1985) 'Economics, politics and potatoes: the changing role of the Potato Marketing Board in Great Britain', Presidential Address, *Journal of Agricultural Economics*, 36, 325–44.

Marx, J. (1981) 'Cloning sheep and cattle embryos', *Science*, 239, 463–4.

Matthews, J. (1982) 'The mechanical farm of the future', *Chemistry and Industry*, 4 September, 647–52.

McBride, B. W., Burton, J. L. and Burton, J. H. (1988) 'The influence of bovine growth hormone on animals and their products', *Research and Development in Agriculture*, 5 (1), 1-21.

McInerney, J. (1984) 'The technology of rural development', *World Bank Staff Working Paper*, 295.

Milk Marketing Board (1989) *The Milk Marketing Board*. Thames Ditton: MMB.

Ploeg, J. D. van der (1986) 'The agricultural labour process and commoditisation', in N. Long, J. van der Ploeg, C. Curtin and L. Box *op. cit*.

Potato Marketing Board (1986) *Survey of Potato Research in the UK*. Oxford: PMB.

Rogers, E. M. (1962) *Diffusion of Innovations*. New York: Free Press.

Rose, H. and Rose, S. (eds) (1976) *The Political Economy of Science*. Cambridge: Schenkman.

Seidel, G. E. (1981) 'Superovulation and embryo transfer in cattle', *Science*, 211, 351–8.

Shoard, M. (1980) *The Theft of the Countryside*. London: Temple Smith.

Ward, N. (1990) 'A preliminary analysis of the UK food chain', *Food Policy*, 15, 429–41.

Wilkening, E. A. (1958) 'An introductory note on the social aspects of practice adoption', *Rural Sociology*, 23, 97–102.

Winter, M. (1984) 'Corporatism and agriculture in the UK. The case of the MMB', *Sociologia Ruralis*, 24 (2) 106–19.

World Animal Review (1978) 'Embryo Transfer', *World Animal Review*, 60.

CHAPTER 5

Retailing, the Food System and the Regulatory State

Andrew Flynn, Terry Marsden and Neil Ward

Introduction

Over the past decade there have been considerable changes in the functions of the state, characterised by the term de-regulation. Whatever the political rhetoric or slogans surrounding deregulation, it is becoming apparent that it does not necessarily mean that regulation disappears, but that it takes different forms (Cerny, 1991). At the same time, while neo-conservative policies, which have been adopted in most advanced societies, may well have broken down traditional Keynesian orthodoxies concerning support for the private sector and collective forms of consumption, growing environmental, food hygiene and health concerns serve to demonstrate that the emphasis on privatisation and individualised consumption only raise new legitimatory problems.

Thus as patterns of state activity change, unfamiliar legitimatory problems for the state emerge. Modes of regulation require social and political support, but this has been neglected by theorists. If regulation theory is to develop it needs to explore at an empirical level the role of the state, of actors and institutions and the terms of the political discourse in the context in which it appears. This chapter is an initial contribution. It will illustrate at the conceptual level the ways in which the state attempts to legitimate itself over time and at the empirical level chart how this occurs through changes to prevailing social and political practices, associated in this case with the British food system.

In the past decade or so we can see some considerable changes within the food supply system, in the power relations between the different sub-sectors, and between these and the state, reflecting both macro shifts in the direction of state policy and, more specifically, the abilities of different interests to reinforce their economic position through political power. An examination of these developments provides us with a vehicle to study the changing nature of the regulatory state.

The restructuring of the UK food system

Who are the key groups of actors involved in the UK food system and how have their roles changed over the past decade? The most important feature of the contemporary restructuring of the food system is the empowerment of the food retailing sector in relation to other sectors; namely farmers, input suppliers and food manufacturers.

Farmers

The agricultural sector is characterised by a large number of producers, each with a minute market share and, therefore, negligible influence over market prices. According to the Ministry of Agriculture, Fisheries and Food (MAFF), approximately 144,000 full-time holdings produce over 97 per cent of total output (MAFF, 1988). The structure of the sector contrasts with those sectors to which farmers are most linked. So, on the one side, the agricultural sector has been increasingly tied to a progressively concentrated input sector through the development of credit links, particularly in the form of leasing and sale back schemes for farm equipment administered by suppliers' own leasing companies. On the other side, in providing the raw materials for the food system, farmers must deal with the oligopolistic buying power of food processors and retailers. Squeezed on both sides, the farm sector receives little over 15 per cent of the value added in the food production process (Harvey, 1987).

Input suppliers

Input suppliers make up the most concentrated sector of the food system, with, for example, around 90 per cent of the UK fertiliser market controlled by three multi-national companies (Norsk Hydro, ICI and Kemira) and almost 60 per cent of the market for manufactured animals feedstuffs controlled by four companies (BOCM Silcock, Dalgety, Pauls and J. Bibby).

Food manufacturers

In the UK, the ten largest food manufacturing companies hold 44 per cent of the total market, although the level of concentration is much higher in particular sub-sectors such as bread and frozen vegetables (Newby and Utting, 1984; Ward, 1990). Most of these companies are wholly or partly British owned and the British market represents about two-thirds of their total sales.

Since the mid 1960s, a key feature of the changing role of manufacturers in the food system has been 'a fundamental shift in the balance of power in the industry away from the suppliers or manufacturers of grocery items and towards the rapidly expanding retail corporations' (Wrigley, 1987: 1284). Of both symbolic and practical importance was the Retail Prices Act of 1964 which prohibited the practice of resale price maintenance (RPM). This had enabled food manufacturers to control the final selling price for their goods. In effect, the practice helped to keep power in the hands of large-scale food manufacturers and at the same time protect smaller, independent grocers from competition from the largest food retailing chains. Large food retailers, in particular, put pressure on the government to abolish RPM, because they were looking to compete on a price basis, taking advantage of lower operating costs (Wrigley, 1992). Once RPM had been abolished, power in the food system moved towards a small group of the largest food retailers who sought to grow further by expanding market share. This they achieved, in part, by passing on to customers the volume discounts they were able to obtain from food manufacturers. Furthermore, the readily identifiable and nationally advertised brand names that had proved so valuable to food manufacturers have come under increasing pressure from food retailers who have sought to exploit their 'own-label' product to compete with the national brands. Here the retailers have also been able to gain from their ability to control how brands are displayed in stores (Davis *et al.*, 1985).

Food retailers

The trend of concentration in UK food retailing is probably the most important process driving the restructuring of market and regulatory relations in the food system. While this goes back to the 1950s, the 1980s have seen the increasing dominance of five retail corporations: Sainsburys, Tescos, Argyll (Safeway), Asda, and Gateway. Their combined share of total grocery sales in Britain rose from 43 per cent in 1984 to 61 per cent in 1990. The relative economic power of the food retailers in the British food system is unusual in international terms. By the mid 1980s, 'profit levels, employment levels, and sheer market and political power of the UK's largest food retailers were sufficient to rival the traditional giants of UK manufacturing industry' (Wrigley, 1987: 1285). This point alone underlines the importance of the UK food system as a *national* concept. Whilst it has been argued that the current global restructuring of capital is eroding national economic regulation and that the agro-food sector provides a good example of this (see Friedland, 1991; McMichael and Myhre, 1991), the dominance of the nationally based retailers in the food system makes the British case crucially distinctive.

Retailing and purchasing practices

As has been argued above, even the highly concentrated food manufacturing sector has suffered from declining economic power in recent decades (Wrigley, 1987; McDonald *et al.*, 1989). This shift has been accentuated by technological innovations in retailing, including changes in the methods of food distribution and handling systems. The employment of food technologists to oversee the development of own label products has enabled retailers to further increase their competitive advantage (Senker, 1990). In conditions of inelastic demand, the consumer end of the food chain has come to govern supply and price, sending signals down the system to less responsive sectors.

The shift in power to food retailers has provoked resistance from other elements in the food system hoping to engage state support through new regulatory arrangements to bolster their own position. Perhaps its most public expression was concern over the buying practices of food retailers, including in the early 1980s charges of unfair buying practices and in the early 1990s concern over the widening British food trade-gap.

Worries that the largest food retailers were able to secure preferential discounts with food suppliers, which represented unfair competition, forcing smaller, independent retailers out of business, were referred to the Monopolies and Mergers Commission (MMC) by the Director General for Trading. The MMC's report (1981) concluded that the practice of securing discounts from suppliers was not harmful to the public interest as long as there was effective competition among both retailers and manufacturers such that at least some of the discounts were passed on to consumers.

However, further concentration in the retail sector followed the MMC report and the issue of discounts and retail concentration again became the subject of regulatory interest with a review conducted by the Office of Fair Trading (OFT) (1985). The OFT's findings echoed those of the MMC and despite a 6.5 per cent increase in the market share of the four largest food retailers, it was concluded that lower buying prices were, in general, being passed on to consumers. Although it could not be shown that concentration in food retailing was not harming the interests of consumers in terms of prices charged, it was recognised that consumer choice had suffered because the number of smaller food retail outlets had declined. This has prompted some commentators to continue their calls for stricter controls over merger within the food retailing sector. For example, Bamfield (1988: 28) argued:

> Regulation does not generally seem an effective way of securing

> competition, but a change in merger policy would seem to be one way in which the increased consumer benefits produced by multiples' battle for sales growth can be safeguarded.

With the exception of Sainsbury's control of some of its meat product supply chains, British food retailers have been reluctant to invest in the farm sector and so complete the process of vertical integration within the food system. This has, in part, been due to the high cost of land for agricultural production and the varying and volatile production time for agricultural products. It is more straightforward to allow a progressively weak, divided and diverse farm sector produce these, and it is those sub-sectors where the production process has been thoroughly industrialised, such as intensive livestock and poultry production, which have experienced the greatest penetration by non-farm capitals. In other sub-sectors, food retailers and manufacturers have been able to extend their control over the production process indirectly, achieving the market relations they desire through 'contract farming'. In Britain the practice where a farmer is contracted to produce exclusively for food retailing or manufacturing companies, has spread rapidly since the early 1970s, such that 'most of the poultry, eggs, pork and bacon, and over 90% of vegetables like peas and beans are grown to the order and specification of the food industry' (Clunies-Ross and Hildyard, 1992: 69).

Through contracts with farmers' retailers are able to emphasise food quality standards and influence the timing of planting, chemical treatments and harvesting of crops. While it can be argued that producing for supermarkets represents opportunities as well as threats to farmers, the premiums offered for meeting quality targets often do not sufficiently reflect the additional demands on farming practices. Harvey notes the problem for farmers is 'that higher quality may become the expected norm for which no premium is payable' (1987: 155) and argues that the challenge for farmers to meet the food retailers' requirements for consistency of food products 'will determine their future profitability as much as policy decisions in the EC' (Harvey, 1987: 156).

In response to these changes, farming groups first began to complain about the so-called 'profitability gap' between the farming and food retail sectors. It was argued that between 1980 and 1990, the retail price index rose by 106 per cent and food prices by 71 per cent, yet prices received at the farm gate had only risen by 46 per cent (Agricultural Supply Industry, 1990). Farming leaders complained that 'the big five supermarket chains make more profit than the whole of British agriculture' (*The Independent*, 1990), and that this was primarily because they 'are able to dictate totally what products they require and to a large extent what price they will pay' (Croft, 1991: 14). Specific complaints in the farming sector were wide ranging. Supermarkets were accused of changing their specifications of fruit and vegetables during a contract, without discussion with the producer; introducing sale or return clauses in supply contracts for highly perishable products; and delaying payments to suppliers (Richardson, 1991; Davies, 1992).

The implications of the economic power of the supermarkets in the food system again aroused concern in the early 1990s after it was argued, first, that British consumers were paying more for basic foodstuffs than consumers in other countries, and second, that supermarket buying strategies were contributing to Britain's balance of payments deficit. It was in this context, whereby, 'the exposed margins of the major British grocery retailers had suddenly become a matter of public debate' (Wrigley, 1992: 1543) that the role of the food retailers in the food system began to be questioned publicly. The supermarkets, though, did not remain passive. Having created favourable market conditions and a dominant position in the food supply system the task was now to sustain it.

In 1987 Safeway had commissioned a study of product sourcing in food retailing carried out by researchers at Stirling University. At the time, Safeway's strategy regarding the geographical sources of its food products was 'broadly neutral'. In other words, the company's approach was 'let us get the product that will sell at the lowest possible price' (A. Grant, 1992: 121). The report was used to demonstrate Safeway's concern about the 'problem' of food imports and to try to identify opportunities for British food manufacturers and suppliers. The report, which was published in March 1991, found that in 1989 Safeway imported £24 million worth of food and drink products and over 50 per cent came from countries with similar climatic, economic and social conditions to the UK (Shaw *et al.*, 1991).

At the same time Food From Britain, the government's food marketing quango, announced that the UK's trade deficit in food and drink for 1990 was £6 billion, 63 per cent of which was accounted for by potentially indigenous produce rather than exotic food stuffs. The food trade deficit represented 42 per cent of the total current account deficit, and Food From Britain argued that reducing the gap was an issue of major importance to the national economy. However, it framed the 'problem' in different terms, suggesting that the UK was 'not on a level playing field with the rest of Europe with significantly lower relative government expenditure on agriculture, food promotion and on food industry resources' (House of Commons Agriculture Committee, 1992b: 2).

In August 1991 the *Sunday Times* published findings of a survey it had conducted on food prices in Europe under the headline of 'Scandal over Britain's high food prices'. It was claimed that British consumers were paying 'up to twice as much for basic foods as consumers in other western countries'. The survey revealed that the average mark up for ten basic food products was 61 per cent in UK supermarkets, compared with 42 per cent in the United States and 22 per cent in Germany, whilst UK supermarket profit margins were up to 8 per cent compared with 2 per cent in Europe and 1 per cent in the US (*Sunday Times*, 1991). The newspaper reported that the House of Commons Agriculture Committee would be investigating the 'mark-up policies of British supermarkets' (*Sunday Times*, 1991: 1). At this stage, farming, consumer groups and press opinion were framing the 'problem' as being one of economic ruthlessness by powerful supermarkets who were making excess profits and at the same time compounding Britain's trade deficit through their buying practices. In November 1991 the Prime Minister chaired a seminar at Downing Street to discuss the problem of the food trade gap which was attended by MAFF officials and representatives from the agricultural, horticultural, food manufacturing and food retailing sectors. They agreed to engage in 'collaborative action' to encourage producers to get together in marketing groups, and retailers to label food products with the country of origin (see House of Commons Agriculture Committee, 1992: 308–9).

When the House of Commons Agriculture Committee began hearing evidence regarding the food trade gap in December 1991, the different actors and agencies involved all had their own definitions of what the 'problem' was. Food From Britain saw the problem as one of its own under-funding resulting in poor export promotion compared to competitors. The food retailers saw the problem, firstly, as one of poor marketing by British suppliers and secondly, of a swing in public opinion towards seeing supermarkets as economically ruthless in their search for profit at the expense of the consumer interests and the national balance of trade. At the same time, British farmers saw the problem as one of excessive supermarket buying power in the marketplace which tied farmers to highly restrictive contracts with poor arrangements for payments. Finally, MAFF saw the issue as one arising from the operation of a free market in food and drink products. The role of government in such circumstances was to ensure a level playing field in regulatory terms in the face of variable levels of foreign intervention and market distortion.

It was this last interpretation of the food trade gap that prevailed. No longer was the focus on the oligopolistic power of food retailers but on an 'irregular European playing field' and the problematic structure of national agricultural marketing arrangements. From being identified as the culprit in the food trade gap, and despite their increasing oligopoly, retailers were redefined as a vibrant sector – the harbingers of competitve capitalism – simply following the signals from the international supply market in which they operated. Pressure for change was thus placed on other parts of the food system, especially producers, to refine their systems of delivery and improve the quality of their produce to make them more attractive to the supermarkets, so reinforcing ties of dependency.

However, the efforts towards market closure by the multiple retailers have been challenged from another direction, by the discount retail sector. British-based discounters generated sales of £4 billion in 1992 compared with £2 billion in 1983. This figure is expected to double by 1996. In 1992 they controlled only 9 per cent of the market but this figure is expected to double by 1995. This growth has been accompanied and fuelled by increasing interest from overseas retailers. Since 1990, German-owned Aldi and the Danish-owned Netto, have established stores in the UK, particularly in the North and Midlands. In 1992, the French retailer Carrefour launched its price cutting Ed discount chain in the UK, while the US warehouse club operator, Cost Co, plans to be trading in three outlets by the end of 1993. Only one of the UK's top three discount chains is UK owned, with the bulk of the discount sales accounted for by Kwiksave, Netto and Aldi.

After a considerable period of market growth, concentration and increasing power over other parts of the food system, by the late 1980s the food retailers were increasingly having to participate in the politics of market maintenance. This was to engage them in a much more diversified set of economic and political contexts.

New patterns of food regulation: from producer corporatism to private interest government

Changes in the increasingly internationalised economic relations of the food system have a political counterpart. New rules, regulations and a changing political context have led to revised patterns of intermediation between the farming community and government, and between the government and food processors and retailers. Whilst the nature of contemporary economic changes are now relatively well understood, the same is not true of the emergent forms and processes of political regulation. More generally, as Cerny suggests:

> The analysis of deregulation and re-regulation is of a state mediating between powerful opposing interests, deregulating here, and re-regulating there, normally trying to change as little as possible while adapting to limitations imposed by wider market or institutional/technological conditions, but occasionally having to impose more extensive changes in the balance of interests which are given priority or special attention. (1991: 192)

The question is how can we conceptually and empirically progress these issues so as to weld together a more meaningful analysis of the state/food sector nexus?

During the post-war years agricultural policy was highly regulated and centralised. The links that developed between the National Farmers' Union and the Ministry of Agriculture have been regarded as the classic case of corporatism in the UK (Grant, 1983; Cox *et al.*, 1985). This enshrined the importance of private producer interests at the expense of other bodies who would have wished to be involved in the making of agricultural policy. Public policy was not open to public participation. For food manufacturers and retailers these arrangements were acceptable so long as they ensured plentiful supplies of good quality, cheap food and food inputs.

The relationship between the state and farmers was to be undermined both politically and economically, however. Entry to the EC disrupted Britain's traditional patterns of food production and supply. Britain had to cope with new forms of internationalisation and this began to test the national forms of producer corporatism. Movement to the European stage of policy-making weakened the relationships between MAFF and the NFU just at the time when the magnitude of agricultural support was to be more seriously questioned. Moreover, faced with fiscal crises successive Conservative governments recognised the need to attack corporatist type relationships. They were seen as privileging anachronistic sectional interests in policy-making and impeding the free working of markets. The maintenance of such relations within Europe was seen, as our discussion of the food trade gap demonstrates, as an impediment to the elusive level playing field.

The traditional form of agricultural producer corporatism has been progressively superseded by new forms of micro corporatism. The state has sought to disengage as much as possible from direct involvement in food regulation, passing the responsibility on to the retailers and, to a lesser extent, the other non-farm parts of the food sector. It is the multiple retailers who become the key actors in the post-productivist food system, and who now have political legitimacy for regulatory control they were largely undertaking already in the exercise of their considerable economic power. Consequently, although public consumption interests may appear to be to the fore, certainly if one accepts the rhetoric of the retailers, they are in fact continually refracted through private commercial interests. In other words it is left to the retailers themselves, who are involved in socially moulding and creating demands, to represent 'their' consumers' interests.

As this analysis implies market structures and regulatory frameworks are inextricably linked. In the heyday of agricultural corporatism, the political and economic weakness of individual farmers was counterbalanced by collective organisation and state intervention over farm incomes and food prices, which in turn protected the economic position of food manfucturers. By the late 1980s the position had shifted dramatically. Retailers were now operating in an oligopolistic domestic market and sought to structure the food market to facilitate flexibility, certainty and product standards in their supplies, and in doing so have increasingly looked overseas. Meanwhile, regulatory structures have been recast to be supportive and flexible towards their interests.

Wrigley (1991) has described the period since the mid 1980s as 'the golden age of British grocery retailing', an era characterised by a 'benign regulatory environment' (1992: 779). The retailers, it should be added, have partly created and then reproduced the benign environment. Statutory legitimation for retailers' regulatory role came with the Food Safety Act 1990. The Act was a response to EC pressures and domestic concern surrounding food hygiene, following a number of health scares in the late 1980s. The passage and the establishment of the Act tended to veer towards the interests of the food industry with a stated aim of protecting 'the needs of an innovative and competitive food industry by avoiding unnecessary burdens and controls' (HMSO, 1990). For example, the Act permitted the selective irradiation of food products, a move favoured by the processors and some of the retailers as it prolonged shelf life while reducing the risks of contamination. Whilst irradiation was the most controversial aspect of the Act amongst food campaigners, more significant in policy terms was the shift in responsibility for food quality control away from the public environmental health inspectorate and towards the private retailers. Local government faced severe financial constraints throughout the 1980s, and with a growing number of food hygiene issues, Environmental Health Officers (EHOs) were spread too thinly to be effective regulators. Moreover, they were not regarded by central government as a key professional group and rarely seem to have been consulted in the preparation of legislation.

It is now the responsibility of food outlets to demonstrate that they have taken 'all reasonable precautions' and shown 'due diligence' in the manufacture, transportation, storage and preparation of foodstuffs. As one managing director of a large retailing firm has commented, even a small manufacturer can:

> gain access to very large markets because all he has to do is produce the product. Now in doing this he gets immense support from his customer. He gets technical advice in producing the product, in maintaining quality standards, in adhering to the Food Safety Act, and we (the retailers) have an obligation to exercise due diligence. (House of Commons Agriculture Committee, 1992b: 111)

In exercising 'due diligence' retailers are likely to take a different approach to that of the Environmental Health Officers, who have tended to focus on point-of-sale inspection rather than monitoring the food manufacturing process (see Painter, 1981). The retailers, in contrast, look into the mixing bowl of food production and manufacture. In doing so, their international procurement strategies may mean they have to transgress national food hygiene and environmental regulations in sourcing countries. Once they have done so, however, they can market products built around their own quality standards.

As part and parcel of the legitimation of its regulatory responsibilities, the retail sector has had to restructure itself at the political level to deal with government. Of central importance here has been the development of the Retail Consortium. Constituted from the representatives of all the major retail companies, in 1992 it merged with the British Retailers Association, the long-standing trades association for retailing. The merger was brought about so as to enhance the representational effectiveness of the sector to government, both at the national and the international level. Increasingly, retailers have to keep one eye on the competitive food chain and another on the Europeanisation of markets and food regulation. As the chairman of the Retail Consortium argued shortly before the merger:

> Legislation and regulation emanating from the EC are rapidly overtaking that from Westminster in their direct and indirect impact on our industry. The past year (1991) has seen numerous proposals in the Social Action programme; protectionism on food issues masquerading as consumer protection; major proposals on eco-labelling and packaging waste; the continuing debate over VAT and excise duties; and many more. (RTA, 1991: 4)

As the responsibilities conferred on retailers have increased over the course of the past decade the sector has also been forced to diversify its representational efforts to include a whole range of concerns associated with trading, planning and the environment, credit supply and social order issues. Like other groups, the Consortium seeks to press its views on government through representations to Ministers and civil servants; briefing meetings with MPs on current legislation; contributing to an all-party group of MPs and peers on the retail industry; and participation and lobbying at the European level in groups such as the European Multiples Federation (GEDIS) and the European Confederation for Retailing (CECD).

These diverse sets of political relations are suggestive of a powerful regulatory and legitimatory role both within the food sector and beyond. In their relations with government the retailers are beginning to formally represent the 'consumer interest'. They are currently influencing directly the development of European-wide standards for food quality, arguing against specific and separate food commodity measures, and for more generalised guidelines. Three-cornered negotiations occur on a range of food quality issues involving MAFF, the retailers and EC directorates. For example, the Retail Consortium has pressed the government to dismantle the monopoly powers of the Milk and Potato marketing boards and to remove the privileges conferred on Caribbean banana exporters. It has also supported the deletion of an EC requirement that produce be labelled to show pesticide treatments (i.e. P number labelling), and it has successfully defended its members' rights to continue to use the term 'free range' on a variety of poultry products.

In these ways we begin to see how retailers are managing the process of competitive and regulatory internationalisation both in the supply and delivery of food, and in its regulation. They are operating both within national government as well as beyond it. Although their retail interests are still largely nationally based, they need to influence off-shore markets and regulations from a position of national strength.

Conclusion

New forms of internationalisation and the increasing power of the consumer end of the food chain are combining to create new forms of national regulation. These are hastening the demise of producer-based corporatism, so much a feature of the post-war national farm policies of most advanced nations, which are giving way to new forms of 'private interest' regulation, whereby the state empowers particular private interests to act on its behalf.

Overseeing food procurement, production and delivery has traditionally been viewed as a major state activity. The emergence of neo-conservative politics in the 1970s assisted the demise of this overt strategic role, and technological advances, combined with the oligopolistic power of food manufacturers and retailers, have reformed the boundaries between private and public interests in food consumption. Whoever controls and then delivers the *rights to consume* becomes a major legitimatory agent in neo-conservative politics, and this axis of concern starts to outweigh the more traditional state concerns associated with increasing primary production or protecting family farms. Having a considerable role in creating 'consumer interests' during the 1980s retailers and the state now have to sustain them politically and socially. Food hygiene scares, concerns over nutritional standards and rising public consciousness about food quality more generally, together with new levels of competition from discount retailers (from home and abroad) mean that the disjunctures between market structures, regulation and the politics of legitimacy have to be continually addressed. Growing internationalisation of food supply and regulation will test the robustness of the British private interest model of regulation.

Regulating new and more variable forms of consumption is a high-profile activity not without political risks. The delegation of power to the retailers produces a new custodialism not only for the food system, but also in terms of the protection and promotion of consumer rights. It remains to be seen whether the regulatory state and the retailers can sustain their new found public responsibilities.

References

Agricultural Supply Industry (1990) 'NFU to meet supermarkets over profitability gap', *Agricultural Supply Industry*, 20 (49), 2.

Bamfield, J. (1988) 'Competition and change in British retailing', *National Westminster Bank Quarterly Review*, February 1988, 15–29.

Cerny, P. (1991) 'The limits of deregulation: transnational interpenetration and policy change', *European Journal of Political Research*, 19, 173–96.

Clunies-Ross, T. and Hildyard, N. (1992) *The Politics of Industrial Agriculture*. London: Earthscan.

Croft, A. (1991) 'Talking point', *Farmers Weekly*, 1.3.91, 14.

Cox, G., Lowe, P. and Winter, M. (1985) 'Changing direction in agricultural policy: corporatist arrangements in production and conservation policies', *Sociologia Ruralis*, 25 (2), 130–54.

Cumming, D. (1990) 'Safety in the food industry; distribution and retailing', 61–7, in F. Miller (ed.) *Food Safety in the Human Food Chain* CAS Paper 20. Reading: Centre for Agricultural Strategy.

Davies, R. (1992) 'Slow-pay supermarkets must be brought to book', *Farmers Weekly*, 15.5.92, 22.

Davis, K., Gilligan, C. and Sutton, C. (1985) 'Structural changes in grocery retailing: the implications for concentration', *International Journal of Physical Distribution and Materials Management*, 15, 3–48.

Friedland, W. (1991) 'The transnationalisation of production and consumption of food and fibre: challenges for rural research', Chapter 3 in R. Almas and N. With (eds) *Rural Futures in an International World*. Trondheim: Centre for Rural Research.

Grant, A. (1992) 'Oral evidence to the Agriculture Committee' 120–6, in House of Commons Agriculture Committee (1992b) *op. cit.*

Grant, W. (1983) 'The National Farmers' Union: the classic case of incorporation?', in D. Marsh (ed.) *Pressure Politics*, London: Junction Books.

Harvey, D. (ed.) (1987) *The Future of the Agricultural and Food System* EPARD Working Paper No. 1, Department of Agricultural Economics and Management, University of Reading.

Hirst, P. and Zeitlin, J. (1991) 'Flexible specialisation versus post Fordism: theory, evidence and policy implications', *Economy and Society*, 20 (1), 1–56.

HMSO (1990) *The Food Safety Act*. London: HMSO.

House of Commons Agriculture Committee (1992a) *The Trade Gap in Food and Drink* Vol 1 – Report and proceedings of the Committee. London: HMSO.

House of Commons Agriculture Committee (1992b) *The Trade Gap in Food and Drink* Vol 2 – Minutes of Evidence and Appendices. London: HMSO.

The Independent (1990) 'Struggling against falling profits', 20.8.90, 5.

MAFF (1988) *Annual Review of Agriculture*. London: HMSO.

Marsden, T.K., Murdoch, J., Lowe, P., Munton, R. and Flynn, A. (1993) *Constructing the Countryside*. London: University College London Press.

McDonald, J., Rayner, A. and Bates, J. (1989) 'Market power in the food industry: a note', *Journal of Agricultural Economics*, 40, 101–8.

McMichael, P. and Myhre, D. (1991) 'Global regulations versus the nation-state: agro-food systems and the new politics of capitalism', *Capital and Class*, 43, 83–105.

Monopolies and Mergers Commission (1981) *Discounts to Retailers*. London: Monopolies and Mergers Commission.

Newby, H. and Utting, P. (1984) 'Agribusiness in the United Kingdom: social and political implications', 265–89, in G. Beradi and C. Geisler (eds) *The Social*

Consequences and Challenges of New Agricultural Technologies. Boulder, Colorado: Westview.

Office of Fair Trading (1985) *Competition and Retailing*. London: HMSO.

Painter, M. (1981) 'Enforcement, a rethink?' *FDIC Bulletin*, July.

Retail Trades Association (1991) *Annual Report*. London: RTA.

Richardson, D. (1991) 'Chain reaction in UK food marketing', *Financial Times*, 3.4.91, 32.

Senker, J. (1990) 'Technology and competitive strategy in food retailing', 83–94, in R. Loveridge and M. Pitt (eds) *The Strategic Management of Technological Innovation*. London: Wiley.

Shaw, S., Dawson, J. and Blair, L. (1991) *Opportunities for British Food Suppliers: Product Sourcing in the Food Chain*. University of Stirling/Safeway.

The Sunday Times (1991) 'Scandal over Britain's high food prices', 18.8.91, 1 and 16.

Ward, N. (1990) 'A preliminary analysis of the UK food chain', *Food Policy*, 13, 439–41.

Wrigley, N. (1987) 'The concentration of capital in UK grocery retailing', *Environment and Planning*, A 19, 1283–8.

Wrigley, N. (1991) 'Is the "golden age" of British grocery retailing at a watershed?', *Environment and Planning*, A 23, 1537–44.

Wrigley, N. (1992) 'Antitrust regulation and the restructuring of grocery retailing in Britain and the USA', *Environment and Planning*, A 24, 727–49.

CHAPTER 6

Agricultural Deregulation: The Case of New Zealand

Paul Cloke and Richard Le Heron

Introduction

It is by now almost passé to emphasise the way in which 'new right' politics and ideologies have been responsible for a wide range of impacts on rural societies in both the developed (see Bell and Cloke, 1989; Flora and Christenson, 1991) and developing (see Ramanadham, 1989) worlds. Much has been written about the political leadership associated with the new right (Cloke, 1992a; Gamble, 1988; Green, 1988; King, 1987), and about how the increasing dominance of market mechanisms and the concomitant rolling back of welfare states and planning apparatus have important implications for rural change (see, for example, Buttel, 1989a; Cloke, 1992b).

There is now a general acceptance that in previous rounds of restructuring the interests of capital accumulation have been served by state intervention in the form of regulating the economy in various ways, but in current rounds of restructuring such interests are facilitated by increasing freedom from regulation of the investment process. This change from regulation to deregulation has, however, been most evident in the service sector of rural economies, with production, particularly in the agricultural sector, being so intertwined with state support as to be regarded as almost immune from the deregulatory process. The frictions of deregulation of agricultural support are well known, due at least in part to the position of agricultural capital and related interests within international, national and local power relations. In many cases a cosy position of corporatism between agriculture and government had until recently been standard, and although this had been verbally challenged by new right politicians in the UK and the USA, the wider deregulatory pressures had not been extended to the agricultural sector to any great extent.

Against this background, the actions of the New Zealand government in sponsoring a speedy programme of withdrawal of agricultural subsidies and other benefits during the mid 1980s (see Willis, 1988; Cloke, 1989; Le Heron, 1991; Britton *et al.*, 1992) serves as a locus classicus for attempts to understand the impacts of deregulatory state practices in the agricultural domain. In this chapter we offer a brief summary of some of the key perspectives from regulation theory and discuss the ways in which the regulationist literature has been used to provide accounts of agricultural change. Our account reveals that when comprehensively applied, regulation theory encourages conceptualisation of the regulation of particular sectors (such as agriculture) in terms of the scope of regulation forms, a range of regulatory sites and the detail of regulatory content. This approach allows the regulatory implications of the economic and state restructuring in New Zealand during the 1980s to be interpreted in a new light. Whereas conventional writings would place emphasis on the deregulation process *per se*, a regulation-inspired analysis recognises the possibility that many unacknowledged and undocumented regulatory arrangements may have been shaping accumulation centred on agriculture.

We then review the specific deregulatory measures instituted by the New Zealand government and place these in the context of New Zealand's location in the wider world food economy. In particular we pose the question of whether deregulation of agriculture is actually possible within one nation state given the interconnected nature of the international political economy. The question derives from the fact that restructuring has introduced a very different regulatory environment with several interlocking and distinctive dimensions. These have involved for agriculture: first, new patterns of governance emanating from enterprise behaviour in the new macro-economic policy environment; second, the overlay of different regulatory infrastructures arising from resource management and sustainability pressures; and third, a complete reorganisation of 'public good' science and technology policy and funding which has seen the establishment of new profit-oriented research organisations. Thus, an exploration of agricultural deregulation is in part an exposé of the reductionist position that has tended to characterise many investigations informed by regulation theory. We conclude that the regulatory respite which found expression in general deregulation has led in the current conjuncture in New Zealand agriculture to a new set of contradictions which are likely to generate persistent tensions over the next decade.

Regulatory theory and agriculture

The regulationist literature is both extensive and fractured into different schools of thought. It was first developed by Aglietta's (1979) attempts to suggest how the social relations of capitalism are reproduced over space and time, given that obvious contradictions occur which seem to jeopardise that reproduction. Subsequently it has been chewed over by a vast array of researchers (see for example, Chouinard, 1990; Cooke, 1989; Dunford, 1990; Florida and Feldman, 1988; Gretler, 1988; Harvey and Scott, 1988; Sayer, 1989; Schoenberger, 1989) who have largely been interested in industrial change in the urban and regional arenas. A key notion to arise from this work, and one which has served to unify the discursive factions associated with regulationism, is that the expansion of the social reproduction of capitalism is never certain, but has to be achieved through a range of social norms, mechanisms and institutions which help to provide relatively stable relations between production and consumption within a particular *regime of accumulation* (see Jessop, 1990).

One of the attractions of the regulationist literature is that attempts may be made to identify these regimes of accumulation in time and space. Aglietta (1979: 71) for example, suggests 'two regimes of accumulation which we call the predominantly extensive and the predominantly intensive' and identifies these in the case of the USA as Taylorism and Fordism:

> Fordism is the state that supersedes Taylorism . . . . It marks a new stage in the regulation of capitalism, the regime of intensive accumulation in which the capitalist class seeks overall management of the production of wage-labour by the close articulation of relations of production with the commodity relations in which the wage earners purchase their means of consumption. (p. 117)

More recently, numerous observers have expounded a further shift in the regime of accumulation, referring to post-Fordist economies, post-industrial societies, post-modern culture and new times (Harvey, 1989). Here the concoction of flexible accumulation, niche marketing and consumption, the rolling back of the welfare-state, the decreasing importance of collectivist bargaining and labourist politics, and the empowerment of the market through processes of privatisation and deregulation, is seen by many as marking both the result of a major crisis of regulation (Lipietz, 1988) and the transition to a new regime of accumulation. The idea of a sea change from Fordism to post-Fordism has been vigorously questioned, and implies not only a transfer to a more flexible form of economic production but also a plethora of changes in the associated norms, mechanisms and institutions which influence the social, political and cultural practices of a particular regulatory period (Cloke and Goodwin, 1992). Nevertheless the idea of a post-Fordist era is now sufficiently well established for us to use these regulationist concepts to interrogate changes in agricultural policy.

Several researchers have begun to use regulation theory in their analysis of agricultural change, but such a direction is not without its critics. Goodman and Redclift for example suggest that:

> while modern agriculture's contribution to fordist consumption via post-war cheap food policies is clear, the attempt to equate agriculture and industry is misguided . . . agriculture's contribution to fordist consumption and accumulation is based on the *failure* to apply 'fordist' principles to the rural labour process. State intervention and its specific characteristics can be traced directly to this failure of industrial capital to *regiment* and *rationalise* productive capacity. Agriculture remains an unstable, volatile sector of activity, with a pronounced tendency in the absence of state intervention towards low returns and over-production crises. (1991: 100–1)

The argument here – that agriculture is something of a special case, with distinctive labour and capital characteristics which do not conform to Fordist norms as found (for example) in manufacturing industries – is mirrored elsewhere (see, for example, Marsden *et al.*, 1993) in the wider suggestion that rural areas are attractive to 1990s entrepreneurs *precisely* because they offer repositories of labour and enterprise which have *not* been subject to Fordist collectivism.

Many other analysts of agricultural change are, however, convinced that regulation theory, with its account of the transformation of regimes of accumulation, can be applied to agriculture, Kenney *et al.* (1989) put this point forcefully and succinctly:

> Regulation theory underscores the key factors important for an understanding of agricultural transformation: the ways in which the farmer is integrated into wider circuits of production and consumption; the effects of external economic processes, such as the development of new technology and markets, on the agricultural system; and the role of the state in [influencing] . . . farmers' political responses to agricultural transformation. (p. 36)

Most of these analyses thus far have focused on the ways in which Fordist industrialisation and the modernisation of family farming may be connected, and on how a transition to post-Fordist regimes of accumulation is occurring in these two areas. Regulation theory thereby offers a perspective on the farm 'crisis' (Goodman and Redclift, 1989) with its associated indicators of higher debt levels, changes in fiscal and monetary policy and in real interest rates, declining land values, declining export sales and commodity prices, and the uneven incidence of farm financial stress (see Buttel, 1989b).

The 'crisis' in US agriculture has been described in detail by Kenney *et al.* (1989, 1991). In their view the Fordist regime represented the outcome of particular struggles and class compromises sparked off by the Great Depression, and created a vast consumer market which agriculture responded to by producing mass commodities of uniform quality. Farmers themselves were further integrated into circuits of consumption both as consumers of industrially processed foods and as consumers of mass-produced inputs such as fertilisers and tractors (see Page and Walker, 1991). The period 1950–73 is described as the Golden Age of US Fordism during which agriculture experienced steady growth in yields, farm income became stable, government subsidies were manageable and the relative cost of food declined.

During the Fordist period, however, internal contradictions were developing which would lead to the crisis of US Fordism and of US agriculture. Initially agriculture benefited from a global food shortfall. The Reagan presidency, however, introduced a raft of monetarist measures in order to fight inflation, resulting in declining land prices and farm incomes and ultimately to a surge of farm foreclosures (see Mooney, 1986). At the same time, the 'crisis' was given an additional dimension by the increasingly vociferous debate on the contribution of farming to industrial pollution.

This perspective sees US agriculture as having reached crisis point:

> The fordist model is now in crisis and the contradictions that it has evolved do not seem resolvable within the logic.... One possibility to consider is how post-crisis agriculture can be made to fit the needs of producers – farmers as well as workers – while reversing the current trajectory of environmental degradation. (Kenney *et al.*, 1991: 185)

The suggestion is that this post-crisis agriculture will steer away from the post-war settlement in which farmers were integrated into Fordist circuits of capital and commodity. There will, however, continue to be contradictions between the aim of reversing environmental degradation and the US government's policy of seeking a 'level playing field' in international trade (through the dismantling of current measures of internal support, import access and export subsidies) which is based on the assumption that its efficient, mechanised and technologically advanced farmers will compete favourably in international markets on these terms (see McMichael, this volume).

A broadly similar account of agricultural transformation in Europe is provided by Sauer (1990) who describes the formation of a Fordist strategy of market regulation for the modernisation of German agriculture and the crisis occurring in this 'one-track growth orientation of industrial policies'

(p. 269) when confronted not only with the economic imperatives of a changing Common Agricultural Policy within the EC, but also with the increasingly pressing debates on environmental damage, on the upgrading of work and activity associated with peasant labour, and on the negative effects of 'unremitting commoditisation and industrialisation of the division of labour at an international level' (p. 270). Sauer sees only a slow growth of post-Fordist alternatives to the Fordist modernisation of farming in Germany, partly because most farms remain tied, both financially and technically to industrialised structures of marketing and production, and partly because of the continuing social relations of family farming which remain culturally tied to the mechanisms and dependencies of Fordist modernisation.

Use of concepts drawn from the regulationist literature, then, allow a clear rewriting of the history of the relations of agricultural production and agricultural policy and point to current farm crises as being the inevitable outcomes of the contradictions inherent in Fordist regimes of accumulation. But what about current and future changes? As is clear from the above, regulationist accounts have tended to stop at the stage of the crisis of Fordism and to be rather vague and speculative about post-Fordist expectations for farming. However, there does seem to be an association between some accounts of future farming policies and the social relations of flexible accumulation emphasised in the post-Fordist account. For example, Commins' account of the restructuring of agriculture in advanced economies concludes by suggesting that:

> we may interpret the implications of this critical juncture in agricultural restructuring as the need for the state to strike a new balance between the continuing requirements of capital accumulation in agriculture and the necessity of maintaining the social conditions – minimum levels of political consensus and quiescence – under which accumulation in general can occur. In the EC's case the compromise involves, on the one hand, a general appeal to productive efficiency within restrictive output limits and diversification of surplus productive capacity in new directions and, on the other hand, the greater institutionalisation of the social or legitimative functions of 'non-productive' farming in modern society. (1990: 71)

Such an account appears to highlight elements of a potentially post-Fordist regime: new social conditions under which accumulation may be reproduced; new, diversified directions for surplus capacity; and legitimation of 'non-productive' farming whether this be geared towards environmental and landscape management or towards other diversified enterprises. Such changes require both flexibility of accumulation conditions and some deregulatory state policy to permit new land uses and even new forms of ecological or environmental production. It could therefore be that a post-Fordist regime of accumulation for agriculture in advanced nations will entail the deregulation of agricultural production and of the use of agricultural land, the diversification of farm enterprise to suit niche-related production and consumption, and the sponsorship of socio-cultural relations in rural areas which increasingly reflect the self-help and exclusivist cultures of the entrepreneur, the craftsperson and the artisan. In this complex arena, new versions of governance involving networking enterprises are likely to appear, breaking down the categories of public and private sectors which were such a dominant features of the post-war boom. It is with this portfolio of expectations that we now turn to the New Zealand case.

New Zealand agriculture

A regulated industry

Any account of agricultural change in New Zealand should begin with a reassertion that contemporary agriculture is international in character, with producers being interconnected with international commodity prices and being subject to strategies of adjustment in response to international food and finance chains (see Schuh, 1986). It follows that the contemporary structures, relations and circumstances in New Zealand agriculture cannot solely be viewed as the outcome of national policies. Rather they are more complex outcomes from the interrelationships between the international political economy and the response and counter-response of national policy, regional policy and economic actors.

As a small nation highly dependent upon its agricultural exports, New Zealand proceeded through the Fordist era with a highly regulated framework of social and economic relations. New Zealand may be regarded as a country on the semi-periphery (Roche *et al.*, 1992) which has developed patterns of production, consumption and welfare akin to those in core nations, while relying on the export of primary-based products in an economy somewhat characteristic of a peripheral nation. It did so firstly (from the late 1930s onwards) through a strategy of isolationism, which gave the agricultural sector a special status by guaranteeing prices for dairy produce and which, more broadly, relied on import licensing and exchange controls to regulate international trade. The outcome of isolationism was an increasing requirement for export growth, and the national economy thus become dependent upon the receipts from agricultural products sold on international markets, first in Britain, and then more widely as Britain's entry into the EC restricted available sales there. The search for new markets was accompanied by a related search for new products to take to those markets, and so there is a long history of diversification in New Zealand's agriculture for this reason. In the 1960s diversification related largely to meat and dairy products, but by the 1970s horticulture had also become an important export sector.

The state's involvement in these changes was as an integral regulator of a national development programme of export-led growth (see Wallace and Lattimore, 1987; Le Heron, 1989; Sandrey and Reynolds, 1990). During the 1960s state resources were made available to support the agricultural export drive. These included low interest development loans and tax concessions and subsidies on fertiliser and transport. By the 1970s the rate of growth in agriculture had slowed partly because of high internal rates of inflation. Accordingly, in 1971 headage payments on sheep were introduced, and were used intermittently throughout the decade as a form of direct income support to the farmers concerned. Market prices for sheepmeat and wool were also underpinned by state funds, and in 1978 the Supplementary Minimum Prices scheme (SMPs) was introduced which guaranteed prices in the livestock sector as a further stimulus to investment. According to Hawke (1978), these were: 'little more than indiscriminate subsidies to farm exporters' which were 'rapidly incorporated into land values and substantially captured by suppliers of farm inputs and processors of farm produce' (para 1.9).

The national development programme also promoted a set of state-centred institutions and infrastructures which were part of the regulation of agricultural production. These included state-supported agricultural research and development, producer and marketing boards for each commodity type, generous credit facilities for farmers (especially from the state-owned rural bank) and extensive farm advisory and product-testing services. Alongside these specific farm-related services, the agricultural sector also benefited from a series of legislative measures which restricted foreign ownership of land and controlled land aggregation in country areas.

This programme was corporatist in nature, relying on a loose but important alliance of government politicians and civil servants, agricultural scientists and economists, and representatives of the farming lobby. Together they defined sectoral targets which were then advertised and 'sold' to farmers as being worthwhile both personally and nationally. As Le Heron *et al.* (1992) explain:

> To make the 'model' work, policies were devised to entice farmers as investors to increase their production, particularly livestock numbers... fluctuating responses by farmers to incentives and uncontrollable influences such as drought and the threat of British entry to the EC, however, forced experimentation with the policy mix. In all, three phases of assistance to the livestock sector appeared, graduating from support for inputs, then to output and finally to price support. During each phase the policy agenda was dominated by productionist issues, though on two occasions, first in the early 1970s

> and then again in the early 1980s, the question of 'farm income' support surfaced as an appropriate policy objective. (pp. 270–1)

Thus by the mid 1980s the New Zealand government had regulated agriculture to the extent of a comprehensive package of intervention policies which were seen as vital incentives to agricultural export production (see Table 6.1). This was part of a well-entrenched dual economy (see Cloke *et al.*, 1990) alongside strong protectionist measures against the import of manufactured goods, designed to encourage home-based manufacturing. McLean (1978) suggests that such a dual economy raised inevitable contradictions within the New Zealand economy, with the high cost of home-produced industrial inputs to agriculture, and of regulated wage and price levels, causing considerable friction between agricultural and industrial capitals.

Table 6.1 New Zealand's package of intervention policies prior to the deregulation of agriculture

Type of intervention	*Chief example(s)*
Input subsidies	Fertiliser subsidies
	Interest rate concessions
	Irrigation subsidies
	Electricity subsidies
Production subsidies	Supplementary minimum prices
Development schemes	Livestock incentive scheme
	Land development loans
Research and services	MAFF health and research
Producer board subsidies	Interest rate concessions
Tax expenditures	Investment allowances
	Export incentives
Industry control	Town milk industry
	Egg industry
Producer board legislation	NZ Mean Producer Board
	Dairy Board
	Apple and Pear Board
State ownership	Rural Banking and Finance Corporation

Source: Cloke (1989: 36)

Deregulation processes and emerging regulatory tendencies

In 1984 the newly elected Labour government instituted a radical programme of 'new right' financial policies in order to create conditions which would allow much greater freedom for the development of capitalist market forces. The Prime Minister (David Lange) and the Finance Minister (Roger Douglas) oversaw a series of measures to deregulate the New Zealand economy: removal of wage and price controls, liberalisation of the financial sector, flotation of currency exchange rates, removal of restrictions on currency flows, reduction of import tariffs, removal of import controls, new taxation provisions, major reductions in public expenditure, and a restructuring of the state sector through corporatisation of state-owned businesses and services. Political scientists in New Zealand (see, for example, Bollard and Buckle, 1987; Boston and Holland, 1990; Collins, 1987) suggest that these reforms represent a somewhat chaotic mixture of ideological direction, pragmatic political response to overwhelming economic pressures and 'muddling through'. It would certainly be misleading to represent these reforms as solely a Labour Party phenomenon even though agricultural areas in New Zealand are traditionally National Party territory. As Cloke points out:

> The previous national Prime Minister, Sir Robert Muldoon, was admittedly a kind of old fashioned state socialist who had resisted the wholesale transfer of responsibilities to the private sector. His successor, Jim Bolger, however, made it clear that a National Party victory in the 1987 election would mean a similar set of agricultural policies to those introduced by Labour, though the scale and speed might have been different. (1989: 37)

Given this political consensus for deregulatory change it was unsurprising that swift and radical changes were applied to policies for agriculture, and within three years of the new government, most of the forms of state support for agriculture had been removed. Table 6.2 lists the main components of deregulation, including the dropping of Supplementary Minimum Prices (worth $505 million in 1983–4) and other subsidies (e.g. $47 million paid out on fertilisers and the progressive raising of Rural Bank lending rates to the current market levels). We should note, however, that this did not constitute a complete deregulation, because the constitution of the producer boards meant that markets, and to a lesser extent prices, were the subject of continuing regulation.

Two issues are particularly important in viewing these changes from the perspective of regulation theory: why and how did they come about – is there a sense that they formed part of a new regime of regulation and accumulation in response to previous inconsistencies and contradictions – and what was the impact of a newly deregulated regime on New Zealand's agriculture? The questions of why and how these changes occurred are difficult to answer precisely. Clearly, the costs of supporting agriculture had become unacceptably high. Pryde (1987) notes that on-farm income support and interest subsidies on government loans cost the state some $2.5 billion between 1980 and 1985, and the Lange government was thus faced with an economic crisis because high public spending over this period had been

Table 6.2 Programme of deregulation reforms 1984–6

June 1984

- ending of the Supplementary Minimum Price (SMP) scheme announced
- producer board accounts at the Reserve Bank to be charged 'commercial' interest rates

November 1984 (budget)

- fertiliser subsidies to be phased out by July 1986
- Rural Banking and Finance Corporation (RBFC) interest rates to be raised progressively to market rates
- irrigation and water supply subsidies lowered
- investment taxation allowance to expire
- noxious weeds subsidy ended
- Farm Vendor Finance Scheme ended
- cost recovery of product inspection re-introduced

December 1985 (economic statement)

- S129 Income Tax Act (10-year clawback) to be repealed
- S188 Income Tax Act ($10,000 loss limitation) to be repealed
- land development tax treatment concessions removed
- livestock standard value system put on similar basis to general business taxation

Source: Cloke (1989: 38)

financed by overseas borrowing, which in turn was causing problems with high inflation and interest rates in New Zealand. The macro-economic solution necessarily meant that state support for agriculture could not be continued.

Added to this seemingly inevitable contradiction in the regulatory regime, there were strong pressures from *within* the previously corporatist channels of decision-making for farmers to receive clearer and more direct signals about world markets in order that the necessary processes of diversification or specialised production could be achieved successfully. Government ministers, and particularly agricultural economists within the civil service, were arguing that the state's positioning as effectively the 'risk taker' in farming had meant that there was less incentive for farmers themselves to attain greater efficiency, and that failure to effect necessary changes in the industry would mean that the New Zealand agricultural sector would become progressively less competitive in world markets. Perhaps more surprising, however, was the degree of support given by Federated Farmers of New Zealand (FFNZ) – the main interest group for farmers and very much involved with previous corporatist decision-making – to the direction of the Lange government's reforms. Roche *et al.* (1992) have studied the motions (or 'remits') discussed at Federated Farmers' annual conference held in 1984, just a fortnight after Labour's victory in the election, and note that 'Regulatory remits called for removal of SMP's, the fixed exchange rate, and other regulatory instruments which insulated farmers from the international price signals' (pp. 24–5 of draft).

During the 1984 election, Federated Farmers had argued for deregulatory reforms, and the subsequent programme of removing subsidies and incentives was welcomed by them, although the uneven impacts of these changes (see below) remained a source of concern. It has been further suggested (see Cloke, 1989) that farming opinion on the reforms was divided along clearly defined lines of self-interest. Smaller and heavily indebted farmers feared that the removal of financial support from the state would jeopardise their livelihood, while some of the more highly capitalised elements of family farming, agri-business and agricultural support services saw deregulation as an opportunity to prosper in a leaner, fitter, New Zealand agriculture.

Other domestic influences were also crucial to the speedy transition to a deregulatory regime. In particular the rising importance of financial and commercial capital in New Zealand exerted particular pressures on the new government *not* to make a special case for the agricultural sector in the overall programme of reducing public expenditure. Again, here, we see the state's role as one of having to choose whether to privilege directly some previously dominant fractions of capital, or in effect to penalise those very fractions in levelling the playing field of accumulation for other rising stars of capital. Such a decision was helped in this case by the willingness of key sub-fractions of agricultural capital to support a rapid and radical change in the regulatory regime.

It has been widely acknowledged, however, that despite these important internal negotiations and constraints it was the economic environment *external* to New Zealand which was the most potent force for change. The government's own Treasury review of land use issues in 1984, for example, admits to pressures imposed by the political economic characteristics of export markets and export competition:

> While New Zealand can be critical of policies applied to agriculture by other governments, and seek to have those policies changed when they affect us adversely, we must in the end adapt to the realities of the external situation. (1984: 11)

The 'external situation' referred to here relates not only to the restrictive practices of the European Community and the consequent restraints on entry to traditionally important market places, but also to the complex negotiations on international trade agreements. New Zealand's closer economic relationship (CER) with Australia is of growing significance, but it is the international dimension of the GATT talks which has consistently been a major influence over recent years. Because of its dependence on agricultural exports, New Zealand is highly sensitive to overseas criticism of the support given to its farming sector. During the 1980s there was a great deal of (hypocritical) complaint that New Zealand was dumping its produce at artificially low prices on to world markets and that these practices threatened the harmony of international trading relations. It was this international scale of political economic force and persuasion which was a crucial backdrop to the reforms in New Zealand's agricultural policy in the mid 1980s.

The second question to be answered about the deregulated agricultural environment in New Zealand concerns the impacts on the farming industry itself. Some key precepts should be stressed here. At the time of the radical changes to policy in the mid 1980s, different agro-commodity chains in New Zealand had different immediate levels of potential for organisational and technological change (Britton *et al.*, 1992). In each of the principal chains major companies and producer boards had already begun to diversify their production to meet the needs of new and changing international markets, but the deregulation of the (agricultural) economy meant both that efficiency and profitability came quickly to the fore as major priorities for all investors, and that capital from various sources was able to circulate more freely in land or land-based production as a commodity.

One clear impact of deregulation was the reduction of direct financial assistance to farmers from the state. Table 6.3 charts the assistance given to pastoral agriculture during the 1980s and shows dramatic declines in both output assistance and input assistance by 1990. However, what has sometimes been represented as a *complete* removal of state support did not, in fact, occur: in particular, state aid to farmers in more hidden areas

Table 6.3 Assistance to pastoral agriculture ($NZ million), 1980–90

	1980	*1985*	*1990*
Output assistance[1]	136	630	35
Input assistance[2]	79	57	18
Assistance to value added factors[3]	189	348	153
Total assistance	405	1,035	206
Total value of output	2,621	4,577	6,148

Notes: 1. NZDB stabilisation; meat industry stabilisation; supplementary minimum prices; inspection, grading and hygiene; town milk subsidy.
2. Fertiliser subsidies, Livestock Incentive Scheme and Land Development Encouragement bonus; agricultural pest control.
3. Advisory services, labour, research and extension, animal health and quarantine, interest concessions, taxation concessions, agricultural organisations, Rural Bank debt write-off, climate relief grants.

Source: Tyler and Lattimore (1990: 72–3)

(advice, concessions, debt write-off etc.) – labelled 'value added factors' in Table 6.3 – was reduced less severely. The notion of an *absolute* cross-over from regulation to deregulation is therefore not supportable given this evidence, and further ambiguity in this area stems from the fact that the Ministry of Agriculture and Fisheries remains a significant government department performing many of the same delivery functions which it did before the reforms (see Le Heron *et al.*, 1992).

Nevertheless, the dramatic reductions in state support have led to various farm adjustment strategies. Farms with high debt-to-equity ratios have been hardest hit and short-term strategies of debt rescheduling, reductions in inputs (particularly use of fertilisers), reductions in stocking ratios and making do with existing (rather than new) machinery have been put in place to avoid foreclosure, sometimes without success (see Figure 6.1). Land and livestock prices have also been deflated particularly in the hill country sheep farms and there is some question now of a retreat in the frontier of New Zealand's pastoral farming (see Britton *et al.*, 1992). A further component of these adjustment strategies is that of diversification into tourist enterprises and an increase in farm household pluriactivity. These trends towards diversification and pluriactivity might be interpreted as familiar spectres of a post-Fordist age. Pluriactivity, however, has been a long-standing practice in New Zealand farming (although it has increased recently – Le Heron *et al.*, 1991) and diversification into 'niche' enterprises will be hampered by a small domestic market place despite the growing influence of tourism. Elsewhere in the developed world, diversification into 'farming the landscape' has occurred via state subsidy, but there is little evidence of this in New Zealand.

A further impact of deregulation has been the potential influence of external capital. The policy reforms of the Lange government supposedly pitched New Zealand's agricultural production fully into the global economy, with the prospect of external agencies taking over land and production and of increased exposure to international commodity interests. There has been significant opposition expressed against new (external) players in the New Zealand land markets, especially from Maori interests and others who take an 'anti-foreigner' stance. The current government reaction to this opposition suggests that they are unlikely to reimpose regulations on the circulation of capital which would impede these trends.

One other response to policy changes which bears a markedly post-Fordist expression has been the restructuring of the meat processing industry in New Zealand. In particular there has been a revival in investor interest in small-scale and more flexible meat processing plants, with some 14 of these in operation by 1990. The plants tend to process frozen boned meat in bulk rather than whole carcasses and rely on high-value, high-technology production techniques. Although union membership has been encouraged at the plants, production takes place over a 16-hour, two-shift day and workers take on up to 20 different tasks each, a degree of labour flexibility which

Figure 6.1 Changes in livestock production, 1982–9

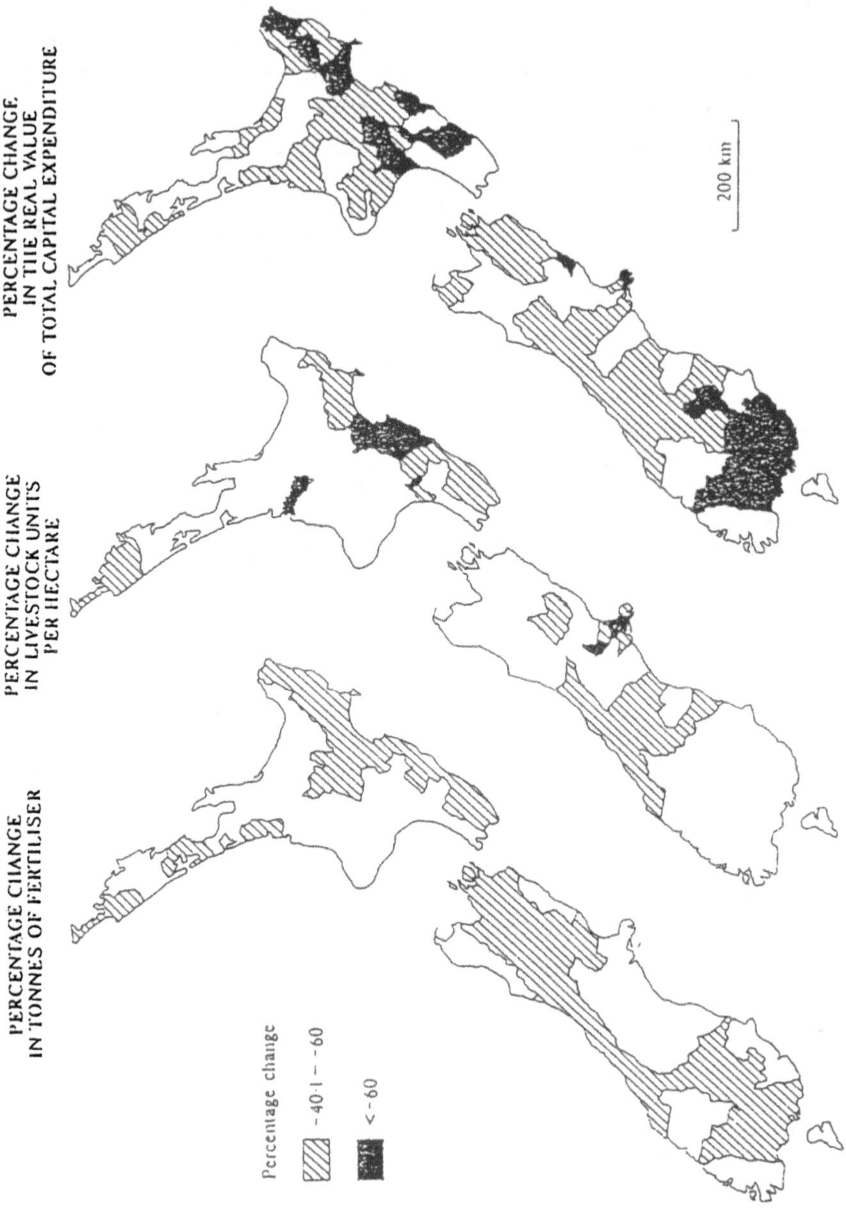

Source: Britton *et al*. (1992: 98)

contrasts strongly with the rigid labour restrictions in force in the more traditional large-scale works. These modern, more flexible plants have resulted in a net loss of jobs in the sector as a whole, and have been able to employ workers at relatively low wages. They appear to epitomise the ensemble of economic, social, political and cultural relations which are thought by some to accompany the flexible regimes of accumulation in post-Fordist new times.

A further dimension to the meat industry example is notable very much in response to the 1991 move of industry ownership into New Zealand hands, with the main co-operative assuming ownership as other players pulled out. The New Zealand Meat Industry Association, a federation of meat companies operating in New Zealand, embarked on a meat industry development plan. The initiative started *outside* the state arena but represented a distinctive regulatory development. It builds on nearly a decade of industry-orchestrated restructuring which has reduced industry killing capacity and the number of jobs in meat works. The main players, grouped under another umbrella (the Meat Planning Council, made up of the large companies and the Meat Producers Board) proposed in August 1993 to divide the key markets amongst the main corporates with 2.5 per cent of total quotas being available for new entrants by a tender process. The 22 small meat companies reacted vigorously, labelling it a 'protective measure for large players in financial strife' (*Evening Standard*, 23 August). An unexpected development was the public announcement by Nippon Meat Packers, Japan's largest meat company of investment in the New Zealand meat industry. The local MP for the area hoping to attract Nippon dismissed the quota system as being 'against the free-market policies promoted by government'.

Overall it is perhaps still too early to say whether these different impacts indicate the likely long-term reaction to agricultural deregulation in New Zealand. There have been some recent indications (Britton *et al.*, 1992) of an upturn in farm investment, livestock numbers and farm improvements but it is unclear whether this is a short-term blip or whether it marks the end of a transitional period of restructuring. This element of doubt arises, at least in part because of a continuing lack of information about the financial state of farm businesses and the income profiles of farm households. Britton *et al.* (1992) identify the following important but unanswered questions:

> How many farm businesses are accumulating, ahead of inflation, and still paying an average wage to household members contributing labour to farm production? What is the situation in farm businesses which are not accumulating enough for long-run household support and business survival? Are these businesses being propped up by the injection of 'free' or 'low cost' family money, cross-subsidies from household earnings gained from non-farm and off-farm work and uncosted

> labour from household members? Do these dimensions to production relations make much difference to the generation, regionally and nationally, of enough farm output to sustain forward processing and value added activity? (p. 114)

In 1992 the New Zealand government completed its restructuring of state sector science and technology provision with the formation of 12 Crown Research Institutes to replace the disestablished departments. These independent organisations have changed the way agricultural research is being conducted in New Zealand (Roche, 1993). Proponents see the payoff as a greater commercialisation of agricultural innovation, while critics suggest the new entities are already exhibiting conservatism in the new policy environment. The general objective of the science and technology reforms is to promote value added export production, within the framework of sustainable agriculture (Science and Technology Expert Panel, 1992). This represents an interesting historical switch in export goals. For nearly 50 years New Zealand's agricultural policy-makers had pursued first product and then market diversification. Refocusing on value added is being interpreted within the confines of existing agro-commodity systems, rather than in terms of developing new inter-sectoral linkages. The case of biotechnology in New Zealand is illustrative of a setback from the deregulation process. The former Department of Scientific and Industrial Research (DSIR) began investigating the potential of biotechnology in 1985 when it set up an embryo transplant laboratory and embarked on genetic mapping and gene sequencing. Funding uncertainties arising from internal restructuring in DSIR and an inability to attract industrial sponsors slowed the state research programme in biotechnology. At the time of changeover to the Crown Research regime, embryo technology research, which is well advanced internationally, could only be described in New Zealand as at the precommercial stage, despite strong scientific opinion that the widespread adoption of embryo technology could raise the productivity of New Zealand's dairy and beef livestock herds by 1 per cent per annum above present rates. In contrast, the 'drought seed' package quickly developed by DSIR Grasslands in 1988–9 is an instance of opportunistic response in the new policy order. Research at Grasslands in the 1970s had identified plant cultivars suitable for the drought conditions of different regions, but the uptake of new seeds released by DSIR was minimal. This reflected to a degree the animal bias in agricultural research and extension in New Zealand. A national survey of farmers in 1985 (the beginning of deregulation in the agricultural sector) revealed that they wanted to see demonstrations of seed performance before they would adopt new varieties. The 1988 drought in Canterbury and the east coast of North Island gave the partially restructured Grasslands the opening to develop a new demonstration strategy (many small plots scattered throughout a region instead of a single large 'distant' research station) and to put in place a new extension infrastructure (complementing the Ministry of Agriculture's post-restructuring specialisation on financial services to farmers). Grasslands set up Grass Line, a consultancy with the objective of promoting the drought seed package. At a local level farmer access to the new technology broke down both the livestock (ahead of plants) bias *and* the hierarchy between scientist and farmer.

It would be a mistake to think that government is uninvolved in the regulation of agriculture through conventional channels and means. Nevertheless it is also very evident that the style of regulation is quite different while the basic tensions between promoting wider interests and objectives and individualist aspirations of farmer-investors remains. The role central government is attempting to play in promoting sustainable agriculture highlights some aspects of the new policy ethos. In a general position statement, that role is described as 'primarily that of encouraging market-led adjustment to sustainable practices' (Ministry of Agriculture and Fisheries, 1993a: 13). In a summary of ten policy instruments available to government a noticeable diffidence about their use can be detected; echoing the adoption of the principles of 'efficient allocation of resources and the full accounting of all costs and benefits accruing to individuals and communities and increasing the capacity of individuals and communities for self-help and encouraging local responsibility for solving problems' (Ministry of Agriculture and Fisheries, 1993a: 13). Perhaps most revealing is the Ministry's answer to its own question 'What next?' – 'MAF can only act as facilitator. The real change has to come from those managing the land' (Ministry of Agriculture and Fisheries, 1993b: 4).

Conclusion

The use of regulationist literatures and concepts has provided an interesting perspective on the agricultural crises occurring in many advanced nations, but in several respects, New Zealand is a different context for political economic change than America or Europe. It is a small and peripheral nation with neither large internal markets nor ready access to large-scale mutual trading groups. Agricultural production had traditionally been geared, therefore, to export markets, and indeed agricultural exports have assumed a dominant importance in the national economy as well as in local employment. New Zealand had thereby been susceptible to external political economic pressures over a long period of its history, and it developed a raft of isolationist measures to deal with this susceptibility. Politically, the New Zealand legislature has sought to evolve a social contract in which high welfare levels have been available to mainstream social groups in both urban and country areas, and this has involved strong state intervention in social and economic spheres.

New Zealand has clearly, therefore, been tied into international food chains and has in the past engaged in mass agricultural production for export markets. Its Statist stance towards support for capital and labour in production processes is reminiscent of some aspects of Fordist regimes of accumulation elsewhere, although there is obviously a scale factor here which precludes other forms of mass production in industry and strong local labourist politics as a prop to the welfare state. Equally clearly there have been internal contradictions in this regime of accumulation. In particular, by the 1980s, the costs of state support for agriculture became too expensive for the national economy, and politically unbearable given the pressures for reform emanating from other capital sectors. It is important to note that the major farming interests in New Zealand also recognised these contradictions and offered broad support for the political measures that were to be put in train to deal with the crisis. Up to this point, then, a regulationist perspective appears compatible with the highly regulated phase of New Zealand agriculture. There does appear to have been a recognisable mode of regulation, integrally linked with a societalisation which spawned hegemonic blocks and socio-political practices and localised coherences in the geography and lifestyles of New Zealand (see Cloke and Goodwin, 1992).

As with other regulationist accounts of agricultural change, however, the post-crisis position is far less clear. Just as it has been difficult to identify a clear post-Fordist coherence in European or American agriculture, so it seems that some of the internal contradictions in capital accumulation in New Zealand agriculture, remain unsolved, and some new contradictions are emerging in the deregulatory regime. There are also clear signs of a more flexible accumulation environment – diversification of product, flexibility in production, greater market niching – and of the associated ensemble of political and economic relations which might be expected to indicate a new mode of regulation. Social and cultural relations in New Zealand, however, raise a number of inconsistencies which deny a smooth transition from Fordism to post-Fordism. First, much of New Zealand's agriculture remains dependent on family farming, and there is considerable uncertainty about how farm households will react to changing conditions. If, as seems likely, the farm household will be adopting strategies that will greatly influence the farm business and vice versa, then we can expect important differences in agriculture from the anticipated response of 'small firms' to a supposedly post-Fordist regime.

A second inconsistency mirrors the concerns expressed in other nations over the potential conflicts between agriculture and the environment. Commitment to a high energy agriculture may weaken not only because of a wish to reduce input costs, but also because of concerns over long-term environmental sustainability. Any such weakening has to be set against the continuing need to improve agricultural productivity so as to maintain the export position in global markets. Clearly, continuing debates about the nature-society relations of intensive agricultural regimes will be an important feature of the post-crisis phase in New Zealand.

Finally, there are currently a number of issues which suggest that a smooth transition to a new socio-cultural order will not be possible in the new deregulatory environment of New Zealand. Aspects of privatisation and deregulation have already had important impacts in service and welfare sectors, ushering in much more of a 'user-pays' society. There is still, however, a broad goal of enhancement of economic and social well-being, and evidence of popular protest, notably by Maori populations but also to a lesser extent by other previously marginalised groups, where this goal appears compromised.

These inconsistencies suggest that the crises of regulatory transition have not yet been fully worked through in New Zealand, and indeed may never be so. New coherences and social hegemony have not yet accompanied political economic change, and it may be that the phase following the Fordist crisis will in fact represent continuing flux rather than the emergence of any particular order. Any coherent sets of relations are likely to be more localised and short-term even in a nation such as New Zealand whose export dependency will continue to be the important economic focus, and regulatory regimes for agriculture at least will continue to be susceptible to external pressures.

References

Aglietta, M. (1979) *A Theory Of Capitalist Regulation: The US Experience*. London: Verso.

Bell, P. and Cloke, P. (1989) 'The changing relationship between the private and public sectors: privatisation and rural Britain', *Journal of Rural Studies*, 5, 1–15.

Bollard, A. and Buckle, R. (eds) (1987) *Economic Liberalisation In New Zealand*, Wellington: Allen & Unwin.

Boston, J. and Holland, M. (eds) (1990) *The Fourth Labour Government* (2nd edition). Auckland: Oxford University Press.

Britton, S., Le Heron, R. and Pawson, E. (eds) (1992) *Changing Places in New Zealand*, Christchurch: New Zealand Geographical Society.

Buttel, F. (1989a) 'The sociology of agriculture: current conceptual status', *Rural Sociologist*, 9, 16–26.

Buttel, F. (1989b) 'The US farm crisis and the restructuring of American agriculture: domestic and international dimensions', in D. Goodman and M. Redclift (eds) *The International Farm Crisis*, Basingstoke: Macmillan.

Chouinard, V. (1990) 'The uneven developments of capitalist states: I Theoretical proposals and an analysis of Canada's assisted housing programme', *Environment and Planning A*, 22, 1291–308.

Cloke, P. (1989) 'Deregulation and New Zealand's agricultural sector', *Sociologia Ruralis*, 29, 34–48.

Cloke, P. (ed.) (1992) *Policy and Change in Thatcher's Britain*. Oxford: Pergamon.

Cloke, P. (1992b) 'Thatcher's countryside', in P. Cloke (ed.) *Policy and Change in Thatcher's Britain*. Oxford: Pergamon.

Cloke, P. and Goodwin, M. (1992) 'Conceptualising countryside change: from post-Fordism to rural structured coherence', *Transactions IBG*, NS17, 321–36.

Cloke, P., Le Heron, R. and Roche, M. (1990) 'Towards a geography of political economy perspective on rural change: the example of New Zealand', *Geografiska Annaler B*, 72, 13–25.

Collins, S. (1987) *Rogernomics: Is There a Better Way?* Wellington: Pitman.

Commins, P. (1990) 'Restructuring agriculture in advanced societies: transformation, crisis and responses', in T. Marsden, P. Lowe and S. Whatmore (eds) *Rural Restructuring*. London: David Fulton.

Cooke, P. (1989) 'Critical cosmopolitanism: urban and regional studies into the 1990s', *Geoforum*, 20, 240–5.

Dunford, M. (1990) 'Theories of regulation', *Society and Space*, 8, 297–322.

Flora, C. and Christenson, J. (eds) (1991) *Rural Policies for the 1990s*. Boulder, Colorado: Westview.

Florida, R. and Feldman, M. (1988) 'Housing in US Fordism', *International Journal of Urban and Regional Research*, 12, 187–210.

Gamble, A. (1988) *The Free Economy and the Strong State*. London: Macmillan.

Gertler, M. (1988) 'The limits to flexibility: comments on the post-Fordist vision of production and its geography', *Transactions IBG*, NS13, 419–32.

Goodman, D. and Redclift, M. (eds) (1989) *The International Farm Crisis*. Basingstoke: Macmillan.

Goodman, D. and Redclift, M. (1991) *Refashioning Nature*. London: Routledge.

Green, D. (1988) *The New Right*. Brighton: Wheatsheaf.

Harvey, D. (1989) *The Condition of Postmodernity*. Oxford: Blackwell.

Harvey, D. and Scott, A. (1988) 'The practice of human geography: theory and empirical specificity in the transition from Fordism to flexible accumulation', in W. Macmillan (ed.) *Remodelling Geography*. Oxford: Blackwell.

Hawke, G. (1987) 'Overview of NZ agriculture', in L. Wallace and R. Lattimore (eds) *Rural New Zealand – What Next?* Agribusiness and Economics Research Unit, Lincoln College, Canterbury, NZ.

Jessop, B. (1990) 'Regulation theories in retrospect and prospect', *Economy and Society*, 19, 153–216.

Kenney, M., Labao, L., Curry, J. and Goe, R. (1989) 'Midwestern agriculture in US Fordism', *Sociologia Ruralis*, 29, 131–48.

Kenney, M., Labao, L., Curry, J. and Goe, R. (1991) 'Agriculture in US Fordism: the integration of the productive consumer', in W. Friedland, L. Busch, F. Buttel and A. Rudy (eds) *Towards a New Political Economy of Agriculture*. Boulder, Colorado: Westview.

King, D. (1987) *The New Right: Politics, Markets and Citizenship*. London: Macmillan.

Le Heron, R. (1989) 'A political economy perspective on the expansion of New Zealand livestock farming, 1960–1984. Part I: agricultural policy, *Journal of Rural Studies*, 5, 17–32.

Le Heron, R. (1991) New Zealand agriculture and changes in the agriculture–finance relation during the 1980s, *Environment and Planning A*, 23, 1653–70.

Le Heron, R., Roche, M. and Johnston, T. (1992) 'The reregulation of New Zealand agriculture and its implications for a restatement of policy and planning agendas', *Progress in Rural Policy and Planning*, 2, 266–81.

Le Heron, R., Roche, M., Johnston, T. and Bowler, S. (1991) 'Pluriactivity in New Zealand's agro-commodity chains', Proceedings, New Zealand Sociology Conference, Discussion Paper No 129. Agribusiness and Economics Research Unit, Lincoln University, Canterbury, 41–55.

Lipietz, A. (1988) 'Reflections on a tale: the Marxist foundations of the concepts of deregulation and accumulation', *Studies in Political Economy*, 26, 7–36.

Marsden, T., Murdoch, J., Lowe, P., Munton, R. and Flynn, A. (1993) *Constructing the Countryside*. London: University College London Press.

McLean, I. (1978) *The Future for NZ Agriculture: Economic Strategies in the 1980*. Fourth Estate Books.

Ministry of Agriculture and Fisheries (1993a) *Sustainable Agriculture*. MAF Policy Position Paper 1, Wellington.

Ministry of Agriculture and Fisheries (1993b) *Sustainable Agriculture for Present and Future Generations*, Brochure Supplement, MAF Policy, Wellington.

Mooney, P. 'The political economy of credit in American agriculture', *Rural Sociology*, 51, 449–70.

New Zealand Treasury (1984) *Economic Management: Land Use Issues*. Wellington: Government Printers.

Page, B. and Walker, R. (1991) 'From settlement to Fordism: the agro-industrial revolution in the American midwest', *Economic Geography*, 67, 281–315.

Pryde, J. (1987) 'Capital and agriculture', in L. Wallace and R. Lattimore (eds) *Rural New Zealand – What Next?* Agribusiness and Economics Research Group, Lincoln College, Canterbury NZ.

Ramanadham, V. (ed.) (1989) *Privatisation in Developing Countries*. London: Routledge.

Roche, M. (1993) 'Public good science fund: crown research institutes and the restructuring of state science research in New Zealand', *New Zealand Geographer*, 49, 42–5.

Roche, M., Johnston, T. and Le Heron, R. (1992) 'Farmer interest groups and agricultural policy in New Zealand during the 1980s', *Environment and Planning A*, 24, 1749–67.

Sandrey, R. and Reynolds, R. (eds) (1990) *Farming Without Subsidies*. Wellington: Government Print.

Sauer, M. (1990) 'Fordist modernization of German agriculture and the future of family farms', *Sociologia Ruralis*, 30, 260–79.

Sayer, A. (1989) 'Post-Fordism in question', *International Journal of Urban and Regional Research*, 13, 666–95.

Schoenberger, E. (1989) 'Thinking about flexibility: a response to Gertler', *Transactions IBG*, NS14, 98–108.

Schuh, E. (1986) 'Strategic issues in international agriculture', *Economic Impact*, 53, 6–13.

Science and Technology Expert Panel (1992) *Long Term Priorities for the Public Good Science Fund*. Wellington: Ministry of Research Science and Technology.

Tyler, L. and Lattimore, R. (1990) 'Assistance to agriculture', in R. Sandrey and R. Reynolds (eds) *Farming Without Subsidies*. Wellington: Government Print.

Wallace, L. and Lattimore, R. (eds) (1987) *Rural New Zealand - What Next?* Agribusiness and Economics Research Unit, Lincoln College, Canterbury NZ.

Welch, R. (1992) *Recent Developments in Embryology of Livestock*. New Zealand Institute of Economic Research, Working Paper 92/21, Wellington.

Willis, K. (1988) 'New Zealand', in P. Cloke (ed.) *Policies and Plans for Rural People*. London: Unwin Hyman.

CHAPTER 7

From State Control to a Managed or Liberalised Market: Dilemmas in the Reform of the Grain Price System in China

Ping Zong

Introduction

Grain price policy has been increasingly recognised as vitally important to economic reform in China since 1979, being a key factor not only in agricultural development and the overall supply and demand for grain, but also in income distribution and the government's budget balance.

For much of the previous three decades, Chinese leaders believed that markets should play a minimal role; instead, output should revert to the state which would then arrange for its distribution. For this reason, grain prices, at least until the end of the 1970s, were centrally administered and the market was strictly controlled.

Since 1978 China has been engaged in systematic efforts to modify its traditional centralised system through greater use of price incentives and the market system. A series of grain price reforms followed this broad policy change, with two major effects. First, the market mechanism was introduced and price signals strengthened in both production and consumption by improving the price incentives and reducing the proportion of the harvest purchased by the state. Agricultural production increased at an average annual rate of 5.9 per cent between 1979 and 1989 (China's Statistics Yearbook, 1991: 346). Secondly, the adjustment of prices had a great influence on income distribution between different social groups in China; average rural income per capita rose from 134 yuan in 1978 to 630 yuan in 1990 (China's Statistics Yearbook, 1991: 295).

In spite of these gains from the reforms, the government has grown increasingly aware of the difficulties in implementing them. One is that although the dual price system (the state market and free market) provided alternative channels for the sale of farm products, the interaction between the state procurement and free market prices weakened the role of prices in regulating grain production, and made it more difficult to achieve the anticipated output. The government also faced severe budgetary problems, and the mounting costs of grain price subsidies became one of the major obstacles to further price reform. Within the system of rationing, prices were kept nearly constant such that each rise of the procurement price resulted in an increase in the government subsidy. Even after May 1991, when in the first major increase in two decades, the retail prices of urban food rations were adjusted upward between 50 and 200 per cent, government still continued to bear a considerable price subsidy through fear of a backlash from urban residents were prices to rise even more sharply.

These problems indicate that grain pricing reform is incomplete although a shift has occurred from the centrally administered price. The current mixed system of central planning, however, continues to hinder the performance and efficiency of pricing in the all important grain sector.

The purpose of this chapter is to present a review of grain price policy over the past four decades; provide a systematic judgement of the degree of market and price control against the prevailing political and economic circumstances; examine the extent and implications of the use of non-market mechanisms for grain production and consumption; and evaluate the impact of price reform on grain production and consumption and the development of agriculture since 1978.

The discussion will proceed as follows. It will first present the establishment of the centrally administered system in the 1950s and the different instruments of government policy for grain employed prior to the reform of 1979. Secondly, it will discuss how this system has changed since the introduction of the economic reform which was intended to return to the market system. Thirdly, some of the factors that constrain further reform will be discussed. Finally, some lessons and conclusions will be drawn from past experience.

The centrally administered system and related policy measures, 1953–78

Many of the contemporary problems of grain supply in China stem from the centrally administered system established in the early 1950s. At the founding of the People's Republic in 1949, the Chinese government was confronted with serious economic problems. In 1950, national population reached 551 million. The urban population was growing dramatically rising from 58 to 72 million between 1949 and 1952 (China's Statistics Yearbook, 1991: 79). But agricultural production had dropped to perhaps two-thirds of the pre-war level (Chen and Galenson, 1969: 89). In this context of worsening shortage, the market prices of grain in rural areas rose and were 20 to 30 per cent above official prices in October 1953. Farmers were, therefore, unwilling to sell grain to the state. As a result, a gap between the state's aquisition and disbursement of grain arose amounting to 3.5 million tonnes during 1952–3 (Cheng and Buckwell, 1991: 43). The government risked being unable to ensure a stable supply of grain to national markets and therefore it moved both to secure the supply and to control consumption.

The non-market mechanism

A system of 'Unified purchase and sale' was set up in the early 1950s, comprising two elements: compulsory purchase to control production and rationing to control consumption. Producers had to sell specified amounts to the state-run food agency which resold them through its local shops to enterprises and urban consumers under a rationing system. Prices were set by the government and a low grain price was adopted.

Before 1953, China had had a mixed economic system. In 1952, private commerce still accounted for 36.2 per cent of wholesale and 57.8 per cent of retail sales. The government had been using prices to influence the marketing of agricultural products. For instance, when the production of cotton had to be expanded to meet the needs of the textile industry, the cotton price was raised in relation to other crop prices. As a result, cotton output increased three-fold between 1949 and 1952. However, while the price mechanism proved to be quite effective in resource allocation, it conflicted with the government's imperatives at that time: a high rate of capital formation and stabilising society. The development of heavy industry was regarded as the key to recovery from wartime destruction and the promotion of industrialisation. But capital was extremely scarce and the level of voluntary saving was far too low to finance the necessary investment. To obtain a sufficiently high saving and investment rate depended, to a large degree, upon the ability to mobilise and extract a significant surplus from the dominant agricultural sector. To this end, the Chinese government adopted a policy of low grain prices to help keep down urban wages, in order to maximise the returns to industry.

Under the unified purchase and sale system, in theory, individuals could sell any surplus at markets after the procurement quota had been fulfilled. In practice, since the state procurement organs purchased as much as they could extract, producers were left with little surplus (Perkins, 1966: ch. 3). Markets were strictly controlled and most agricultural product prices were fixed by the state. With the government exercising almost complete control of trade, from the procurement through to the retail stage, but also of the transport network, direct private trade essentially disappeared.

The compulsory purchase price policy was implemented during 1953–7 and achieved its primary objectives. First, it secured for the state sufficient grain from the farmers. For the period from 1953 to 1959, total state procurement of grain accounted for 27 per cent of total output (*People's Daily*, 25 October 1959: 6; Donnithorne, 1967: 354). Secondly, it greatly contributed to the process of industrialisation by increasing the disparity between industrial and agricultural prices, through the state setting low prices for agricultural products in relation to the prices that farmers had to pay the state for industrial products. The proportion of industrial output in the total national output value increased from 34.4 to 61.9 per cent between 1952 and 1978 (China's Statistics Yearbook, 1991: 47).

But compulsory purchase also created many problems. One was that the heavy burden of supporting the low grain price fell on the government and farmers. Consumers no longer bore any risk of the fluctuation of grain prices: no matter what their income was or whether they were in work or not, people living in the urban areas received their grain ration from the state at low prices. Farmers' incomes, however, suffered. By 1978, compared with the 615 yuan of the average annual per capita income in urban areas, the average annual per capita income of rural producers was only 74 yuan and about a quarter of grain producers had incomes below 50 yuan (Yang and Ming, 1991: 10; China's Statistics Yearbook, 1991: 269).

Moreover, the excessive transfer of agricultural income to the industrial sector seriously affected agrarian development. The very low compulsory purchase price acted as an invisible tax on agriculture. Thus, while formal taxes amounted to less than 7 per cent of the value of total agricultural production (Donnithorne, 1967: 338), it has been estimated that the accumulated capital benefit to the state through low grain prices was nearly one-third of the net value of agricultural production between 1953 and 1978 (Yang and Ming, 1991: 10).

The non-price measures

Under the unified purchase and sale system, the role of prices in resource allocation was greatly reduced. Many non-price instruments, such as quantitative control of output, procurement planning and other political factors, including organisational changes and ideological exhortation, came to play an important role.

The control of production

The grain procurement quota was the principal measure used by government to control farm production directly. The size of the quota was determined on the basis of average yield from which seed and the farmers' self-consumption requirements were deducted. The residual was then treated as marketable output, with the bulk of it considered as the quota to be sold to the state at the state procurement prices.

Increases in output were due to qualitative controls, rather than any price incentive. In 1953, in response to the food crisis of that year, there had been over-procurement which caused great hardship and widespread resentment among the farmers. In 1955, therefore, the government adopted a new policy called 'The three fixes' to encourage producers to increase grain production: 'fixed production' signified that a standard production quota would be assigned to each piece of land used for growing grain: 'fixed purchase' referred to quota for compulsory sales to the state; and 'fixed sales' to the rations to be supplied to grain-deficient farmers. This policy required that the quota be set with reference to the 'normal yield of land', which was the amount to be produced in an ordinary year. Once it was set, the quotas were not to be revised for three years. In the interim, not more than 40 per cent of any increase in production could be taken by the state (Perkins, 1966: 50–2). Through this ceiling on farmers' liability for compulsory sales, the government sought to provide greater incentive to farmers to increase grain production. In the following years, the average total grain purchased fell from 59.1 million tonnes during 1958–60 to 43.7 million tonnes during 1961–5. Net grain purchases (i.e. the total purchased minus the grain resold by the state to farms) likewise fell from 40.1 to 29.2 million tonnes per annum over the same period. The total and net purchasing ratios declined from 34.9 to 25.5 per cent and from 23.5 to 17 per cent respectively (Cheng and Buckwell, 1991: 46).

The second approach to the control of production was through organisational change, particularly collectivisation. Prior to 1955, agricultural collectivisation had occurred gradually and at a small scale, with roughly 60 per cent of rural households having joined local mutual aid teams by 1954. These developments may have boosted output: the growth rate of grain was 8.5 per cent in 1955 and 4.8 per cent in 1956, and rural direct grain consumption per capita rose from 190 kg in 1954 to a peak of 205 kg in 1956 (Sicular, 1988: 458).

In mid 1955, the state stepped up the pace and level of collectivisation. Only 18 months later, about 90 per cent of households had been grouped together in Agricultural Producer Co-operatives (APCs). The pressures were stepped up further in 1958 when the state attempted to use its collectivising policy to develop agricultural production. APCs were further developed into the People's Communes. These higher-level co-operatives each embraced two to three hundred households which now received compensation on the basis of their labour contribution and not on the basis of any land or tools brought with them. About 90 to 95 per cent of land was to be cultivated collectively (Perkins, 1966: 74). Inevitably such upheaval disrupted production and supplies. Urban per capita grain consumption declined by 15 per cent between 1954 and 1956, and the People's Commune movement aggravated the shortage of grain during 1959–61. Moreover, efforts to boost grain production were at the cost of a precipitate decline in certain subsidiary occupations like vegetable cultivation, and rearing hogs and poultry (Terry, 1988: 254). The overall result was a decrease in the sensitivity of farm production to economic signals and an increase in its sensitivity to political currents (Perkins, 1966: 62–8).

Thirdly, grain production was also promoted by enforcing mandatory sown area targets. Before the sowing season the state decided on the areas for the principal crops. Cropping quotas were reported to cover more than three-quarters of China's cultivated area. Restricted by this kind of planning, the farmers were unable to make their own management decisions in such a way as to allocate resources efficiently and to obtain maximum benefit from their resources. All of these measures were supplemented by ideological means. The government believed that moral incentives were an essentially practical way of getting people to take a more active part in production. Producers were constantly urged to put their own interests behind those of the people and of the state. On the other hand, political pressure was placed on producers: for example, failure to fulfil the compulsory purchasing quota was regarded as a serious political matter.

The control of demand

Demand for grain was also administered largely through non-price measures. Although compulsory purchase helped the government to control the supply, this alone could not ensure an equilibrium with aggregate demand. To control the demand for grain, a nation-wide rationing system at fixed retail price was established in 1955 and has been maintained since that time.

Grain in China was the first item to be strictly rationed in the mid 1950s, and it made up nearly 30 per cent of food expenditure and over 15 per cent of total consumption expenditures for an urban worker. Moreover, the income elasticity of the demand for food grain for Chinese urban dwellers was estimated by a Japanese authority at less than 0.2 at that time (Ishikawa, 1960: 139–85; Cheng, 1982: 204). This fact would suggest that control of monetary income alone had little effect on the consumption of food grains. The only way to reduce consumption under a centrally planned system was through rationing.

Local rationing of grain for urban residents began in 1953, and it was made nation-wide in 1955. Allocations varied according to age and type of work. Each family received a certificate that listed its total ration of grain and allowed it to purchase grain at designated stores and at a fixed price.

Initially, in the mid 1950s, state retail prices of grain and other food products were set just marginally above their planned purchase prices. Thus retail grain prices in large and medium-sized cities were 5 to 15 per cent higher than the state purchase price (Wang, 1985: 61; Sicular, 1988: 269) and the state commercial department made a slight profit from its trade in grain. Subsequently, however, although the state purchase prices were adjusted several times, rationed grain prices were less frequently changed. For example, in 1961, although the state purchase price was raised 27 per cent nation-wide, the retail price of grain supplied under the rationing programme remained unchanged. Despite the fact that rationed grain prices were gradually raised during the early and mid 1960s, the state still sustained losses on its grain commerce, as part of its strategy of transfering resources intersectorally from agriculture to industry. Rationed grain prices for the urban population were not even high enough to cover the cost of procuring the grain from the farmers, let alone the additional costs of transportation and handling (Xuyi *et al.*, 1982: 125–6; Terry, 1988: 477).

Price measures under a non-market mechanism

During 1953–78, grain production was mainly managed by non-price measures. Nevertheless, prices did have some influence.

In early 1955, with the quota level already high, the state could not continue to raise it to increase state grain purchase. The alternative of increasing the purchase price would have conflicted with the priority of industrial development. Therefore, the state adopted another approach. Prices for certain manufactured inputs to agriculture were reduced by about 30 per cent. These price revisions had some positive effect on production. However, since the use of modern inputs was low, the supply response was undoubtedly smaller than that of raising output prices.

Grain price increases were not entirely excluded. In the late 1950s, procurement prices were raised in peripheral areas and poor mountainous regions. The second large-scale price adjustment by the state was in the early 1960s. At the beginning of 1961, due to the Great Leap Forward, the People's Commune movement and natural calamities, grain production declined sharply, and there was widespread hardship and mass starvation. The government was forced to shift its development strategy and turned to various price measures and material incentives to encourage agricultural production and marketing. In 1961, the index of average price for major grains was raised by 33.2 per cent and by an additional 5.9 per cent in 1966 (Figure 7.1). Subsequently during the Cultural Revolution, however, although the need for price adjustments was recognised, state quota prices for grain remained virtually frozen from 1967 through 1970 and again from 1973 through 1976 for political reasons.

In 1960 the state also began to pay a 10 per cent price bonus to producers for deliveries above a set amount. This price bonus programme was eliminated in 1962 (Sicular, 1988: 461), but was re-introduced in 1965. In

Figure 7.1 Index of the state procurement prices for grain products, 1953–78 (1953 = 100)

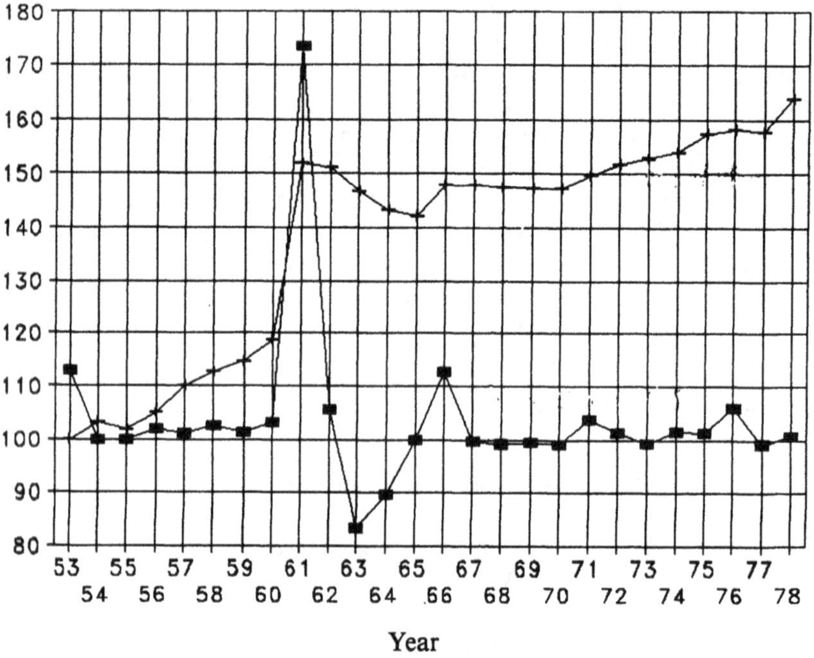

Notes: +—+—+ = State procurement price index (1953 = 100)
■—■—■ = Annual rate of increase (%)

subsequent years, not only were price bonuses increased, but farmers were also given encouragement sale awards which entitled them to certain manufactured commodities in short supply in return for deliveries of agricultural products to the state (Lardy, 1983; Sicular, 1988: 461).

Change since 1979

The Chinese leadership prior to 1978 believed that market controls and centralised planning would efficiently co-ordinate the economy. However, a highly centralised command system was never fully put into effect and the production of grain for a long time underlined the resulting stagnation. By 1978, the gross value of agricultural products was merely 125 billion yuan and average per capita income was less than 160 yuan (China's Statistics Yearbook, 1991: 54, 295). Although the aggregate demand and supply of grain were under government control, the system only guaranteed minimum subsistence levels to most people. Even then, in 1979, about 100 million people, representing about 10 per cent of China's population, did not have enough food (Butterfield, 1979; Cheng, 1982: 215). The slow growth of agricultural production caused imbalance in the economy and in turn constrained the growth of the industrial sector. Thus, the average annual growth of industrial output, which had increased rapidly in the early 1950s, declined from 34.8 per cent from 1950 to 1952, to 18 per cent from 1952 to 1957, to 2.44 per cent in 1976 (China's Statistics Yearbook, 1991: 395).

Following Mao's death, an 'ideological emancipation' movement emerged in 1978, with the slogan 'practice is the sole criterion for testing truth'. The new leadership re-evaluated past policies. The key ideological differentiation from Mao's thoughts was in taking economic development as a central task and in stressing the need to 'obey objective economic laws'.

Major economic reforms were decided by the Central Committee of the Chinese Communist Party in December 1978. Although the initial action was confined to rationalising the planning system, the priority of development was substantially revised from heavy industry to the following order: agriculture first, then light industry and then heavy industry. The new leadership also called for increased reliance on 'economic levers', such as prices, taxes, monetary and financial policy to guide the economy. Such material incentives and price mechanisms were regarded as more reliable than exhortation and coercion to motivate people to work hard.

Economic reform, accompanied by agricultural price adjustment, started in the countryside and can be divided into three stages: first, increasing price incentives; secondly, the trial of market mechanism; and thirdly, the establishment of a dual price system.

Increasing price incentives, 1978–84

Weakening the state compulsory quota system: price adjustment

The first stage of reform taken by the state was to raise grain procurement prices by a large margin in order to stimulate grain production and encourage deliveries of grain to the state, as well as to raise rural income rapidly. In 1978 and 1979, prices for quota deliveries of key crops were increased substantially (Table 7.1). Seasonal and quality price differentials were also widened. Overall, the annual rate of increase of prices between 1978 and 1984 was 4.53 per cent. The government concurrently expanded bonuses for above-quota deliveries which, when multiplied by the prevailing higher quota prices, meant that over this same period above-quota prices rose 36 per cent for grains. In addition, the government expanded a variety of material incentive programmes under which producers were awarded the right to purchase low-priced or scarce commodities such as chemical fertilisers, in return for delivering farm products to the state.

Meanwhile, in order to further strengthen the role of price incentives, the state also took steps to relax the control of procurement purchase. First, the

Table 7.1 The adjustment of state quota procurement prices, 1978–90

Unit: RMB/100KG

Year	*Indica paddy*		*Japonica paddy*		*Wheat*		*Corn*		*Soyabean*		*Average increase as %*
	Yuan	*Increase as %*	*Yuan*	*Increase as %*	*Yuan*	*Increase as %*	*Yuan*	*Increase as %*	*Yuan*	*Increase as %*	
1977	19.62	0	Na	Na	26.86	0	18.18	0	32.60	0	Na
1978	19.62	0	Na	Na	27.22	1.3	17.60	−4	40.12	23.1	Na
1979	23.14	17.9	29.72	0	32.96	21.1	21.44	21.8	46.14	15	18.95
1980	23.14	0	29.72	0	31.44	−5	21.44	0	46.14	0	0
1981	23.14	0	29.72	0	31.44	0	21.44	0	69.21	50.0	12.5
1982	23.14	0	29.72	0	31.44	0	21.44	0	69.21	0	0
1983	23.14	0	29.72	0	31.44	0	21.44	0	69.21	0	0
1984	23.14	0	29.72	0	31.44	0	21.44	0	60.00	0	−3.25
1985	31.32	35.4	39.38	32.5	44.14	40	29.32	36.7	61.50	2.5	29.41
1986	31.40	2.5	40.48	2.8	44.20	1.3	30.44	3.8	69.00	12.2	4.52
1987	34.64	10.3	42.38	4.7	44.28	0.2	32.02	5.2	69.00	0	5.12
1988	34.68	0.1	44.26	4.4	47.66	7.6	32.20	0.6	69.00	0	2.6
1989	44.74	29.0	56.16	26.8	50.70	6.4	34.20	6.2	69.00	0	14.9
1990	44.80	0.1	56.42	0.5	50.90	0.4	34.20	0	90.00	30.4	6.28

Source: The Ministry of Commerce Institute of Commercial Economic Research, 1990

Table 7.2 Grain production, gross procurement, state procurement and free market trade

Unit: million tonne

Year	Total prodn mt	Gross procurement mt	Gross procurement As % of TP	State procurement Quota mt	State procurement As % of GP	State procurement Above-quota mt	State procurement As % of GP	Free market mt	Free market As % of GP
1978	305	51	16.6	38	75	13	25		
1979	332	60	18.1	35	58	21	35	4	7
1980	321	61	19.0	34	56	23	38	4	7
1981	325	68	21.1	30	44	33	49	5	7
1982	355	78	22.0	30	38	42	54	6	8
1983	387	102	26.5	30	29	67	66	5	5
1984	407	117	28.8	30	26	77	66	10	9
1985	379	108	28.4	79	73	12	11	17	16
1986	392	115	29.4	63	55	32	28	20	17
1987	403	121	30.0	53	44	42	35	26	21
1988	394	120	30.4	50	42	Na	Na	Na	Na
1989	408	121	29.7	Na	Na	Na	Na	Na	Na
1990	446	140	31.4	Na	Na	Na	Na	Na	Na

Source: China's Commercial Statistical Yearbook, 1985: 191, 547; 1988: 55; 1989: 613, 620, 714. China's Statistical Yearbook, 1985: 547; 1991: 346, 587.

range of commodities under state procurement was reduced from 180 to 39 and eventually to 21. Secondly, the state increased its above-quota purchases. Thus reducing the proportion of grain purchased at quota price from 75 to 44 per cent between 1978 and 1981 (Table 7.2).

Strengthening the functioning of market co-ordination

Market trading had been tightly controlled in China and grain sales were prohibited outside of state agencies. Since 1979, these market controls have been relaxed. Markets rapidly developed in both urban and rural areas, their number increasing from 38,000 in 1979 to 48,000 in 1983 (An, 1986: 453). By 1980, all products except cotton were allowed to be traded commercially after state delivery quotas had been fulfilled. The expansion of the free market provided an alternative channel for the sale of farm products, often at prices exceeding those offered by the state. A significant consequence was the reduction of the state monopoly in grain markets. In 1982, the grain sold through market channels accounted for 8 per cent of the purchased grain in the whole country (Table 7.2).

Price adjustment triggered

These new price policies were quite successful in the initial stages of reform. Grain output grew at an average annual rate of 4.3 per cent between 1978 and 1984 when it reached a historical high of 407.3 million tonnes. Deliveries of grain output to the state increased from 17 per cent in 1977 to 20.3 per cent in 1982 (Table 7.2). Rural real incomes also grew rapidly: from 1978 to 1984, the average net income of someone employed in agriculture increased 2.7 times, from 134 yuan to 356 yuan largely due to the increase of grain prices (An, 1986: 454). Farmers' living standards rose proportionately. From 1978 to 1984, the average consumption expenditure of someone in agriculture increased 2.4 times from 116 to 273 yuan (An, 1986: 454).

The budgetary problems and inversion of prices

Despite the completion of these adjustments during 1978–84, the government found itself confronted with severe budgetary problems. With production expanded, the government was required to buy ever-increasing quantities of grain at the higher above-quota prices. The price subsidy for grain, which had been roughly 0.04 yuan per kilogram in the late 1950s and early 1960s (Xue, 1983: 45), leapt to 0.2 yuan per kilogram in 1979. On edible oil, the subsidy was 1.6 yuan per kilogram. Food subsidies that year amounted to 11.5 billion yuan which accounted for the bulk of a record budget deficit of 17 billion yuan. The cost of subsidies continued to mount accounting for more than a fifth of government expenditure during the early 1980s and peaking at 28.3 billion yuan in 1984 (Table 7.3).

The government had increased above-quota prices in order to encourage farmers to produce more. At the same time, according to the existing quota

Table 7.3 State revenue, expenditure and food subsidies, 1978–90

Unit: billion yuan

Year	*Total state revenue*	*Total state expenditure*	*Government's deficit*	*Consumer food Value*	*Subsidies As % of TSE*
1978	112.1	111.1	1	Na	Na
1979	110.3	127.4	−17.1	11.5	9.0
1980	108.5	121.3	−12.8	17.2	14.2
1981	109.0	111.5	−2.5	25.0	22.4
1982	112.4	115.3	−2.9	24.3	21.1
1983	124.9	129.3	−4.4	26.3	20.3
1984	150.2	154.6	−4.5	28.3	18.3
1985	186.6	184.5	2.2	26.1	14.1
1986	226.0	233.1	−7.1	24.7	10.6
1987	236.9	244.9	−8.0	25.9	10.6
1988	262.8	266.8	−4.0	26.4	9.9
1989	294.7	304.0	−9.3	Na	Na
1990	331.2	345.2	−1.4	Na	Na

Source: China's Statistics Yearbook, 1991: 209; International Bank for Reconstruction and Development, 1991: 146

system, it was obliged to buy as much as farmers wished to sell in both years of shortage and years of surplus. Thus, even when temporary surpluses of grain emerged in 1982 and 1984 and free-market prices began to dip below state-quota prices, the government still had to buy the surplus grain at the higher above-quota prices. In fact, the government propped up the excess higher prices and continued to give the wrong signal to producers to expand production in conditions of surplus.

Overall, the changes of 1978 to 1984 in pricing policy, although important, did not reflect a radical break from the past, but rather an evolution in the process of price and agricultural development. This is reflected in two aspects. First, the operation of the agrarian economy remained firmly under state supervision. Although grain prices were adjusted dramatically, they were still fixed by the state and formulated in the planning office of the Ministry of Commerce, rather than in the real market place. Secondly, grain production was still administered by non-price measures. Although price administration had been relaxed, the state procurement and rationing system remained unchanged.

Nevertheless, the flaws in the old system had been recognised and a new incentive system for grain producers had been provided. The foundation for the second stage of the reform of the grain price system had been laid.

The trial of market mechanism, 1985

In response to these budgetary problems and in accord with the government's wish to accelerate the price reform towards the market system, the Unified Purchase System was replaced by one of Voluntary Contract in early 1985. No longer would the government give farmers a compulsory delivery quota. Grain would be purchased by contracts negotiated with farmers before the sowing season. If the amount of voluntary contract purchase did not reach the state's planned targets, the state would buy additional grain on the free market. Farmers could choose freely whether or not to sign contracts with the state or dispose of their products on the market. The state no longer promised to purchase grain beyond the contract amount at above-quota prices. Only if market prices fell below the old quota price would the state guarantee to buy additional grain, but then only at the old quota prices.

Planned procurement for other farm products was to be gradually eliminated and replaced by a market allocation. State commercial departments, thus, would increasingly buy and sell at market or near market prices. Through market participation, the state would meet its needs to supply to urban areas, industry and export based on the plan. Through market participation, the state would also exert influence on market trends.

The voluntary contract prices, it was decided, would be set equal to 30 per cent of the quota price plus 70 per cent of the above-quota price (Gao, 1989). In this way, the two former kinds of state prices were merged into a single system, as part of what was hoped to be a transition from planned prices to a market price system. The new programme was also very important because it meant that mandatory quotas for grain were to be eliminated, to be replaced by a programme of voluntary contract and market purchases. Thus the traditional purchase and sale system ceased to exist and pricing reform entered a new stage.

But the reform encountered a series of problems in the first year. The most difficult to solve was that the state was unable to fulfil its planned purchase through voluntary contracts. What happened was that in areas where the state contract purchase price was higher than market prices, producers would actively contract with the state. But in areas where the contract purchase price was lower than market prices, producers were unwilling to contract with the government.

Between 1984 and 1985 grain deliveries declined from 117 to 108 million tonnes. With only 72 per cent of the total grain being fulfilled by contracts (China's Statistics Yearbook, 1991: 589), which was well below the expected level, the state was forced to give up this programme at the end of 1985 and reverted to mandatory purchase.

The immediate reason why the new price policy failed was that contract prices were not competitive with market prices. But the reforms also ignored the fact that the key to adjusting producers' behaviour was not the average procurement price, but the above-quota prices, that is, the marginal prices received for additional output. Such marginal prices determined the profitability of increasing or decreasing production levels. The effect of combining the above-quota and quota prices was to cut marginal prices by 10 per cent. Naturally it would have deterred producers, especially in new grain production areas. The effect was magnified because of the historical discrepancy in quota levels between regions. In the past, regions with low quotas had been able to sell more at above-quota prices and thus receive a higher average price, while those with higher quotas had received a lower average price. Usually, it has been the newer grain production areas that were most strongly oriented to selling grain to the state and their original quotas were low, so they could get greater marginal returns from the above-quota price. However, under the voluntary contract price, the more grain an area exported to other regions, the greater the loss it incurred. Provinces with a comparative advantage in grain production were thus reluctant to increase output.

The underlying reason why this trial failed was thus due to established institutional structures, which although formally relinquishing compulsory delivery remained wedded to it in practice. The huge trading system remained in the government's hands and played contradictory and self-defeating roles in the movement towards free markets. On the one hand, it directly participated as independent accounting units in marketing activities. On the other hand, it still represented a need to fix the markets according to the state's plan.

The dual pricing system and policy, 1986–

The failure of the trial of the market system in 1985 led the government to retreat. The voluntary contracts for grain soon became mandatory again. The problems mentioned above prompted greater administrative intervention in grain procurement. At the end of 1985, to ensure contract fulfilment, the state imposed strict restrictions on the state contract purchase. The delivery contracts were not voluntary but obligatory quotas under a new name. In reality, contracts and the process for determining the quota for producers differed little from the old procurement system. The total state purchase of grain was subject to a dual pricing system, with one part purchased on the state market according to the state contracts and at prices centrally set, and the other, on the free markets at prices set by market forces.

In principle, the government still hoped to rely increasingly on market measures to stimulate grain production. Thus, the initial purpose of the dual pricing system was to effect a gradual transformation of the over-centralised system of grain price control through the introduction of the market mechanism. Yet there are major arguments for the dual pricing system per se and not just as a transitional phase. Before its introduction, the various planned prices were determined exclusively by different levels of the planning system. However, with the establishment of the dual pricing system, dual markets were introduced, and the state market was no longer the only trade channel for grain producers. On the other hand, the government's ability to enforce quota was weakened by decentralising the production plan and by reducing the quantities of the state contract purchase. At the same time, market forces were strengthened.

The principal advantage of the dual pricing system is that it reduces the political risks in price reform. Because a large-scale adjustment to the highly distorted grain price structure would entail drastic income distribution, it would be likely to arouse strong opposition. Under the dual pricing system, the existing pattern of income distribution was preserved by maintaining low planning prices for quota allocations while the distorted price was partially adjusted by introducing market prices. Thus, the dual pricing system was regarded as a transitional device and part of the process of gradually transforming the old system into the new one.

In practice, in order to improve incentives for grain production, the government adopted a series of new measures. At the end of 1985, the state announced it would reduce the amount of contract purchase and enlarge the role of negotiated prices in the market. Over the two years 1986 and 1987, the government reduced nationwide planned delivery contracts for grain by 11 per cent (Table 7.2). The contract quota reductions meant that the state allowed producers to sell more grain at negotiated and market prices.

The further price adjustment

Continual price adjustments have been made to deal with the distortion of grain prices and the average annual rate of increase in grain prices between 1985 and 1988 was 9 per cent. At the same time, in 1987 the state instituted material incentives for contract deliveries of grain, which included cash advances and high-grade chemical fertiliser and diesel oil at low state list prices. However, the expected boost to production and deliveries to the state did not materialise, thus revealing shortcomings in the dual pricing system.

Under the dual price system, the much higher market prices attracted producers to sell on the free market rather than specifically produce more. Perversely, therefore, the higher prices operated as a strong incentive not to fulfil their quota obligations. In addition, because the basic contract quota levels differed between crops, higher market prices adversely affected cropping patterns by giving farmers an incentive to switch land from crops with high quotas (such as grain) to those with low or no quotas (such as cotton).

Constraints and dilemma on further reform

Various problems have arisen mostly due to contradictions in the pricing system. A major problem is the contradiction between the mandatory procurement purchase system and the market mechanism. Thus, prices as a means of resource allocation need to be flexible, but prices as a means of income distribution are required to be fixed within the present social-political system. The other major problem is the contradiction of interests between various groups in society, as some people have benefited from the increase in prices while others have lost out.

Thus, when the grain price reform proceeded to the stage of the dual pricing system, the state faced a dilemma. It wanted to let prices play a bigger role in grain production and marketing, but this would risk social stability. Therefore, in order to keep the society stable and ensure sufficient supply of grain to the market, it was ultimately reluctant to give up the control of price administration, even though this would lead to more rigidity in the price structure and worsen its own finances. Hence, the reform of grain prices at present only proceeds in the area of price adjustments. So far, although price adjustments have been substantial, the effects have been very limited, largely because they have failed to keep pace with both the rising costs of production and the sharply rising prices of other farm products where (unlike grain) price controls have been relaxed. Thus, although the objective of price adjustment is to push the development of a market mechanism, the grain price system has hardly been affected.

A move towards market regulation is advocated by many economists and an intensive argument about the changes needed and their likely consequences are hotly debated. However, many of the political and social factors that constrain further reform seem not to be fully realised. People have long been used to the old command system and they are unaccustomed to market mechanisms. The whole state machine is used to conducting economic affairs by means of mandatory plans and administrative control. This has led to an acute contradiction between administrative and market mechanisms. It has also resulted in a conflict between farmers and the state. There is obvious evidence of that in early 1985, when, because of the shortfall in contract purchasing, the government reimposed compulsory purchase. Subsequently, there has been widespread failure amongst farmers to fulfil their quota obligations.

The rudimentary state of the market is also a real obstacle to the transformation from the old system to a new one. Price reform requires favourable conditions, but the whole economic environment is immature. Market imperfections in China are multiple, but with the following three underlying features. Firstly, markets are disarticulated and regionally isolated. Secondly, the operation of the market is severely constrained by poor communications and difficult access to relevant market information. Thirdly, the inter-regional flow of grain is handled mainly by the state food agency and local government food companies. Apart from these fundamental market imperfections there are other decisive factors which impair the development of the market: 1) the imbalance of aggregate grain supply and demand; 2) the inadequacy of physical infrastructure, such as roads and means of transport; 3) the absence of necessary legal regulations for a market economy; and 4) the continued existence of a system of consumer rationing for grain.

With the increase of price subsidies in recent years, budgetary problems have become another obstacle to further reform. Because of the gap between state purchase prices and free market prices, the government is confronted with a dilemma. If it tries to make the procurement price as competitive as the market price, the financial burden would become intolerable. On the other hand, if the government attempts to limit procurement prices in order to contain food subsidies, the farmers' incentive to produce grain and to fulfil their obligations would be impaired. Thus, in a sense, a move towards the market-oriented system, to a large degree, depends on how much financial subsidies the government can provide to support price reform. This of course depends upon the government's revenue, the bulk of which (40–60 per cent) comes from the profits of industrial and commercial enterprises (China's Statistics Yearbook, 1991: 209, 210; 1984: 419). But the alternative path of increasing grain prices would also put a strain on government revenues as this would raise the cost of production, which in turn would squeeze firms' profits.

It can be seen that many problems stem from the old pricing system. This system has created a policy environment which constrains further reform. So far changes have only attempted to liberalise the administrative controls without touching the policy environment. Therefore, it seems inconceivable that there can be liberalisation of administrative controls without simultaneous reforms of the policy environment.

Conclusions

This historical review of the grain pricing system provides a clear illustration of the course of reform from centrally administered planning to a market system. On the one hand, since 1978, China has attempted to move towards greater reliance on the price mechanism. Specific measures include the reduction of state procurement, the relaxation of control over markets, increased state purchase prices and the introduction of a dual pricing system. These reforms, to a considerable degree have changed the approach of the state management of grain production. On the other hand, China still has a high degree of state intervention in grain pricing and it has not yet succeeded in creating a mechanism in which prices can become self-regulatory.

Perhaps the main reason why such a new mechanism has been hard to establish is the debate on what kind of market model - state managed or liberalised market - should be adopted. At one time, the view that 'The planned economy is primary and markets are supplementary' was the dominant one. Later, the view that 'The state regulates markets, and markets guide enterprises' was proposed by others. All that is conveyed by this view is that the government's role in grain pricing should be emphasised. This view was supported by the fact that national governments played an increasingly important role in economic activities in many developed countries after the Second World War. But they ignored the same important fact that many developed countries not only have experience of government intervention in economic activities, but also of market regulation in the development of their economies. In such circumstances, government intervention is usually based on a developed and mature market system, within which enterprises can actively respond to government policy. This is what China is looking for, but it lacks a mature market system. In this situation, further relaxation of price controls and reduction of the state's intervention in production and marketing are preconditions for the success of grain pricing reform.

Recently, the model of the market-operating mechanism was announced by the 14th National Congress of the Chinese Communist Party (October 1992). Although the desirability of a move towards a liberalised market is fairly widely accepted, there is debate on the current objectives of the reform and how far and how fast they should proceed. The current objectives of economic reform for rural China are to transform the dual pricing system into a single one as early as possible and to establish such a price mechanism that prices are determined by market forces, rather than set by the state. In order to achieve these aims, the key to success is the improvement of the economic environment which calls for an improved grain supply, increased grain taxes and a dismantling of the rationing system. The reasons are as follows:

First, in order to realise the shift from prices being set by the state to prices being determined by market forces, one of the most important considerations is to achieve a relative balance of supply and demand. However, absolute shortfalls in grain supply are a common phenomenon in China. In this situation, to avoid prices being raised sharply and to reduce the impact of market prices for grain on social stability. China could import the necessary additional amount to fulfil demand.

Secondly, an increase in grain tax to replace the invisible tax of low grain prices, is also an indispensable measure. Adjustments towards market conditions imply that grain prices would be increased. In this case, it is impossible for the government to eliminate all price subsidies and as explained above, there is a need to continuously provide financial subsidies to support the grain price reform. Under these conditions, an increase in grain tax would offset the impact on state revenue of increased price subsidies.

Thirdly, the rationing system should be completely abandoned. Many problems stem from the state purchase prices being adjusted when rationing prices remain unchanged. What the government worries about is that the change in rationing prices will possibly cause social and political unrest. In order to continue to maintain living standards, and political and social stability, this measure should be preceded by gradual reductions in the amount of rations and increases in prices for rationed grain, coupled with wage improvements.

Although these matters need to be explored further, two concluding observations can be made. First, on the basis of past experience, such reform would seem possible. Apart from the import of grain and the increase in grain tax, China's government has already taken steps to reduce urban per capita ration allotments for grains and to increase substantially the rationed retail grain prices in 1991 and 1992, for the first time in over two decades (The State Price Bureau Price Information Centre, 1992). This adjustment basically achieved the aim of parallel increases in procurement prices and the urban sale price without provoking serious opposition. China should seize the moment to realise the goal to wean the urban population from the rationing system once and for all. Secondly, this reform to a great degree depends on a changed socio-economic environment. This would include an altered role for the state in the economy, changes in the position of producers and consumers, and the reform of other economic policies, such as wage policy, financial policy, monetary policy, tax policy and employment policy. Since economic reform is a systematic programme and since there are various contradictions between these factors, it can be predicted that China has still a long way to go to the goal of reform in grain pricing policy.

References

An, X. J. (1986) 'Pricing system reform for agricultural products and price policy adjustment in China (1979–1984)', pp. 449–65, in A. Maunder and U. Renbory (eds) *Agriculture in a Turbulent World Economy*. Oxford: Institute of Agricultural Economics, University of Oxford.

Butterfield, F. (1979) 'China's modernisation said to cause 1989 deficit', *New York Times*, 5 June 1979.

Chen, N. R. and Galeson, W. (1969) *The Chinese Economy Under Communism*. Edinburgh: Edinburgh University Press.

Cheng, C. Y. (1982) *China's Economic Development and Structural Change*. Boulder Colorado: Westview Press.

Cheng, L. Y. and Buckwell, A. (1991) *China Grain Economy and Policy*. CAB International Press.

China's Commercial Statistics Yearbook (1985, 1988, 1989) China's Commercial Department.

China's Statistics Yearbook (1983, 1984, 1991) The State Statistic Bureau, China's Statistical Publishing House.

Donnithorne, A. (1967) *China's Economic System*. London: George Allen & Unwin Ltd.

Gao, X. M. (1989) 'Present situation and reform of grain purchase and marketing system in China', *Developing Communication* (internal), no. 12.

Guo, S. T. (1988) *Shortage and Policy Decision in Chinese Food Problems*. The Chinese People's University Press.

International Bank for Reconstruction and Development (1991) *China: Options for Reform in the Grain Sector*. Washington DC: The National Technical Information Services.

Ishikawa, S. (1960) *Capital Formation in China*. Tokyo: Tokyo Book Store, 139–85.

Lardy, N. R. (1983) 'Agriculture prices in China', World Bank Staff Working Paper, no. 606, Washington DC.

Lin, J. Y.F. (1990) *Reforming the Agricultural Sector in China*. National Centre for Development Studies, The Australian National University.

Liu, Z. F. (1982) *Price Handbook*. China Finance and Economics Publishing House.

Perkings, T. U. (1966) *Market Control and Planning in Communist China*. Cambridge Mass.: Harvard University Press.

Sicular, T. (1988) 'Grain pricing: a key link in Chinese economic policy', *Modern China*, October.

Stone, B. (1988) 'Relative food grain price in the People's Republic of China', in J. W. Mellor and R. Ahmed (eds) *Agricultural Price Policy for Developing Countries*. Baltimore: Johns Hopkins University Press.

The State Price Bureau Price Information Centre (1992) 'An important measure of the price adjustment', *China Prices*, no. 4.

Wang, D. H. (1985) 'A course of lectures on agricultural prices: grain and oil-seeds prices', *Price Theory and Practice*, no. 2 and no. 3.

Xue, M. Q. (1983) 'Problems of stabilizing and adjusting prices since 1979', *Economic Research*, no. 6.

Yang, Q. R. and Ming, Y. L. (1991) 'Chinese grain policy study', in China's Grain Policy Research Reports by the China Agricultural Department, unpublished.

You, L. J. (1985) 'On the road to price reform with the Chinese characteristics', *Economic Research*, no. 2.

Yu, C. J. (1991) *Chinese Grain Economy and Policy*, Redwood Press.

CHAPTER 8

The National Politics of International Trade Reform: The Case of Germany

Gizelle Hendriks

Introduction

The German Federal Republic has to bear a two-fold responsibility for the contemporary crisis of the European Community's Common Agricultural Policy (CAP) and its embroilment in the Uruguay Round negotiations within the General Agreement on Tariffs and Trade (GATT). First, in the 1950s and 1960s, German policy-makers imposed their own traditional agro-political model on their EC partners and, secondly, they overcame the resistance of other member states to the setting of Community-wide agricultural price levels above those of most member states and well above world market prices. These early policy decisions have severe financial repercussions on the Community budget and have resulted in agricultural surpluses whose disposal has provoked serious international trade conflicts. Throughout, Germany's role in the evolution of the CAP has been consistent, beginning with demands for the adoption of a highly protectionist agricultural policy, through an abrasive attempt to veto a Commission proposal for lower prices in June 1985, down to efforts to influence contemporary reforms in line with German needs. It was only when the MacSharry reform was tabled in July 1991 and under the influence of concurrent GATT negotiations that Germany reluctantly agreed to a major overhaul of the CAP. However, even this hesitant adjustment to economic reality did not indicate a change of heart, but has come about because of external pressures and the overriding German national interest in a successful outcome to the GATT negotiations.

Background to Germany's agricultural policies

It is important to realise some of the specific features of the background to Germany's agricultural policies. First, it has a long tradition of agricultural protectionism which originated in the 1870s. High tariffs against cheap imports were introduced under Bismark, who was anxious to maintain the support of the landed ruling classes. Since then, German agriculture has enjoyed massive state intervention to protect farmers from foreign competition, and this underlying philosophy found expression in Germany's post-war agro-political strategy.

Secondly, there has been a close collaboration historically between German governments and the agricultural sector underpinned by close operational contact between the ministry of agriculture and the farm lobby. This alliance which re-emerged after the Second World War despite the drastically altered context has resulted in a high degree of interest homogeneity between ministerial administration and the agrarian élite.

Thirdly, political support for the rural sector transcends party-political lines. The right-wing and centre parties nurture farming interests because of their reliance on farmers' votes; the left (although occasionally abrasive in its criticism of the CAP) feels the need to accommodate the interest of Germany's numerous small-scale producers; whereas the Greens stress the ecological importance of the agricultural sector.

Fourthly, the powerful German church has a vested interest in the preservation of rural Germany as a guarantor of social stability promoting family life and ensuring a broad spectrum of property ownership. Thus the church reveals an almost complete identification with the sort of agrarian fundamentalism promoted by Germany's conservative and liberal parties.

Finally, the weakness of consumer organisations reflects the traditional tolerance of the German public to special support measures for farmers and the reluctance of trade unions to take up the interests of consumers. In sum, agricultural support in Germany is based on a broad national consensus.

Germany and the formulation of the Common Agricultural Policy

In the immediate post-war years agricultural policies in Germany were dominated by food scarcity and the need to reconstruct the devastated farm sector. Furthermore, Chancellor Adenauer instinctively felt that an artifically large peasantry would support conservative governments. These considerations led to the introduction of special 'Import and Storage Boards' whose intervention ensured that German farmers were guarded from outside competition and enabled farm prices to remain above those of the world market and above most of its partners in the EC. Prior to the Treaty of Rome, Germany's need to boost its export trade had determined the source and volume of agricultural purchases. However, with the inauguration of a common agricultural market in Europe, the 'selection' of imports from strategically or economically important countries would no longer be acceptable. As a result, Germany initially resisted the establishment of the CAP and, once it was realised that this was untenable, attempted to impose its own agricultural policies on the Community. The Bonn government was aware that any European arrangements for the agricultural sector would need the support of the German farm lobby.

The post-war agricultural interest organisation, the *Deutscher Bauernverband* (DBV) representing nearly 90 per cent of all German farmers, had viewed the imminent integration in the agricultural sector with suspicion. When in 1952/3 a report published by the farm union[1] revealed lower income figures for agriculture than for the industrial sector, the lobby demanded 'parity' with industry. Identifying with the farmers' cause, the German government, in September 1955, passed the Agricultural Act (*Landwirtschaftsgesetz*) 'to equalise the social situation of people working in agriculture with that of comparable professions'.[2]

The objectives of the Act were to:

1. ensure a reasonable standard of living for farmers;
2. raise productivity in this sector;
3. stabilise agricultural markets;
4. ensure food supplies at reasonable prices.

The inception of the Agricultural Act aroused great interest across Europe.[3] Two years later, its basic ideas and principles were faithfully reflected in Article 39[4] of the Treaty of Rome which defines the objectives of the CAP. The founding fathers of the German Agricultural Act of 1955 were thereby indirectly instrumental in the formulation of the basic principles which have been guiding the CAP for over 30 years.

The general ambiguity and vagueness of the Rome Treaty on future agricultural policy made for divergent interpretations subsequently and left considerable scope for choosing specific measures through which to integrate agriculture - stipulating merely that member states must 'develop the common agricultural policy by degrees during the transitional period' (Art. 40(1)). This suited Bonn which wanted to see its existing national market organisation continue until such time as the final common organisation of agricultural policy as agreed. The avoidance of specific commitments at this stage enabled Germany to postpone possible economic disadvantage resulting from new regulations - for example, a reduction in its domestic price levels. In fact, the authors of the Treaty of Rome merely postponed contentious issues, and the struggle for the CAP began in earnest in the 1960s.

After protracted negotiations, between January 1962 and December 1964, the Council of Ministers, eventually agreed on the central policy tool of the

CAP.[5] In an effort to achieve the overriding objective as outlined in Article 39 of the Treaty of Rome, namely the safeguarding of farm incomes, the Community adopted a price support system which became the hallmark of the CAP. Farm incomes were to be ensured by a support price policy (annually determined by the Council of Ministers), a variety of protective devices at EC frontiers to protect Community products against cheaper agricultural imports and a system of intervention buying whereby any excess of supply over demand was bought up by the Community agents at the pre-determined price level.

Common prices were and are a fundamental part of the CAP. However, given the different price levels in the six member states, this was obviously an area of conflict. German domestic prices were the highest in the six member states; cereal prices for example were 30 per cent higher than in France. Consequently, Germany initially refused to realign its domestic price level with those of the other member states, because that would have meant a drop in its national price level. For several years, Bonn led a ferocious battle in defence of its farmers. It was only when France, in the autumn of 1964, set a time limit for the agreement of a common price level to be reached by December of that year, that Germany reluctantly and at the last minute agreed to the harmonisation of agricultural prices. Nevertheless, the FRG emerged as victor from these negotiations on two counts.

First, although Germany had to lower its own price level slightly, some of the other member states, particularly France, had to accept a considerable rise in their domestic price level. Furthermore, Bonn succeeded in neutralising opposition to the agreement from a crucial segment of its electorate by the dangerous precedence of paying German farmers EC-funded compensation. Although German agriculture had thus been brought into the common market out of overriding European considerations, it remained under the influence of a traditionally powerful domestic agricultural lobby.

Secondly and most importantly, because of German pressure the Community had settled around the German price level – the most protectionist in the Community – and, in subsequent years, had to face the legacy of German agricultural protectionism.

The CAP in operation

The 1960s and 1970s saw widespread and rapid technological innovation in European agriculture and, underpinned by high producers prices, farm output escalated. The instruments on which the CAP operated might have been viable, had the Community continued to be a major importer of agricultural goods. However, a system of high support prices in a protected market encouraged production at a time when demand remained relatively static. The resulting growing surpluses needed an outlet: the Community, which in the 1950s had been a large net importer, by 1975 had not only reached self-sufficiency in all temperate-zone products but had become one of the largest exporters of key agricultural products. The growth in output seemed to falter in the mid 1970s but then resumed its relentless trajectory. Between 1973 and 1984, the self-sufficiency rate for cereals rose from 91 per cent to 118 per cent, for butter from 98 per cent to 124 per cent and for sugar from 100 per cent to 141 per cent.[6] The EC was developing a considerable export capacity. Indeed, its level of agricultural exports was now second only to that of the United States. This set it in direct competition with other agricultural exporters, above all the United States.

The open-ended intervention system – that is, buying off any excess of supply over demand, thus ignoring the operation of market forces – had to be financed from Community resources. Since CAP prices perpetually towered above those of the world markets, agricultural expenditure was dominated by export refunds. The costs of these subsidies rose dramatically and the Community budget expenditure on agriculture more than quadrupled between the 1970s and 1980s: from ECU 4 bn in 1973 to ECU 29 bn in 1988.[7] During the 1970s and 1980s agricultural expenditure represented between 60 and 80 per cent of the Community's budget.

At the same time, the collapse of the Bretton Wood system and the fluctuation of exchange rates had an immediate and unforeseen impact on the Community's common price level and hence on the CAP budget. The CAP was constructed on the principle of common pricing, expressed in the EC monetary unit – originally the Unit of Account and, since 1979, the ECU – and then translated into the national currencies. In the event, however, truly common prices were a short-lived phenomenon in the Community. In August 1969 the French Franc was devalued by 11 per cent against the European Unit of Account and a few weeks later, in October, the Deutschmark was formally revalued by 8 per cent. In principle, each country would have had to change its agricultural rates of exchange to take account of the new value of their currencies. However, whereas Germany was concerned about the immediate income loss to its farmers, France wanted to protect its consumers from inflationary pressures. In order to minimise the impact on agricultural trade flows and prices, border taxes were applied to cover the gap.

Originally it was hoped that the reintroduction of the border taxes would be a temporary measure. However, one of the most serious macroeconomic crises of the 1970s was the complete breakdown of the fixed rate parity system and the resulting volatility of exchange rates which had important consequences for the Community's trade in agricultural products. The Community sought to isolate agricultural prices from fluctuations in member states' separate rates by using the Monetary Compensation Amount (MCA) system of taxes and levies in intra and extra-EC trade. In strong currency countries MCAs act as an export subsidy and import levy to keep prices above the common price level and are known as positive MCAs; in countries with a depreciating currency, MCAs act as an import subsidy and an export tax and are called negative MCAs. It is important to realise that since 1973 the system has been entirely funded by the EC and by 1977 MCAs comprised 14.5 per cent of the total agricultural budget.[8]

The device enabled a reconciliation between German agricultural interests and the CAP. The so-called 'green' rates are normally decided once a year as part of the price fixing. This means that national governments are able to exert considerable influence over the value of their 'green' currencies and they have an important degree of control over the internal price level. The Bonn government soon appreciated that the support of German agriculture could now be provided under the auspices of the CAP, and the German farm sector has flourished accordingly. Indirectly, the combination of relatively high prices and positive MCAs has benefited other sectors too. The food industry (production, processing, trade, hotels) consists of some 300,000 enterprises employing nearly 3 million people. Some 4,500 traders in agricultural machinery, the electrical and chemical industries, distributors and small tradesmen have all become strong allies of the farmers. As a result, German policy-makers have consistently and adamantly insisted on the perpetuation of a system which avoids an appreciating Deutschmark leading to a reduction in farm incomes. Irrespective of the costs to the Community budget and despite serious conflicts over the continuation of MCAs with both the Commission and France, Germany has deliberately used the system as a means of determining the level of its domestic product prices. In fact, it has been argued[9] that the system effectively restored the original difference in prices (before the harmonisation phase in the 1960s) between the Federal Republic and its EC partners.

Although the MCA system was reformed in 1984, as part of the progress towards European monetary integration, the need for German green rate revaluation was side-stepped by the evolution of the 'strong currency correcting factor'. While the reform involved an agreement to dismantle all existing positive MCAs and to avoid the creation of new ones in the event of a change in currency parities, there was an agreed correcting factor which was to be increased in proportion to any revaluation of the strongest currency in the ERM, namely the Deutschmark. The linkage between the new 'green' ECU and the Community's most rapidly appeciating currency has created an in-built upward price trend during periods of currency fluctuations within the Community.

A further strain on the CAP emerged in the late 1970s, when the EC became a major exporter and the CAP mechanism sharply reduced the Community's agricultural import needs. This reversal of the Community's earlier position in agricultural trade drew criticism from other agricultural exporters, particularly the United States. External pressures on the Community to cut its agricultural subsidies came to a head in the Uruguay

Round of GATT negotiations which started in 1986. The US called for an abandonment of a regulated market system, a demand resolutely opposed by the EC.

The EC reforms the CAP

Since the mid 1970s the CAP has been subject to cautious reform attempts initiated by the Community itself in response to chronic budgetary problems. The build-up and destruction of surplus food, the direct and indirect costs of the high price policy, the budgetary implications of the MCA system at a time when the number of farmers was rapidly falling, made reform a pressing issue. These debates came to a head in the early 1980s when, for the first time, the EC accepted that unlimited agricultural support had to give way to quantitative control on production.

The need for reform and the budget crisis could no longer be denied, even by Bonn. Germany's previous stance of pressing for high prices now gave way to efforts to promote and shape any corrective measures to budgetary reforms that threatened the incomes of German farmers. Three examples may illustrate this shift:

The Minister of Agriculture, Kiechle, and the farm lobby were aware that an income-orientated price policy could only be maintained if production could be limited.[10] Kiechle, who is a Bavarian, has an expert knowledge of the milk sector and he was influential in securing the introduction of production quotas for the dairy sector. The quota system was pushed by him despite the fact that a large number of interest groups and political actors, including trade and industrial organisations, consumers, unions, the SPD and the Greens, voiced opposition or reservations. The powerful farm union, the DBV, however, after consultation with the Minister, came out in favour. Farmers' support for the introduction of quotas was a trade-off for the promise of higher prices. There is evidence to suggest[11] that the German Minister was then able to influence both the Commission and other member states as to the desirability of the system which was agreed by the Council of Ministers in 1984.

The bluff of Bonn's 'reform strategy' was called in June 1985, when Germany vetoed a Commission proposal which involved price cuts for cereals. Kiechle's table-thumping stance, invoking vital national interests to block agreement on the 1985/86 price package provoked a Community crisis. In an attempt to uphold continuity in the implementation of reforms approved in 1984, the Commission, in January 1985, had proposed a drop in cereals prices of 3.6 per cent. Faced with Kiechle's categorical resistance to the proposal, the Commission, after several months of unsuccessful negotiations, presented a compromise proposal in an attempt to meet German demands. On 12 June 1985, Germany, for the first time in the history of its EC membership, vetoed the Commission's compromise proposal.[12]

The tough German negotiating stance was fuelled by Bonn's determination to stand firm by its farmers.

Nearly three years later Kiechle was once again successful in shaping reform according to his own concepts. Despite the previous efforts to contain the CAP, agricultural expenditure soared once again and by 1987 the Community faced an acute budgetary crisis. At an emergency summit in February 1988 a comprehensive reform package was approved after a year of intense debate. This involved the application of 'stabilisers' to curb expenditure on market and price support. These measures were combined with structural policies: withdrawal of land from agriculture (a set-aside scheme) and provisions for early retirement for farmers. Two earlier attempts to solve the agricultural and budgetary crises – at the Brussels and Copenhagen summits in June and December 1987 – had failed over Chancellor Kohl's categorical refusal to accept cuts in agricultural prices. In January 1988, however, Germany took over the presidency of the Council and it was now Bonn's responsibility to direct the reform debate. The effect was to weaken the original stabiliser plans as presented by the Commission. The production limit on cereals in particular was loosened. Despite protests from other member states, particularly Britain, Bonn's compromise package, centering on an EC cereal production of 160 million tonnes, found acceptance with the majority of member states.

Bonn's role in the agricultural reform debate so far has been consistent: in order to protect farm incomes, the FRG has not only agreed to, but has pressed for, measures which, while curbing overproduction, would leave scope for price increases during the annual farm price reviews. The February 1988 emergency summit certainly brought some temporary relief for the Community's pressing agricultural financial and structural problems. As well as the agricultural decisions, a new source of revenues was created for the EC, a new basis was adopted for EC budget keeping and structural funds were doubled. The outcome was something of a diplomatic triumph for the German presidency. However, the reform of 1988 presented no change in Bonn's agricultural philosophy, as more recent developments demonstrate.

The MacSharry reform

The MacSharry reform of July 1991 involved an important change of direction for the CAP as it included, for the first time, the concept of decoupling payments, that is to say a break in the link between price support and production. According to the Commission, it represented the 'most fundamental reshaping of the CAP since its inception 30 years ago'.[13] The reforms were to be introduced by 1993 and to be fully operational by 1996. The key features were major reductions in prices particularly for cereals which, because cereals are an input into animal production, triggered a cut in livestock product prices as well. In addition, there were stronger supply control measures (e.g. set-asides in cereals, lower milk quotas). But substantial compensation for price reductions were also involved, indicating that the reform proposal was less a turning point than originally perceived by most observers.

Initially the reform was tabled in response to internal difficulties over the CAP, in particular its costs. However, this step and subsequent ones must be seen against the background of the GATT negotiations which started in 1986 and which became deadlocked at the end of 1990 over the issue of reductions in agricultural subsidies. The US and the Cairns group of 14 agricultural exporting countries were calling for a radical reduction in agricultural support. Only after protracted negotiations did the Community show a willingness to reduce some of its protectionism. But views differed greatly on the extent to which subsidies should be reduced. A year after the failure of the Round in December 1990, GATT Secretary General Arthur Dunkel, on 2 December 1991, tabled a compromise paper with a view to concluding the negotiations by 15 April 1992. The hallmark of the paper was reductions over five years of 36 per cent in farm subsidies and 24 per cent in the volume of agricultural exports by the Community.

The internal pressure on the CAP, in the form of the MacSharry reform plan, the external pressure from international trading conflicts, both of which came to a head in early 1992, caused a serious dilemma for Bonn. As a significant export country, the second largest in the world, Germany had a vital interest in the liberalisation of world trade, and by implication in the success of a GATT package which not only covered farming for the first time but also embraced services and intellectual property.

When Chancellor Kohl returned from the economic summit of the seven richest nations (G7) in July 1991, GATT was in the forefront of his mind. Two previous G7 summits had made a commitment to resolve the farm trade problem but with no effect, and further failure would be an embarrassment for Germany who was to host the following G7 summit in July 1992 in Munich. To define the German position in GATT and to work out Bonn's position in the CAP reform debate, Chancellor Kohl instructed his farm minister, Kiechle, to report on the agricultural situation. During a special cabinet session on 9 October 1991 a compromise was worked out on the CAP. While the principle of reform was not contested, the MacSharry Paper as it stood could not be accepted either. As a result, Bonn worked out its own guidelines. It was decided that any reform, particularly involving price reductions, had to be accompanied by a 'package of measures' (a concept which originated in the Ministry of Agriculture)[14] and which should comprise not just price cuts but income compensations, set-aside quotas and flanking measures. In detail, the Federal Republic resolved that:

(1) Cuts in support prices would only be accepted on the basis of income compensation. Producers, moreover, must be able to look forward to a positive and vigorous development in market prices.

(2) The income compensation must be continuous and guaranteed. It also must not discriminate against larger holdings. (The last point was made not just in consideration of Germany's larger farms in Schleswig-Holstein, but particularly in consideration of the new situation after unification which has altered Germany's agricultural structure.)
(3) The compensatory payments must not be part of the negotiating package in GATT.

The novelty of the German position was that for the first time Bonn was ready to consider price cuts, that is, cuts *before* the quota threshold. This was obviously done under the influence of GATT and in response to international criticism.

The compromise thus reached was apparently supported by all: the ministries of economics, finance and agriculture and even the farm lobby, although they, in their official statement published September 1991, had come out in outright rejection of the MacSharry reform. The DBV knew, however, that reform had to happen, as the only hope of re-establishing market equilibrium eventually, and therefore allowing a more rigorous price policy. In keeping with the lobby's previous reform positions, moreover, as long as there were income compensations, the DBV might be prepared to accommodate some reform measures.

It was hard for Germany to adopt a unified political position, a concept which would do justice to its industrial interests in the GATT round and its agricultural population, on whose voting potential the government heavily relied. In the spring of 1992 there were two very important Länder elections in agricultural regions: Baden-Württemberg, Kohl's own region; and Schleswig-Holstein, which has predominantly large farms. Kohl was under pressure from both the farm lobby and his own CDU/CSU party. In the event, the two regional elections were marked by a sharp rise in votes for extreme right-wing parties and a humiliating defeat for Kohl's party in Baden-Württemberg.

Furthermore, Germany for the first time faced serious resistance to its agricultural policy from industrial and economic circles. Traditionally, there had been a close alliance between industry and agrarian interests, originally cemented by Bismarck. In fact, there had been almost a conspiracy by the government, political parties and industry against any possible backlash from consumer associations against the CAP and agricultural policies. This alliance now appears to have broken down. Already in 1987, the Federation of German Industry, had come out, though cautiously, in favour of agricultural reform.[15]

With GATT negotiations at stake, German industry began to exert pressure on the federal government. The Federation of German Industry wrote several times to the Federal Chancellor, urging him to use his power and authority on his EC partners who might still hesitate to meet US demands. It warned of 'devastating economic effects' on the national economy which derives 32 per cent of income from exports.[16] The presidents of the six economic research institutions in Germany put him under similar pressure warning of a renewed period of protectionism, reminiscent of the 1930s.

Industry also found support from the FDP controlled Economics Ministry which traditionally urged a market-orientated reform course and articulated a strong interest in liberalising world trade. The FDP chairman returned from Washington in February 1991 with the message that it was Chancellor Kohl and not Kiechle who was seen by US opinion to hold the key to a successful conclusion of the GATT round, because only Kohl could persuade France to give up its opposition to a reduction of export subsidies. Apparently Kohl was warned: 'If the GATT Round fails, you will be identified as the one to blame.'[17] Möllemann, the Minister of Economics, declared 'the break-down of GATT would be a catastrophe'.[18] Every fourth job in Germany depends on its export performance. It has been estimated that a reduction of Germany's exports by only 2 per cent, would result in 1 million unemployed.[19]

Kohl, however, seems to have been fully aware of the significance of the GATT Round. He appears to have made use of his '*Richtlinienkompetenz*', that is to say his right, according to Article 65 of the Basic Law (the German Constitution), to set policy guidelines and he instructed his cabinet that 'The GATT Round must not end in failure.'[20]

In the event the Uruguay Round deadline of 15 April 1992 expired without accord and was postponed indefinitely. At the same time little progress was made in the CAP reform debate. Germany, while not contesting the substance of the planned reform, found the price cuts as demanded by the Commission unacceptable. MacSharry, the Commissioner for Agriculture, however, defended the Commission's reform plan and resisted attempts by member states' delegations to water down the price reductions.[21] The Portuguese Presidency drew up several compromise documents maintaining the main points of the MacSharry Plan, but providing for more flexibility in price cuts. The proposals were given a cool reception, however, with the national delegations merely agreeing to continue the debate.

In its fourth attempt to reach an agreement, the Portuguese Presidency tabled a proposal, the key element of which was a reduction of cereal prices, not by 35 per cent as originally proposed by the Commission, but by 27 per cent and with full compensation for farmers who took land out of production (whereas the Commission in its original proposal had set a ceiling on the area on which compensations would be paid).[22] The reduced cut in cereal prices was disavowed as inadequate by the Commission but was still too severe for Germany, whose opposition ensured a continuing stalemate.[23]

The CAP reform debate eventually came to a conclusion in a marathon session of agricultural ministers that started on 18 May 1992. During the previous 18 months and through 16 Council sessions, the ministers had moved from unanimous opposition to the Commission's proposal to a search for a compromise based on the original MacSharry reform plan. After intense debate, the Agricultural Council reached an agreement on 21 May, approving a radical overhaul of the CAP. The eventual compromise involved a price reduction of 29 per cent for cereals and compulsory set-aside of 15 per cent of arable land. Although the price cut was higher than the German government had wanted, there was satisfaction with the compensations that had been negotiated which included set-aside compensations for all farmers and the extension of the milk quota system until the year 2000.[24] Kiechle insisted that compensation payments would have to continue 'indefinitely' to make up for drastic cuts in cereal prices.

For the first time Kiechle had resisted the powerful domestic lobby who demanded that he 'veto' the price package as he had done in 1985. He had won important concessions, however, including the right to keep paying income support measures for 1992 to replace the 3 per cent VAT rebate paid to German farmers between 1985 and 1991 and originally negotiated as a national measure to compensate them for a revaluation of the Deutschmark in 1984. The most important concessions concerned set-aside compensation.[25] Furthermore, the reform package would have to be accepted in GATT 'as the bottom line', with the compensation payments being 'quite simply non-negotiable'.[26] The Commission did send a clear warning to the United States with the statement that:

> our trade partners must recognise the extent of the step taken by the Community today and its contribution to the stabilisation of world markets. The Council decision on reform can *provide the necessary impetus to conclude shortly the Uruguay Round* provided that the other parties to these negotiations are prepared to be realistic, pragmatic and to pay in return our contribution.[27] (original emphasis)

Conclusion

In the event, it was to be another year and a half before the GATT round was completed. Detailed bilateral negotiations between the EC and the USA on agriculture achieved a compromise whose terms on the EC side were largely based on the modified MacSharry reforms.

Germany's role had been crucial in the reform debate. Used to support its farm population by an income-orientated price level and high tariffs which had been Germany's prime objectives for over a hundred years, it was hard for Germany to agree on drastic price reductions. Chancellor Kohl stressed that the CAP reform had 'created the conditions for a successful conclusion of the GATT negotiations'.[28]

Reform of the CAP was possible – but only under the following two conditions: first, the agricultural population had to be paid off, not just in the short run, and not on a degressive scale, but with a view to re-establishing market equilibrium so that within that framework a more price-orientated policy could be pursued in the future. This was in keeping with Bonn's traditional strategies. Secondly, the policy, that is to say the CAP, came in direct conflict with other overriding German interests, such as GATT. German willingness to reform the CAP therefore was due to overriding wider interests and was pursued with maximum consistency by the Chancellor. There are plenty of examples in the 1950s and 1960s, when the construction of the custom union and the establishment of the EC was such an overriding interest, so that sectoral needs – in this case, agriculture – had to be subjugated. Another example was during the late 1980s/early 1990s when German Unification was at stake and Bonn needed the Community to support Unification as a legitimate objective of Bonn's policies. Reform of the CAP was therefore only possible under the pressure of these overriding German interests and under Kohl's influence of priority.

Notes

1. Lücker, A. (1987) 'Dreissig Jahre Landwirtschaftsgesetz der BRD', in P. Urff and H. Meyer (eds), *Landwirtschaft, Umwelt and ländlicher Raum*, Nomos, Baden-Baden, p. 31.
2. 'Landwirtschaftsgesetz', in *Bundesgesetzblatt* (BGB1), Jg. 1955, vol. 1, Bonn, p. 565.
3. Lücker, A. (1987) 'Dreissig Jahre Landwirtschaftsgesetz', *op. cit.*, p. 36.
4. The objectives as set out in Article 39 of the Treaty of Rome were to:
   - increase agricultural output;
   - guarantee a satisfactory standard of living for farmers;
   - stabilise markets;
   - guarantee supply;
   - provide supplies to consumers at reasonable prices.
5. This was the so-called Agricultural Code based on three principles: of a uniform internal market, of Community preference and of financial solidarity.
6. EC Commission, *The Agricultural Situation in the Community*, Report, various years.
7. EC Commission, *The Agricultural Situation in the Community*, Report, various years.
8. Strauss, R. (1983) 'Economic effects of MCAs', *Journal of Common Market Studies*, XX1(3), p. 273.
9. Rodemer, H. (1980) *Die EG-Agrarpolitik – Ziele, Wirkungen, Alternative*, Tübingen.
10. Bulletin der Bundesregierung, 3 January 1984, p. 5 and 7 June 1984, p. 604.
11. Petit, M., de Benedictis, M., Britton, D., de Groot, M., Henrichsmeyer, W. and Lechi, F. (1987) *Agricultural Policy Formation in the European Community: The Birth of Milk Quotas and CAP Reform*, Amsterdam, Oxford, New York, Tokyo.

12. Hendriks, G. (1989) 'Germany and the CAP: national interests and the European Community', *International Affairs*, 65(1), pp. 75–87.
13. EC Commission, *The Development and Future of the Common Agricultural Policy*, Proposals for the Commission of the European Communities, Brussels 9 July 1991, COM (91) 258.
14. Interview by author, Ministry of Agriculture, Bonn, 5 March 1992.
15. Bundesverband der Deutschen Industry (1987) *Agrarpolitik - Denkanstösse fur eine markwirtschaftliche Reform*, Köln.
16. *Financial Times*, 22 April 1992.
17. *Wirtschaftswoche*, 1992, 46(11), p. 18.
18. *Frankfurter Allgemeine Zeitung*, 4 March 1992.
19. Interview by author, Ministry of Economics, 5 March 1992.
20. Interview by author Bundeskanzleramt, 4 March 1992.
21. *Europe*, 11 March 1992, p. 6.
22. *Frankfurter Allgemeine Zeitung*, 28 April 1992; *Financial Times*, 29 April 1992; *Independent*, 30 April 1992.
23. *Financial Times*, 7 May 1992.
24. *Financial Times*, 21 May 1992; *Europe*, 22 May 1992, p. 7.
25. *Financial Times*, 22 May 1992; *Süddeutsche Zeitung*, 23/24 May 1992.
26. *Financial Times*, 23/24 May 1992.
27. *Europe*, 23 May 1992, p. 7.
28. *Europe*, 27 May 1992, p. 11.

CHAPTER 9

GATT, Global Regulation and the Construction of a New Hegemonic Order

Philip McMichael

Introduction

The continual stalling of the Uruguary Round was not simply because the parties could not agree to a new code of agricultural trade relations. It was also because the GATT talks marked a new theshold in the history of the world capitalist economy. This is the subject of this chapter. I will argue that the appearance of agricultural policy and trade on the GATT agenda is a clue to a new organisational juncture in agricultural political economy. This includes three significant transitions in the world economy: first, the decline of US hegemony; secondly, the emergence of a new international division of agricultural labour, as transnational food companies (TNCs) develop global sourcing capacities; and thirdly, the erosion of national institutions, including farm support policies now under pressure from TNCs favouring a free agricultural trade regime. While these trends are related they are not necessarily mutually reinforcing. In particular, the post-hegemonic US policy of agricultural trade liberalisation may intensify the new division of agricultural labour to its disadvantage.

The proximate reason for the GATT focus on agricultural liberalisation is an ostensible shift by the US from a mercantilist to a liberal farm policy. Originally agriculture assumed an exceptional status in GATT. At US insistence in 1955, agricultural trade was excluded from consideration in GATT codes, thus protecting US farm supply policies from import competition. Since the mid 1980s the USA has sought to deploy GATT against government regulation of agricultural imports, the stated rationale being that this will enhance global agricultural efficiency. The policy change expresses the growing dependence of US farmers on export markets, as a result of the institutionalisation of 'green power'[1] in US foreign policy. Its immediate target is the European Common Agricultural Policy (CAP) of subsidising cheap farm exports that have penetrated US foreign markets. In short, US policy is concerned with reforming international trade rules, as a condition for improving the US balance of trade via 'green power' within a general post-national free-trade regime (see McMichael, 1993).

However, the irony is that international trade liberalisation may jeopardise US green power. In the long run, the unprotected northern (metropolitan) farmer may not be as competitive with lower-cost southern peripheral producers (Buttel, 1989: 68). This possibility stems from other world-economic shifts identified earlier: the restructuring of the world division of agricultural labour under the aegis of the transnational food companies. The emergent division of labour centres on agricultural exporters in the south (many of which belong to the Cairns Group[2]) specialising in the production of agro-industriual inputs (especially interchangeable feed crops), and high-value food crops such as meat products and fruits and vegetables (see Friedmann, 1991a). Much of this trend embodies transnational companies' global sourcing arrangements (under contract with southern producers) and food-processing investments. The current conjuncture juxtaposes, as it were, a residual *national* (green power) strategy of the USA, with an emergent *global* strategy on the part of the transnational food companies. The question arises: if a free-trade regime favours the TNCs over US green power, why is the US state deploying the GATT to liberalise world agricultural trade?

It is tempting to quip that this is the end-game of a declining hegemon, with no choice but to play to its historic strength in agriculture by reforming out-moded trade rules, out-moded because they have nurtured rivals to US green power. While there is an element of truth to this proposition, the politics of GATT are considerably more complex. As I shall argue below, the restructuring of American agriculture within the context of the green-power agro-export strategy has re-oriented farm support policies towards the (world) market sphere, and away from preserving a coherent national (family) farm sector. Policy instruments (such as the Export Enhancement Program) use neo-mercantilist tactics to promote GATT liberalisation measures deemed to ensure a US role as 'breadbasket of the world'. US administration support of GATT derives from monetarist impulses, to eliminate expensive farm subsidies and allow 'comparative advantage' to have its way in international commodity trade. This is a strategy aimed at undermining national regulatory institutions, legitimised by free-trade doctrine. Arguably, given the ability of TNCs to construct their own patterns of competitive advantage in the world economy, US green power could well prove to have been a residual, political construct rather than a viable world-economic force. The implicit trend in this possible scenario – from national to global organisation of agriculture – raises questions also about the salience of national economic sectors in the world economy.

Agriculture is arguably the most common national economic sector, both by default and by design. That is, nation-builders have universally targeted *extant* (or indeed newly settled) rural producers as the source of transfers of food, funds and labour to the urban-industrial sector. In the period of modern nation-state formation within the framework of the first food regime this relationship developed reflexively (Friedmann and McMichael, 1989). That is, the 'nationalisation' of commercial agriculture anchored the modern state system, appearing first in the new settler states as the model of subsequent nation-building in the metropolitan, and then peripheral, states. This movement was rooted in the rise to global hegemony of the most powerful settler state, the USA. We are presently witnessing the decline of this form of 'nationalised' agriculture, and with it, the reformulation of the nation-state system under a general shift away from national coherence towards national competitiveness that increasingly drives all national political-economic strategies (Cerny, 1991; McMichael, 1991).

This chapter will explore these issues by first outlining the relationship between US green power and the GATT negotiations; second, examining the TNC role in restructuring world agriculture; and third, considering the implications of a GATT regime for the world food economy, especially in terms of agriculture's political role.

US green power: post-hegemonic strategy?

In this section I argue that green power as a post-hegemonic strategy is problematic. It is a legacy of the mercantilism of post-war arrangements making agriculture an exception to trade liberalisation. The GATT, established in 1947 in conjunction with the Bretton Woods financial institutions (World Bank and IMF), was confined to liberalising trade in manufactured goods among contracting parties. Restrictive agricultural trade practices, such as import controls and export subsidies, were institutionalised in Articles XI and XVI respectively. These measures were largely in response to the United States' demand in 1955 that GATT rules not apply to domestic farm policy, reflecting the particular character of the post-war order.

Post-war international political economy embodied the dual, and ultimately contradictory, principles of national regulation and freedom of enterprise. Under American hegemony, the institutional conditions for the former promoted the latter. The Bretton Woods institutions, underwritten by the US dollar as the international reserve currency, provided the financial and multilateral scaffolding for the elaboration of different forms of national regulation on the one hand, and foreign direct investment on the other hand. International regime theory characterises this combination as 'embedded liberalism' where 'multilateralism would be predicated upon domestic interventionism' (Ruggie, 1982: 393).

The national regulation of capitalism derived from the US strategy of securing European and East Asian national capitalism in the context of the Cold War (Block, 1977: 10), legitimised by an *idealised* model of US development. In this model the agricultural sector, articulated with industry, was a key to the accumulation process, rather than simply being a resource base for industry and the state (Friedmann and McMichael, 1989). With some variation, the model spread globally via green revolution technology. As Leclercq argues, this form of national regulation of agriculture which 'stimulated the input industries and processing sectors of the agro-industrial complex and encouraged the diversification of Brazilian agricultural exports', in the late 1960s 'recalls similar processes which occurred in United States' and European agriculture after the Second World War' (1989: 277).[3]

The viability of the model of national regulation was rooted in the dollar/gold standard. The gold standard required stable national trade accounts as a condition of low interest rates to secure the capital accumulation process. Relatively balanced trade in turn put a premium on national economic regulation, so that the ideal conditions for capitalism and 'development' came to be associated with those elaborated by, and within, the nation-state (Phillips, 1977). Within this model, based as it was on key farm and labour constituencies of the national polity, protection of socio-economic sectors was legitimised through Keynesian policies of national regulation. This national form, stemming from the national movement of the late nineteenth century and the class movement of the early twentieth century, has been characterised as 'a certain set of labour control practices, technological mixes, consumption habits, and configurations of political-economic power . . . called Fordist-Keynesian' (Harvey, 1989: 124).

National regulation depended on the Bretton Woods international regulatory system. While this system sustained new domestic social structures of accumulation based in compacts between organised labour and capital (Cox, 1987; 1991) and family-farm supports, at the same time it institutionalised the US model of accumulation on a global scale. This had two aspects that concern us here: first, the US agricultural model and second, the general principle of freedom of enterprise.

The US agricultural model stemmed from adjustments made during the inter-war period (1933) in response to the economic crisis, which was particularly severe in agriculture. President Roosevelt's federal commodity programmes (supported by federal credit) were geared to reviving the national accumulation process by restroring farm purchasing power. In addition, they stabilised farm production and institutionalised commodity specialisation both in production and in the organisation of the farm lobby (Buttel, 1989: 49–50). In 1935 the Agricultural Adjustment Act was amended, via Section 22, to allow the Secretary of Agriculture to bar agricultural imports undermining a price-support programme: 'Since the USDA was setting domestic prices above world market prices, it was necessary to close the borders to lower-priced foreign goods' (Bovard, 1991: 159). Thus the import control side of mercantilist agricultural policy was implied in farm supports. The export side stemmed also from farm supports. Stabilising farm prices under conditions of rising costs of new technological inputs institutionalised overproduction and systems of government-managed agricultural surpluses (Wessel, 1983: 22–3), to be disposed of via the US food aid programme.

Within the framework of the *Pax Americana*, the US model of capital- and energy-intensive agriculture was exported via the Marshall Plan to Europe, and later via the green revolution to the Third World (Cleaver, 1977; Tubiana, 1989). In each case this model anchored national farm sector development (Friedmann and McMichael, 1989), and/or severely limited exports of basic grains and some tropical products, via the protectionism of the metropolitan model (Friedmann, 1991a; forthcoming). The model transformed both production and consumption relations overseas, acting as a conduit for US wheat, maize and soya exports which were politically managed via both the Kennedy Round negotiations whereby 'American soya complemented European cereals in the feed of European livestock' (Tubiana, 1989: 26) and the PL480 programme of food aid to the Third World. The latter solved the problem of disposal of US surpluses once Europe began protecting its cereals sub-sector (Friedmann, 1982).

Alongside the construction of national forms of capitalist political-economy, the international institutional framework facilitated freedom of enterprise and trade, which Arrighi has termed the 'substantive' dimension of US hegemony (1982). Both the Marshall Plan and the green revolution were vehicles for foreign investment, rendering new domestic farm sectors increasingly dependent on imports of oil and agricultural technologies, such as inorganic fertilisers, hybrid seeds, farm machinery and so forth. At the same time, the specialised character of the agricultural model encouraged a transnational integration of specialised agricultural sub-sectors, notably in the commodity chain linking feedstuffs producers with livestock industries (Berlan, 1991). In each case, newly constructed national agricultural sectors in both north and south incorporated the global relations inherent in the US agro-food model, and in turn constituted a new arena for transnational argibusiness.

In this context it is not surprising that, under conditions of crisis in the US balance of payments in the late 1960s, the State Department identified export agriculture as a strategic trade weapon. Rising costs of empire (including an expanding Eurodollar market beyond US control) and a severe trade deficit led to the establishment of the Williams Commission, which formulated a green-power strategy. The Commission Report of 1971 recommended the USA specialise in high technology (capital equipment, armaments and computers) and agricultural export commodities such as food and feed grains (Wessel, 1983: 162–3). This resulted in a policy shift, from national agricultural commodity supply management (via the food aid programme, organised around farm price supports in excess of world market prices and production quotas) to a demand management policy. Geared now to commercial, rather than concessional, exports, demand management provided export incentives to farmers and sought trade liberalisation to maximise US 'comparative advantage' and to reduce production costs, especially petroleum inputs (Tubiana, 1989: 38; Revel and Riboud, 1986: 91–8).

President Nixon undermined the Bretton Woods system by devaluing the dollar and, reinforced by the massive US/Soviet grain deal of 1972, an export push began. US wheat exports increased 90 per cent in the first four years of the 1970s and grain prices by 400 per cent (Wessel, 1983: 163). From 1969–71, when the US had about a third of the world trade in grains, its share increased to about 60 per cent in 1980–1 (Insel, 1985: 897; Johnson, 1989: 178). The opening of the Soviet bloc to the grain trade (accounting for 60 per cent of the increase in world grain imports) was as significant as the US export juggernaut in the 1970s (accounting for 60 per cent of the increase in world grain trade), each shift being instrumental in merging the Cold War blocs and ending the post-war food regime (Friedmann, 1991a; 1991b).

The resulting export dependency is clear in the 425 per cent increase in US farm exports since 1970 (Krebs, 1988: 19) and in the restructuring of US production, where specialised monoculture has expanded and now more than one acre in three is for export production of three primary low-value products (LVPs: wheat, corn and soyabeans). In the 1970s the proportion of farm land committed to export production rose from one-half to two-thirds, and hired labour increased from 25 per cent to 50 per cent of farm labour (Strange, 1988: 40–1). In short, the green-power strategy of the 1970s fundamentally transformed American agriculture via a policy shift in which supply management and the stability of family farming yielded to a trend of agricultural capitalisation via internationalisation. The dual logic of this shift is clear: both a restructured American farming and the food companies emerging within and sponsoring this process of internationalisation, require a free-trade regime.[4]

The breakdown of the Bretton Woods system and the post-war food regime ushered in an unstable era of world-economic reconstruction. Unregulated financial markets combined with unregulated American farming, which responded to sharp price rises in food between 1972 and 1974, fuelling a 60 per cent expansion in the world grain trade from 1974 to 1980. The peak in 1980/81 at 215 million tons, was 'almost exactly three times the volume of 1960/61'. The structure of the grain trade had altered significantly: once modest importers, 'Developing countries, including China, were importing 73 million tons, the USSR 39 million tons, and Eastern Europe 12 million tons. The EC was a *net exporter* of 4 million tons by this time' (Hathaway, 1987: 13). Whereas in the 1950s the south took 10 per cent of all wheat imports, by 1980 this had increased to 57 per cent (Grigg, 1986: 248).

The rivalry of the EC and USA in supplying an increasingly food-dependent south elevated the market as the vehicle of ostensible American agricultural comparative advantage via green power. Southern food dependency underpinned the shift from US food aid to trade. This shift was anticipated in 1962, when the Kennedy administration lowered support prices to world price levels to permit unsubsidised exports (Revel and Riboud, 1986: 62), leading to a gradual decline in the role of food aid in US exports, which bottomed out in the early 1970s. But the comprehensive Agricultural Act of 1973 (of the Senate Agriculture Committee), which removed production constraints on American farmers, was not simply a formal change in the mechanism of disposal of farm surpluses. It was a qualitative shift in the goals of US policy.

Until the 1970s, US farm policy focused on stabilising farming within a nationally regulated system of accumulation, with exports/food aid as a by-product of the domestic management of surpluses. As the analysts of US green power remark:

> One of the apparent paradoxes in U.S. agricultural policy, then, was that for the twenty-five years that marked the greatest development of production in its history, the United States sought only to protect its domestic market rather than to shape world commerce to its advantage. (Revel and Riboud, 1986: 59).

In 1970 the Nixon administration established a set-aside scheme complementing a policy of unrestricted production secured by continuing direct aid payments to farmers. In addition, the pegging of the support price (loan rate) under the world price directly encouraged export production and 'changed the intervention agency, the CCC (Commodity Credit Corporation), from a stockpiling organization into a bank issuing warehouse warrants for crops' (Revel and Riboud, 1986: 91). In short, the new agro-export policy reshaped American agriculture as much as it represented the emergence of a post-hegemonic export strategy geared to free-market policies. Ironically, EC protectionism, taking its cue from post-war US policy, represents the greatest challenge to this agro-export policy.

Recent US strategy has evolved within this context: from establishing green power via the market in the 1970s, to attempts in the 1980s to enforce it through deployment of a GATT free-trade regime against the Europeans and the Japanese. One condition for the US administration taking the lead in liberalising farm policy has been the considerable restructuring, through economic polarisation, of the farm constituency. But this did not happen overnight. In the 1970s, the dramatic change in American farm policy, as well as in patterns of world food trade, produced ambiguity and anxiety in the farm belt. Responding to farmer concern with the run-down of public grain stocks, the Democratic administration's 1977 farm bill instituting a new grain reserve regulation scheme 'reflected the conflicting desires to return to domestic interventionism and to continue with free market policies' (Revel and Riboud, 1986: 95). This reintroduction of federal support prices undercut the export drive by raising American crop prices above world prices, such that by 1985 the US share of the world wheat market had fallen to 29 per cent from 68 per cent in 1979 (Bovard, 1991: 160). American agriculture assumed the position of residual supplier to the world market (Insel, 1985), having re-established a reserve stock system.

This 'interruption' of economic liberalism expressed the residual power of forces associated with the national regulation era in American farming. On the one hand, politicians were still accountable to the family farm constituency in the late 1970s (prior to the farm crisis resulting from the policy shifts in the early 1980s). On the other hand, the domestic grain/meat complex remained 'the privileged sector' requiring price stability in feedstuffs via the reserve stock (Revel and Riboud, 1986: 98).

However, the farm crisis of the 1980s shifted the balance of forces in favour of the large producer and the food companies. Credit restrictions, the rising dollar and rising farm support prices from 1977 legislation undercut the booming export economy. The proximate cause of the crisis was the sharp rise in farm price supports between 1977 and 1982: 'Between the 1981–82 and 1985–86 market years, American wheat exports declined by 50 percent, cotton exports by 75 percent, corn exports by 40 percent, rice exports by 33 percent' (Bovard, 1991: 160). For producers, the crisis was a debt crisis analogous to the debt crisis in the Third World (Green, 1987). That is, the 1970s agro-export policy was supported financially by the state, primarily through its privileging of the Federal Land Banks,[5] which outstripped the commercial banks and life insurance companies as lenders as the decade wore on (Mooney, 1988: 131). The land banks' strategy reduced farm economy dependence on internal financing, introducing speculative debt-financing (Strange, 1988: 136).

American farmland values more than quadrupled during the 1970s, with debt more than tripling (Strange, 1988: 22). Under these conditions, where bank credit favours cash volume via increasing scale and intensity of production (Mooney, 1988: 125) land concentration rose as farm ownership patterns skewed in a shake-out not so much of 'farmers who farm . . . (but) of farmers who own' (Strange, 1988: 126). The large owners, fully capitalised and thoroughly specialised, are products of government commodity support programmes. In 1984, '15 per cent of farms producing three-quarters of the output obtained 70 per cent of direct government payments' (Commins, 1990: 65). The trends in land concentration are clear in all three low-value crops depicted in Figures 9.1, 9.2 and 9.3. Large producers, who held 83 per cent of the bad debt in 1983, were relatively privileged when it came to debt collection (Wessel, 1983: 57). This was precisely because of the size and consequence of their debt, given the reconstitution of farm credit programmes, where larger producers out-competed low-income farmers for finance in an increasingly privatised farm-loan market (Strange, 1988: 139–43).

Figure 9.1 Wheat by acres harvested (no. of farms in thousands)

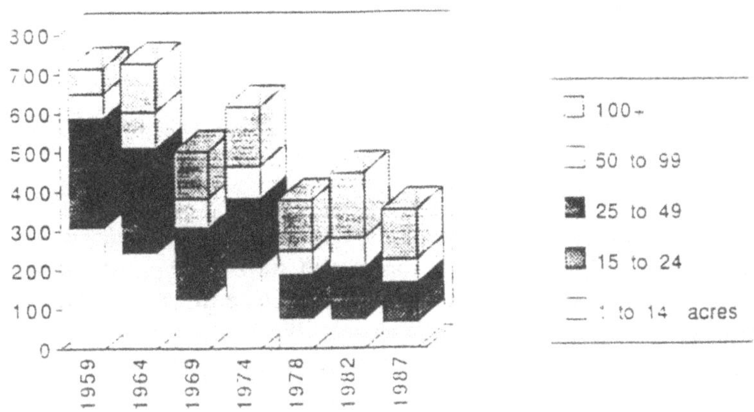

Figure 9.2 Corn by acres harvested (no. of farms in thousands)

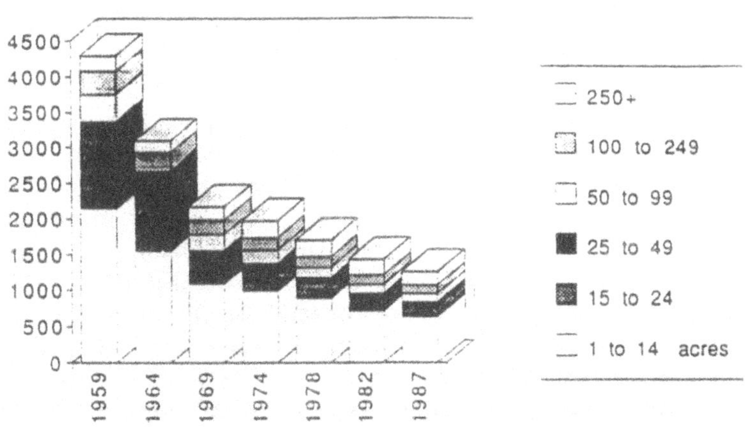

Figure 9.3 Soybeans by acres harvested (no. of farms in thousands)

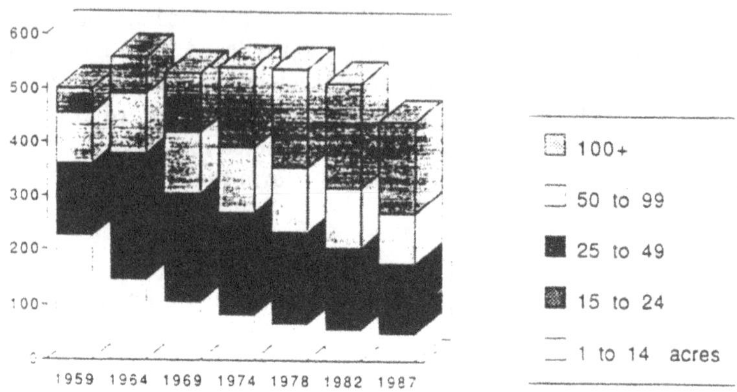

Source: Compiled from Aggregate US Agricultural Census Data by Chul-Kyoo Kim

The shift in farm credit delivery, from predominantly state-supplied (and increasingly centralised) credit in the 1970s to the Reagan policy of replacing Farmer's Home Administration loans with state-guaranteed private loans (Mooney, 1988: 159; Strange, 1988: 143), marked a threshold in farm policy presaging current liberalisation pressures. Not only was it indicative of a change from a rural welfare policy to one of socialising the cost of private expansion, it also signalled the passage in the power of agricultural credit facility to private banks, simultaneously beneficiaries of US monetarist policies which, by inflating the dollar, allowed southern agro-exports to out-compete US farmers in the world market as a debt-repayment strategy (Krebs, 1988: 21). By 1985, American crop prices were as much as 37 per cent higher than those of rival producers (Bovard, 1991: 160). In short, the realignment of forces towards the transnational private banks across this period coincided with the dismantling of the substance of the US national farm programme.

1985, the year of the Plaza Accords, was a turning point in management of the world economy as far as the USA was concerned. Confronted with a massive trade deficit and national debt, the US government proposed a new, export-expanding international trade policy, with support to devalue the dollar from the Group of Five's (France, Germany, Japan, the UK and the USA) Finance Ministers and Central Bankers (Feketekuty, 1990: 94). Externally, the sluggishness of multilateral agreement on reforming international trade led the USA to adopt an aggressive unilateralism via activation of Section 301[6] against trade practices deemed unfair by the GATT, in large to kick-start a new round of GATT negotiations. Internally, among other things, the Food Security Act of 1985 sought to reduce federal expenditures and arrest the downturn in American farm exports. In this specific context, the farm bill's focus on recovering US green power constructed an unusual consensus among farmers and agribusiness interests (Browne, 1988: 231).

While the 1985 farm bill reduced support prices (loan rates) to make exports more competitive, the commodity lobbies (representing the bulk of government programmes) ensured target-price deficiency payments to farmers remained relatively high to guarantee farm income. At the same time, continuing set-aside programmes allowed competitors the opportunity to fill the gap of foregone production (Browne *et al.*, 1992: 84). As Bovard stresses, these federal benefits inflate land prices and therefore production costs, 'while doing nothing to increase farmers' productivity or efficiency', thus 'providing Australian and South American farmers with a big advantage over American farmers' (1991: 162). In effect the US government was both subsidising inefficiency and compensating by subsidising exports via the newly established Export Enhancement Program (EEP), the average cost of which equals 62 per cent of the value of exports (Bovard, 1991: 167).

The EEP was directed particularly at the EC, to whom the USA sent the message: either

> initiate policy reforms in accordance with U.S. priorities, or the U.S. would use the EEP to subsidize exports to recapture world market shares for wheat, feed grains, and selected livestock products in direct competition with the Community. (Ames, 1990: 286)

To that end, EEP commodities have been used to target markets in the Soviet Union, China, North Africa and the Middle East.

The fundamental goal was to use the EEP as a tool of the US negotiating strategy in the newly constituted GATT Uruguay Round to challenge competitors' subsidies and other 'unfair' trade practices (Ackerman and Smith, 1990: 7–8). The 1990 US Farm Bill continued to support an agro-export offensive, shifting the initiative partly to producers. Deficiency payments (farm income supports) were denied on 15 per cent of a farmer's basic acreage (beyond land set aside), and this portion has risen to about one-third now. This, in addition to a marketing loan policy, encourages producers towards direct participation in the world market and away from reliance on government transfers (Lynch, 1991: 47).

The context of the new GATT round was the rising protectionism and bilateralism of the early 1980s, associated with the world economic recession.[7] The possibility of a new round gave northern states room to counter domestic protectionism.[8] The USA initiated the current round, in part to 'reconstruct its export-oriented free-trade coalition to bolster domestic support for international trade agreements' (Schott, 1990: 4), an associated strategy being to deploy the forces of international liberalisation against entrenched domestic support of increasingly costly farm programmes (Paarlberg, 1992). It is widely believed that trade liberalisation would enhance the farm commodity exports of the USA and the members of the Cairns Group, while European and Japanese agricultural trade balances would deteriorate (Rayner *et al.*, 1990: 7). Interestingly enough, this strategy would reverse the historical process, whereby farm sectors in the EC and Japan were reconstructed as nationally protected sectors under US post-war hegemony. US sourcing, of technical inputs, feed and food grains was central to the adoption of the model of production and consumption associated with the American agro-food system. The US liberalisation thrust fundamentally seeks to refurbish and extend such transnational integration (for instance, via continuing oilseed exports to the EC, and food and feed grain exports to Japan). As an inherent feature of the US agro-industrial model, such consolidation is perceived as a way of arresting US trade deficits.

Although the rhetorical goal is free trade based in 'comparative advantage', the substantive aims of the US administration in this GATT round have been quite neo-mercantilist. That is, green power appears to have become a 'breadbasket of the world' strategy, rather than simply pursuit of national comparative advantage in a multilateral trading system. In order to achieve this goal, the USA stepped up pressure through the modified 301 and Super-301 clauses of the Omnibus Trade Act of 1988, whereby the USA claims right of retaliation against unfair trade policies – now determined by US rather than by GATT principles (Winters, 1990: 1301). It includes cross-retaliation clauses, linking trade policy issues across the sub-sectors of goods, services and intellectual property rights: so that violation of trade practices in one sub-sector can trigger retaliation in another.

In other words, the US administration has had the benefit of flexibility in pursuing its international trade policy. Under the umbrella of the Uruguay Round, dedicated to liberalisation, it has deployed both trade retaliation and the EEP to cajole illiberal partners and to outcompete them in third markets, respectively. It is, of course, quite a contradictory set-up – where liberalism is enforced via neo-mercantilism, reduction of costly farm programmes is countered by expensive export subsidies and in turn export subsidies inflate domestic prices rendering US grains less competitive in world markets. Evidence that the neo-mercantilist strategy is more than a retaliatory device against EC/Japanese protectionism was provided by the Bush administration's export offensive announced in September 1992. Even if the $1 billion in export subsidies was an election-year gimmick, ostensibly to gain Farm Belt support, its targets were new markets traditionally supplied by Cairns Group free-traders Australia, Canada and Argentina (*Wall Street Journal*, 8 September 1992).

The ultimate contradiction, of course, is that while the US government plays out its green-power strategy to enhance its world market position and to eventually bring prices into line with costs via farm policy reforms, it is arguably undermining the long-term sustainability of this strategy. Inflicting damage on rival exporters via these expensive and inflationary tactics may not stem the longer-term likelihood of competition from cheaper southern producers under contract to the transnational food companies, especially under a free-trade regime.

TNCs and world agricultural restructuring

Current restructuring of world agriculture is expressed in part in the emerging international division of agricultural labour analogous to the reallocation of some manufacturing operations to the south in the 1970s (Frobel *et al.*, 1979). Simply put, it rests on a division within agriculture between low-value and high-value products, where trade in low-value temperate cereals and oilseeds is dominated by the north, and trade in high-value products is distributing increasingly to southern agro-exporters. It is perhaps best captured in the exchange between the United States and Mexico, where, in 1986, Mexico's exports to the USA (the world's largest food importer) exceeded $2 billion, much of which was fruit, vegetables and beef, and in turn Mexico's imports totalling about $1.5 billion, largely grains and oilseed (George, 1988: 143). While for southern states this is often an unstable trade (see Raynolds *et al.*, 1992) it is an emergent pattern - most clearly seen in the significant role played by new agro-exporters in the beef trade (Brazil), pork (China and Hungary), poultry (Brazil, Hungary and Thailand) and, more widely dispersed, in fruit and vegetables exports (Hathaway, 1987). The instability of this division refers to the more fundamental process at work: a widespread internationalisation of agriculture that potentially abstracts place by subordinating producing regions to global production and consumption relations organised by transnational food companies.

The extension of a new international division of labour to the agro-food sector is not so much an evolutionary process as a conjunctural phenomenon. It reflects the new crisis of (the south in) the world economy as a result of the 1980s debt regime. It is linked to the so-called new international division of industrial labour that emerged as the Bretton Woods order broke down. That is, the 'decentralisation' of industrial capital in the 1970s was a condition of the current 'decentralisation' of agro-food capital. Southern states overextended themselves with debt-financing by petro-dollars recycled through new international capital markets, matched by offshore northern corporate venture capital. 1980s monetarism ended easy credit conditions, imposing debt service on the south via draconian IMF conditionality agreements, including intensified agro-exporting. More than this, the apparent reproduction of a new 'colonial' division of labour whereby the north exports technology and services, and the south exports agro-food products (but is also now food dependent on the north) signals a new threshold in the organisation of the world economy.

The new juncture is one in which agriculture is less a national-societal anchor. Its role as a foundation of the nation-state system is changing. It now increasingly anchors a system of global accumulation in food products. Further, the TNC strategy of incorporating regions into global production and consumption relations is simultaneously a strategy of undermining the institutional bases of national farm sectors (see for example, Ufkes, 1993; McMichael, 1993). This directly symbolises the transition underway in international political economy. It is not simply a question of the economic viability of family farming programmes. It is also that these farm-based institutions, which nurtured agribusiness by stabilising national patterns of consumption of farm commodities in direct and indirect (agro-industrial) form, have become obstacles to the transnational strategy and structure of the food companies. They are obstacles because, for example, domestic price supports not only raise prices of agro-industrial inputs, but they also disadvantage food processors and grain traders in the world market.[9]

Transnational corporations stand to gain overall from a free-trade regime, since it would enhance and reward capital mobility and reduce costs precisely by de-regulation of national farm policies. Some 14,000 American companies (including IBM, GM, Honeywell, American Express) formed the Multinational Trade Negotiation coalition in May 1990, to de-regulate national economies (*New York Times*, 20 November 1990). Global firms in general support the GATT multilateral approach to liberalisation (Milner, 1990: 171). In fact, the original US proposal to the Uruguay Round was drafted by Cargill's former senior vice president, also a former officer of the US Department of Agriculture (Wysham, 1990: 771). Food companies, grain traders and the chemical industry all generally favour using the GATT to phase out farm programmes, eliminating supply management and driving down prices by exposing producers to world-wide differential labour costs (Ritchie, 1990: 27). Some agribusiness interests work with the US Foreign Agricultural Service on liberalisation issues, and indeed there is an expanding involvement of agribusiness in public affairs efforts to increase American food product exports (Browne, 1988: 115). To this extent, the organising principle of the world economy is shifting from nation-state to capital, as transnationals seek to exploit the differentials and scale of global economic circuits.[10]

The historical conditions for this shift in the agro-food sector stem from the process of agro-industrialisation, especially in the relationship between farming and downstream industries. Not only is the food *industry* the largest American industry (Revel and Riboud, 1983: 115), but also its centralisation in a few mega-food companies puts them in a commanding position *vis-à-vis* producers. This is especially the case where the food companies can exercise contradictory global capacities, in product sales *for* producers, and in bringing competitive pressures *against* producers. To the extent that family farm supports historically limited the wholesale reorganisation of northern land-based agriculture along mass-production lines, agribusinesses have pursued two alternative accumulation strategies of 'substitutionism'[11] and global sourcing: one being the condition for the other.

Mechanisms of vertical integration, such as contracting arrangements and direct agribusiness production, developed within the national regulation context, where the articulation of farm programmes with industrial and food service sectors established mass marketing. In the USA, vertical marketing arrangements rose from 22 per cent of total agricultural output in 1970 to 32 per cent in 1980, this (continuing) trend being closely related to farm specialisation and concentration (Goodman *et al.*, 1987: 85). Beyond this, in the grain trade, Morgan found that American farm co-operatives sell 70 per cent of their export-bound grain directly to the grain traders (1980: 311), and Kneen found that Cargill's method of beating the volume limits imposed by the Canadian grain pools and Wheat Board was to reorganise transport facilities via 'unit trains' offering variable rates to large farmers with volume sales (1990: 91).

The extension of these arrangements on a global scale is the basis for the food companies' pressure to dismantle national farm policies. This is both a trading, as well as a production, strategy, in so far as some agribusinesses are interested in direct investment in agriculture. On a global scale, new institutional forms of mass marketing of commodities produced under contract in multiple locations are emerging, especially in the global fruit and vegetable industry (Watts, 1990). Returning to the Mexican example, because it portends a future under free trade, in the 1980s the food industry grew at an average annual rate in excess of all manufacturing. Moreover, growth in food processing was overwhelmingly concentrated in export production, growing faster than overall agricultural trade (Shwedel and Haley, 1992: 48). The context has been Mexican economic deregulation, offering new opportunities for foreign investors, often in joint ventures with Mexican capital or with other foreign capitals. An example is the Trasgo group, a vertically integrated poultry operation targeting Japanese consumers, combining domestic, US and Japanese capital, focusing on local market experience, technology and knowledge of the Japanese market, respectively (Kuenzler, 1992: 47). Del Monte, a vigorous supporter of the North American Free Trade Agreement (NAFTA), and anticipating land-holding regulations, is currently experimenting with large-scale commercial production of tomatoes via private land companies managing the *ejidatarios* (small producers settled on nationalised land) (Carlsen, 1991b: 29).

Under increasingly de-regulated conditions, US (for example, Bird's Eye, Green Giant, Pepsico, General Foods, Kellogg's Campbell's, Kraft), Japanese (for example, *Sogo Shosha* such as Mitsui, Mitsubishi, C. Itoh, Sumitomo) and European (Unilever, Nestlé) companies are investing at an increasing rate in production and processing operations (Shwedel and Haley, 1992: 49). US investment in Mexican food processing, after declining 17 per cent annually through the 1980s, rebounded by 81 per cent in 1989, coinciding with changes in foreign investment regulations allowing 100 per cent ownership and use of *maquiladora* (assembly zones with entrepot status) as sites for domestic sales (Carlsen, 1991a: 21). Japanese *Soga Shosha* (commodity firms) provide organisations and management of traditional low- and medium-technology industries being phased out of Japan and relocated to Mexico, essentially reconstructing Mexican (agro)-industry to complement the Japanese economy (Ramsamooj, 1991: 15). Meanwhile, as the NAFTA has evolved, the average Mexican tariff has been reduced from 27 per cent to less than 8 per cent, encouraging imports from North America (Kuenzler, 1992: 44).

Perhaps presaging the 1990s, the Mexican Foreign Secretary proclaimed in 1991: 'Mexico is one of the newer trading powers of the world that has helped to maintain the pace for bringing about an ambitious reform of the world trading system' (quoted in Fenley, 1991: 41). In other words, Mexico's embrace of trade and investment liberalisation in the NAFTA (claimed by the US ambassador to the GATT to be consistent with, and linked to the GATT system: *Reuter*, 2 April 1992) expresses emergent relationships between food-product importers like the USA and Japan and new agro-exporters like Mexico that are the foundation for the new economic forces supporting establishment of a GATT free-trade regime. And here Japan is becoming more consequential because of its unique resource dependence, intensified by its industrial export offensive, not to mention its extraordinary affluence. Between 1986 and 1988, Japanese foreign investment in food processing more than tripled, exceeding the overall growth rate in Japanese direct foreign investment (Riethmuller, 1992: 25). Yen appreciation, Japanese government taxation policy, as well as the expectation of trade liberalisation in agricultural products, have encouraged rising offshore investments. These range, for example, across Thai poultry production and food processing (where costs are 10 per cent of those in Japan), in Hungarian food processing (apple juice), in Australian and US beef production, and in vegetable production and processing and soybean processing in the USA (Riethmuller, 1992; Buell *et al.*, 1988).

The beef industry is a paradigmatic case, not simply because it is a key global complex integrating feed and cattle producers and processors, but also because it is expected to continue expanding as a global industry. Where US per capita beef consumption has declined from 94.2 lbs in 1976 to 72.7 lbs in 1988 (Gorman, 1989: 47), Japan's beef consumption is predicted by the Japanese Ministry of Agriculture to increase by 50 per cent from 1988 to 2000 (Sato, 1991: 81). In this context, Australia is emerging as a significant site of grain-fed beef for the East Asian markets, especially since new beef agreements were signed by the governments of Japan, Australia and the

United States in 1988 (Gorman and Mori, 1990). For Japanese investors, the advantages of the Australian beef industry are its ability to ship fresh chilled beef (in contrast to frozen beef from the USA), lower production costs of grain-fed beef, an alternative supply zone to the USA, and the opportunity for Japanese firms through joint ventures to influence the organisation of production and processing to tailor cuts to the Japanese consumer preference. Australia's share of Japanese markets for chilled beef grew from less than 10 per cent in 1986 to more than 50 per cent in 1989 (Gorman and Mori, 1990: 42, 46). Like Mexico, the context for this reconstitution of Australian agriculture has been its drastic de-regulation over the past decade (Lawrence, 1987), where declining world prices for wool and wheat have pushed farmers into beef and feed production (for the parallel case of New Zealand, see Cloke and Le Heron, this volume). Illustrating my earlier point about the more fundamental process of internationalisation, Japanese reconstruction of supply zones is ultimately region-neutral in north/south terms, whether in US and Australian beef (where modern slaughtering and meat-packing plants have been relocated near feed and livestock supplies), Thai poultry and food processing, or Mexican fruit and vegetable production processing (see McMichael, 1992b).

Offshore investment and new export strategies complement one another. Regarding the latter, declining US beef consumption provoked an aggressive export strategy by US beef producers in the 1980s, when large producers joined agribusinesses in the Meat Industry Trade Policy Council to press for GATT-based trade liberalisation (Ufkes, 1993). Part of this strategy involved investment in the emerging Australian grain-fed beef industry by ConAgra and Cargill, matching investment by Japanese TNCs (for example, C. Itoh and Mitsubishi). In turn, these new investments reinforced the growing pressure in the Uruguay Round on metropolitan states to de-regulate their farm sectors.

Implications of a GATT regime for the world food economy

This section considers the impact that a GATT free-trade regime might have on the world food economy and its implications for US green power. Liberalisation is likely to intensify current restructuring trends in the world food order. For the north, whose temperate products are protected by farm policies, liberalisation would in the short run raise basic foodstuff prices (grains, livestock products and edible oils) to the advantage of northern producers (particularly US producers, and those of selective Cairns group members such as Argentina, Australia, Canada and Brazil), and to the disadvantage of net food-importing southern countries (UNCTAD, 1990: 47). For the south, green revolution technology, once geared towards the construction of national agricultural sectors in the middle-income states, has virtually institutionalised the production of inputs and/or commodity substitutes for global agro-industrial complexes and niche-market exports[12] (Barkin *et al.*, 1990; Friedmann, 1991a). That is, southern farm sectors are likely to progressively lose any national coherence they might have had – again Mexico is a telling example (see Raynolds *et al.*, 1992). Overall, current restructuring trends are governed by a complementary specialisation in high-value 'non-traditional' exports from the south and low-value cereals exports from the north, exacerbating southern food dependency (McMichael, 1992a).

At present, southern food dependency is sustained through managed surplus dumping. The US 1985 farm bill sought to diminish 'the US role as residual supplier by reducing drastically – in many cases by 50 percent or more – the price of U.S. products on world markets, thus expanding U.S. exports by gaining a larger share of the market' (US Congress, 1989: 25fn). In fact, one of the architects of the farm bill argued: 'if we do not lower our farm prices to discourage these developing countries from aiming at self-reliance now, our world-wide competitive position will continue to slide' (quoted in Watkins, 1991: 41). As an extension of this goal, a US-led movement within the Uruguay Round was committed to reducing the 'special and differential treatment' rules that existed within GATT to protect southern producers as part of their particular development needs (Watkins, 1991: 47). The point is that within the emerging division of labour, even if world market prices rise as surplus management declines with liberalisation,[13] the expansion of southern agro-exporting under the imperatives of the debt regime compounds the limits on conversion to domestic basic food production to supply ever-growing urban populations.

A GATT free-trade regime is likely to have three *immediate* effects. First, it would privilege large-scale producers (mostly in North America) that have benefited disproportionately from price support programmes (Wessel, 1983: 65, 107; Kneen, 1990: 90). For US producers, farm policies and green-power policies have institutionalised a comparative advantage that would continue in the short run in an open market. Secondly, in the longer run, it would further centralise economic power in the hands of the TNCs involved in the food industry. And thirdly, liberalisation would further erode the national coherence of the states committed to enforcing this new free-trade regime.

These likely effects are qualitative in nature, rather than simply quantitative trade measures, especially as the Uruguay Round identified reform of domestic farm policy as a requirement for international trade reform (for elaboration, see McMichael, 1993). Where GATT initially aimed to liberalise trade in manufactured goods among participating members, the recent Round addressed a broader set of economic relations prefigured by the TNCs. Attached, and related, to farm liberalisation is the issue of subordinating contracting parties to the internationalisation of investment, services and intellectual property rights. The new GATT rules would offer non-discrimination and reciprocity to individual members of a more liberal order, on condition that they enforce internationally defined standards of trade, environmental regulation, property rights and so on. The guiding principle is that 'any nation that decides to impose limits on the rights of foreign companies, for environmental or social reasons, can be retaliated against for creating a "restraint of trade"' (Schaeffer, 1990: 14). This portends a reorganisation of global production relations at the expense of (especially southern) national economic and political sovereignty (Raghavan, 1990: 69, 75). Indeed, comparative advantage theorists argue that efficient global food production requires international fora such as GATT 'to help counter domestic political pressure for increases in agricultural protection' (Anderson, 1983: 328).

Turning to the question of what is in a GATT regime for the United States, two issues need attention: first, the institutional role of a GATT regime, and secondly, the implications for the green-power strategy. In a period of US hegemonic decline, what is interesting about the Uruguay Round is its distinctive constitutional focus, for example on developing formulae and political criteria regarding trade and regulation measures (Winters, 1990). The constitutionality of GATT becomes the enforcement mechanism whereby the USA could deploy the GATT to legitimise a free-trade regime in lieu of fashioning its own rules for the world order, as hegemon. Under this arrangement, member states would assume responsibility for securing the world market, simultaneously submitting to world market rule as dictated by suprastatal institutions like the IMF, the World Bank and GATT. Here, national regulation is formally subordinated to mechanisms of global regulation (for elaboration of this concept, see McMichael and Myhre, 1991; Friedmann, 1991b; McMichael, 1992a). Some of these mechanisms are already institutionalised in redistributions of power within states, from social/sectoral ministries (for example, agriculture, education, social services) to the central bank, and trade and finance ministries (Bienefeld, 1989; Canak, 1989; Cox, 1991). These mechanisms are, however, asymmetrical within the state system, since the institutions themselves continue to embody the principles established under US hegemony, especially freedom of enterprise (Arrighi, 1982), which would reinforce emergent north/ south hierarchies.

Freedom of enterprise, however, is a double-edged sword for the USA, since the food companies intensify competition between US and alternative producers in world markets. This could take the form of price or product competition. For example, in the 1980s US soybean exports lost 50 per cent of their market share with competition from Brazil and Argentina and from alternative oilseeds such as rapeseed, cotton seed and groundnuts (Rosson *et al.*, 1989; Crowder, 1990). As far as wheat is concerned, the USA is currently no more competitive in world markets than Europe, under the CAP (Phillips, 1990). Nevertheless in a free-trade regime the US research, transport and marketing infrastructure is believed to favour US wheat producers, especially given the sheer volume of US supplies on the world market (Revel and Riboud, 1986; Charvet, 1990: 179). However, the productivity of US agriculture could itself become a liability, where there is already evidence that large importers, such as China, Eastern Europe and Egypt, may exert their own market power to obtain the most favourable terms of trade among competing export regions co-ordinated by the transnationals (*International Wheat Council*, 1988, report 16; Pick and Park, 1991).

Compared to Europe, the USA is also believed to have a competitive advantage in animal feeds such as secondary cereals and oil products (Lambert, 1990). However, with biotechnology developments and the internationalisation of intensive animal protein production, feedstuffs competition has intensified as Brazil, China and Thailand rival traditional cereal exporters like the ex-settler states. Grain substitutes, such as cassava, corn gluten feed and citrus pellets have become important export commodities (Hathaway, 1987: 30) and, as substitutes, they furnish new competitive strategies for the food companies (Friedmann, 1991a).

The US green-power strategy is based on more than just trade competition. It also presumes a strong upward trend in cereal demand in southern countries as new class diets centred on animal protein products emerge, and that technological capacities under rain-fed conditions limit local cereal production (de Janvry *et al.*, 1989: 33). In the 1980s the fastest growth in southern agricultural imports has been in feed grains rather than food grains. In a study of 41 southern states, the newly industrialising countries (South Korea, Singapore, Indonesia, Mexico and Brazil), which constituted 24 per cent of the population, accounted for 47 per cent of cereal imports (de Janvry *et al.*, 1989: 10). Whether other countries will follow suit and whether this kind of intensive agro-food model can sustain itself in the long run, are of course big questions. But it is clear that the USA is banking on the intensive livestock complex as the foundation for green power. This is the case not simply because the US state perceives American agriculture to have a comparative advantage, at least in terms of its complementary role in the world agricultural trade, [14] but also because the dietary implications of the US agro-food model are becoming universalised via the activities of the TNCs in a context of rapid urbanisation.

A counter trend, however, is the new internationalisation that may eventually undercut the current complementarities in the world food economy. US predictions are elaborated to some extent from recent trends that have emerged within a framework of continuing national agricultural regulation in the north. As I have argued, this framework is under attack from the TNCs and/or the GATT negotiations. Perhaps more to the point, the universal spread of low-wage production stems from the dismantling of systems of national regulation. Mass production for regulated high-wage economies is no longer an adequate model. Thus flexible forms of specialisation complement mass production forms as corporate strategies refocus on global and/or regional segmented markets that replace national markets. Global production strategies, privileging certain producing regions within the global organisation of the food companies, is the outcome.

While it is true that the institutionalisation of green power has concentrated American farming and complemented foreign livestock industries via feed exports, there are signs of alternative possibilities in the world food economy. First, global sourcing provides food companies with a flexibility that is belied by heavily capitalised American farmers. A GATT regime, with its sanctions against agricultural protection, would intensify the competitive possibilities inherent in transnational strategies of accumulation. Secondly, the reintegration of feed and feed-lot production zones evident, for example, in Thai poultry and Australian beef production – both of which have successfully rivalled traditional US poultry and beef exports to the East Asian markets (McMichael, 1992b) – challenges the pattern of regional specialisation linking US feed production with foreign livestock producers that anchored the second post-war food regime (Friedmann and McMichael, 1989). Interestingly enough, this has been the context within which the US intensive beef sub-sector has been restructured recently, in part to supply new specialty markets for meat products (which is why Japanese corporate investment has been involved). This has encouraged the relocation of automated meatpacking plants near the huge feedlots (on the sparsely populated High Plains) associated with newly specialised feed-grain producers and the importing of cheap immigrant and native-born migrant labour to perform the high-turnover, unskilled jobs on the livestock 'disassembly line' (Stanley, forthcoming). Thus, agro-industries are being reconstructed around global accumulation strategies, rather than national economic complexes.

Conclusion

It is now possible to argue that the institutionalisation of green power combined two potentially contradictory tendencies. On the one hand, the US green-power strategy consolidated a new complementary international division of labour still based in residual national agricultural sectors, of which the international livestock/feed complex is perhaps the paradigmatic case. On the other hand, the green-power strategy centralised agribusiness capital as the basis for food TNCs, whose ultimate interest is in global market rule at the expense of nationally organised sectors. A GATT free-trade regime appears likely to favour the former in the short run, but perhaps the latter in the longer run.

In the short run, liberalisation is likely to reinforce US predominance in markets for food and feed grains, because of its infrastructural as well as spatial advantages (Franklin, 1988: 35), but also through the specific terms of liberalisation, by allowing the USA to manipulate dollar grain prices by exercising acreage controls, which were excluded from GATT under the 1989 Geneva Accords (Hine *et al.*, 1989: 392). Nevertheless, the US 'breadbasket/restauranteur[15] of the world' strategy is already under competitive pressure, as feed and specialty meat production are recombined in feed-supply zones, ruminants being 'efficient converters of low-grade roughage to high-grade protein' (Coyle, 1990: 52). The liberalisation of beef imports into Japan, for instance, achieved through US Super 301 pressure pursuant to a GATT regime, also has been the context in which TNC global sourcing of beef has been consolidated. In the long run, the further reorganisation of world agriculture within the parameters of global, rather than national, forms of regulation of production and comsumption is the likely outcome of a GATT-based free-trade order. This potential food regime, while by no means uncontested (McMichael, 1992a), would mark a corporate hegemony secured by states institutionialising market rule and a recursive reactionary politics, governed by the discourse of globalisation.

Notes

1. The term 'green power', not to be confused with environmental politics, refers to world market dominance in agricultural commodities, especially grains (c.f., Revel and Riboud, 1986). I emphasise its emergence as an agro-export strategy by the US government.
2. The Cairns Group, within the Uruguay Round, comprised Argentina, Australia, Brazil, Canada, Chile, Colombia, Fiji, Hungary, Indonesia, Malaysia, Philippines, New Zealand, Thailand and Uruguay.
3. Interestingly enough, the Brazilian form of the agro-industrial model is not simply a replication of the US and European agricultural modernisation strategies, but represents an advance in so far as the Brazilian state has encouraged processed agricultural exports, as opposed to the low-value exports associated with traditional agricultural exporters like the USA (see Friedmann, forthcoming).
4. Morgan (1980: 307) cites a 1975 USDA Report that:

   > U.S. grain exporting is dominated by five grain companies that account for about 85% of the total volume, Cargill's 1974 share of American grain exports being 42% for barley, 32% for oats, 29% for wheat, 22% for sorghum, 18% for soybeans, and 16% for corn – on average, Cargill and Continental each handling about a quarter of total U.S. grain exports.

   By the end of the 1970s, the six great grain/oilseed trading companies (Cargill, Continental, Bunge, Dreyfus, Andre & Co., and Mitsui/Cook) exported 96 per cent of all US wheat, 95 per cent of its corn, 90 per cent of its oats and 80 per cent of its sorghum (Krebs, 1988: 19). Revel and Riboud add that between 1970 and 1975, these companies 'exported 80 percent of Argentine wheat, 90 percent of Australian sorghum, and 90 percent of the wheat and corn from the European Community' (1986: 118).

5. During the 1970s tax-exemption was made available for land purchasing via loans from the Federal Land Bank, which allowed loans of up to 95 per cent of land values (Strange, 1988: 21–2).
6. Section 301 was part of the Trade and Tariff Act of 1974 (amended in 1979, 1984 and 1988) and authorises the US Trade Representative to enforce US international trading rights, as recognised in the GATT, against violations of those rights.
7. According to Producer Subsidy Equivalent estimates of the OECD, between 1979/81 and 1984/86 the average rate of government assistance to agriculture across seven OECD countries increased from 29.3 per cent to 38.2 per cent, and, for nine OECD countries, from 34 per cent in 1984 to 51 per cent in 1986, declining to 45 per cent in 1988 (Rayner *et al.*, 1990: 5).
8. Later, the US trade negotiator, Carla Hills, would reiterate: 'As long as there are no international rules it is hard to tell the elected representatives of our people that they cannot protect the national interest' (*The Economist*, 15 December 1990).
9. Browne claims, for example, that to an important extent, agribusinesses 'no longer condone the idea that farm legislation is a legitimate producer prerogative' (1988: 110). It is important to note, however, that agribusiness companies do not have a homogeneous outlook on trade policy, in part because they have different organisational formats depending on their specific histories and point of entry into the food system. They frequently diversify vertically and horizontally by commodity as products undergo change: 'Cargill, for example, not only manages nonagricultural businesses, it also merchandises grain, processes meat, mills corn and wheat, refines corn sweeteners and various oils, produces seed, and manufactures animal feed' (Browne, 1988: 112).
10. The point here is that firms that operate via global capital circuits are influencing the content and organisation of national economic circuits. For example, in the Newly Industrialising Countries (NICs) transnational corporations are responsible for a significant percentage of industrial output: according to UN Center on Transnational Corporations studies, 33 per cent of Argentinian, 44 per cent of Brazilian and 39 per cent of Mexican industry is under TNC control. Further: 'On their own books, as internal transactions, they carry as much as one-quarter of all world trade' (Piel, 1992: 652).
11. 'Substitutionism' is the term used by Goodman, Sorj and Wilkinson (1987) to conceptualise the industrialisation of the food product as a strategy of capital accumulation via value-adding.
12. High-value products accounted for 83 per cent of southern agricultural exports during 1970–87. Processed exports have undergone the most rapid growth and accounted for almost half of southern high-value exports in 1986/87, most of which go to northern markets (Burfisher *et al.*, 1991).
13. Liberalisation would formerly eliminate subsidised over-production and government-assisted exporting. Nevertheless, technologically assisted over-production is unlikely to disappear (Watkins, 1991: 46). This could limit the predicted price rise.
14. Recent USDA research suggests that overall US/LDC global trade patterns are complementary in agriculture, where the USA was found to be especially globally competitive in coarse grains, food grains, and flour and meal (Vollrath and Scott, 1991).

15. Strange (1988) coined this term in reference to the significance of feedstuffs in US exports.

Acknowledgement

The author acknowledges financial support from New York State Experimental Station research grant No. 159406.

References

Ackerman, K. Z. and Smith, M. E. (1990) *Agricultural Export Programs. Background for 1990 Farm Legislation*. Washington, DC: USDA-ERS.

Ames, G. C. W. (1990) 'US-EC agricultural policies and GATT negotiations', *Agribusiness*, 6(4): 283–95.

Anderson, K. (1983) 'Growth of agricultural protection in East Asia', *Food Policy*, 8: 327–36.

Arrighi, G. (1982) 'A crisis of hegemony', 55–109, in S. Amin, G. Arrighi, A. G. Frank and I. Wallerstein (eds) *Dynamics of Global Crisis*. New York: Monthly Review Press.

Barkin, D., Batt, R. and DeWalt, B. (1990) *Food Crops vs. Feed Crops: the Global Substitution of Grains in Production*. Boulder, Co: Lynne Reiner.

Berlan, J-P. (1991) 'The historical roots of the present agricultural crisis', 115–36 in W. Friedland, L. Busch, F. H. Buttel and A. Rudy (eds) *Towards a New Political Economy of Agriculture*. Boulder, Co: Westview Press.

Bienefeld, M. (1989) 'The lessons of history and the developing world', *Monthly Review*, 41(3), 9–41.

Block, F. (1977) *The Roots of International Economic Disorder*. Berkeley: University of California Press.

Bovard, J. (1991) *The Farm Fiasco*. San Francisco: Institute for Contemporary Studies.

Browne, W. P. (1988) *Private Interests, Public Policy and American Agriculture*. Lawrence: University Press of Kansas.

Browne, W. P., Skees, J. R., Swanson, L. E., Thompson, P. B. and Unnevehr, L. J. (1992) *Sacred Cows and Hot Potatoes. Agrarian Myths in Agricultural Policy*. Boulder, Co: Westview Press.

Buell, B., Levine, J. B. and Therrien, L. (1988) 'American food companies look yummy to Japan', *Business Week*, June, 61–2.

Burfisher, M. E., Missiaen, M. D. and Blackman, A. (1991) 'Less developed countries' performance in high-value agricultural trade', *Staff Report*. Washington, DC: USDA-ERS.

Buttel, F. H. (1989) 'The US farm crisis and the restructuring of American agriculture: domestic and international dimensions', 46–83 in D. Goodman and M. Redclift (eds) *The International Farm Crisis*. New York: St. Martin's Press.

Canak, W. (1989) 'Debt, austerity and Latin America in the new international division of labor', 9–27 in W. Canak (ed.) *Lost Promises: Debt, Austerity and Development in Latin America*. Boulder, Co: Westview Press.

Carlsen, L. (1991a) 'Reaping winter's harvest', *Business Mexico*, May, 20–3.

Carlsen, L. (1991b) 'New products, new markets', *Business Mexico*, July, 28–9.

Cerny, P. G. (1991) 'The limits of deregulation: transnational interpenetration and policy change', *European Journal of Political Research*, 19, 173–96.

Charvet, J-P. (1990) 'Cereal producer strategies in the major exporting countries in the face of collapsing world prices', *International Social Science Journal*, 124, 169–80.

Cleaver, H. (1977) 'Food, famine and the international crisis', *Zerowork*, 2, 7–70.

Commins, P. (1990) 'Restructuring agriculture in advanced societies: transformation, crisis and responses', 45–76 in T. Marsden, P. Lowe and S. Whatmore, (eds) *Rural Restructuring. Global Processes and the Responses*. London: David Fulton Publishers.

Coyle, W. T. (1990) 'The changing structure of Japanese agricultural trade', 49–55, in *World Agriculture Situation and Outlook Report: Forces for Change in the 1990s*. Washington, DC: USDA–ERS.

Cox, R. W. (1987) *Production, Power and World Order. Social Forces in the Making of History*. New York: Columbia University Press.

Cox, R. W. (1991) 'The global political economy and social choice', 335–49, in D. Drache and M. S. Gertler (eds) *The New Era of Global Competition: State Policy and Market Power*. Montreal: McGill-Queen's University Press.

Crowder, B. M. (1990) 'Government programs for soybeans', *National Food Review*, 13(1), 32–6.

de Janvry, A., Sadoulet, E. and White, T. K. (1989) *Foreign Aid's Effect on U.S. Farm Exports Benefits or Penalties*? Washington, DC: USDA–ERS.

Feketekuty, G. (1990) 'U.S. policy on 301 and Super 301', 91–103, in J. Bhagwati and H. T. Patrick (eds) *Aggressive Unilateralism*. Ann Arbor: University of Michigan Press.

Fenley, L. (1991) 'Promoting the Pacific Rim', *Business Mexico*, June, 40–1.

Franklin, M. (1988) *Rich Man's Farming: The Crisis in Agriculture*. London and New York: Routledge.

Friedland, W. (forthcoming) 'The global fresh fruits and vegetable system: an industrial organisation analysis', in P. McMichael (ed.) *Agro-Food System Restructuring in the Late-Twentieth Century*. Ithaca: Cornell University Press.

Friedmann, H. (1982) 'The political economy of food: the rise and fall of the postwar international food order', *American Journal of Sociology*, 88S, 248–86.

Friedmann, H. (1991a) 'Changes in the international division of labor: agri-food complexes and export agriculture', 65–93, in W. Friedland, L. Busch, F. H. Buttel and A. Rudy (eds) *Towards a New Political Economy of Agriculture*. Boulder, Co: Westview Press.

Friedmann, H. (1991b) 'Regulating capital on a global scale', *Studies in Political Economy*, 36, 9–42.

Friedmann, H. (forthcoming) 'International relations of food', in B. Harriss (ed.) *Food*. Oxford: Basil Blackwell.

Friedmann, H. and McMichael, P. (1989) 'Agriculture and the state system: the rise and decline of national agricultures, 1870 to the present', *Sociologia Ruralis*, XXIX(2), 93–117.

Frobel, F., Heinrichs, C. and Kreye, O. (1979) *The New International Division of Labor*. New York: Cambridge University Press.

George, S. (1988) *Till Debt Us Do Part*. Washington, DC: Institute for Policy Studies.

Goodman, D., Sorj, B. and Wilkinson, J. (1987) *From Farming to Biotechnology*. Oxford: Basil Blackwell.

Gorman, C. (1989) 'Roundup time for teriyaki beef', *Time*, March, 13, 47.

Gorman, W. D. and Mori, H. (1990) 'Competitive position of Australian grain-fed beef in the Japanese market', 42–9, in *Pacific Rim. Agriculture and Trade Report*. Washington, DC: USDA-ERS.

Green, G. P. (1987) *Finance Capital and Uneven Development*. Boulder, Co: Westview Press.

Grigg, D. (1986) *The World Food Problem*. Oxford: Basil Blackwell.

Harvey, D. (1989) *The Condition of Postmodernity*. Oxford: Basil Blackwell.

Hathaway, D. E. (1987) *Agriculture and the GATT: Rewriting the Rules*. Washington, DC: Institute for International Economics.

Hine, R. C. K., Ingersent, K. A. and Rayner, A. J. (1989) 'Agriculture in the Uruguay Round: from the Punta del Este Declaration to the Geneva Accord', *Journal of Agricultural Economics*, 40(2) 385–96.

Insel, B. (1985) 'A world awash in grain', *Foreign Affairs*, 63, 892–911.

Johnson, D. G. (1989) 'The current setting of U.S. agriculture', 173–90, in G. Horwick and G. J. Lynch (eds) *Food, Policy and Politics. A Perspective on Agriculture and Development*. Boulder, Co: Westview.

Kneen, B. (1990) *Trading Up. How Cargill, the World's Largest Grain Trading Company, is Changing Canadian Agriculture*. Toronto: NC Press, Ltd.

Krebs, A. V. (1988) 'Corporate agribusiness: seeking colonial status for U.S. farmers', *Multinational Monitor*, July–August, 19–21.

Kuenzler, L. T. (1992) 'Foreign investment opportunities in the Mexican agricultural sector', *Business Mexico*, special edition, 44–7.

Lambert, F. (1990) 'Is European agriculture competitive in the face of its North American competitors? An analysis based on a comparison of producer prices', *Economie-Rurale*, 196, 23–31.

Lawrence, G. (1987) *Capitalism and the Countryside. The Rural Crisis in Australia*. Sydney and London: Pluto Press.

Leclercq, V. (1989) 'Aims and constraints of the Brazilian agro-industrial strategy: the case of soya', 275–91, in D. Goodman and M. Redclift, (eds) *The International Farm Crisis*. New York: St. Martin's Press.

Lynch, L. (1991) 'U.S. food and agricultural policy', 47–9, in *Developing Economies. Agriculture and Trade Report*. Washington, DC: USDA-ERS.

McMichael, P. (1991) 'Food, the state, and the world economy', *International Journal of Sociology of Agriculture and Food*, 1, 71–85.

McMichael, P. (1992a) 'Tensions between national and international control of the world food order: contours of a new food regime', *Sociological Perspectives*, 35(2), 343–65.

McMichael, P. (1992b) 'Agro-food restructuring in the Pacific Rim: a comparative-international perspective on Japan, South Korea, the United States, Australia and Thailand', in R. A. Palat (eds) *Pacific-Asia and the Future of the World-System*. Westport, Conn.: Greenwood Press.

McMichael, P. (1993) 'World food system restructuring under a GATT regime', *Political Geography*.

McMichael, P. and Kim, C.K. (forthcoming) 'The restructuring of the agricultural systems of Japan and South Korea in comparative and global perspective', in P. McMichael (ed.) *Agro-Food System Restructuring in the Late-Twentieth Century*. Ithaca: Cornell University Press.

McMichael, P. and Myhre, D. (1991) 'Global regulation vs. the nation-state: agro-food restructuring and the new politics of capital', *Capital and Class*, 43, 83–105.

Milner, H. (1990) 'The political economy of U.S. trade policy: a study of the Super 301 provision', 163–80, in J. Bhagwati and H. T. Patrick (eds) *Aggressive Unilateralism*. Ann Arbor: University of Michigan Press.

Mooney, P. (1988) *My Own Boss? Class, Rationality, and the Family Farm*. Boulder, Co: Westview Press.

Morgan, D. (1980) *Merchants of Grain*. Harmondsworth: Penguin.

Paarlberg, R. L. (1992) 'How agriculture blocked the Uruguay Round', *SAIS Review*, 12(1), 27–42.

Phillips, A. (1977) 'The concept of "development"', *Review of African Political Economy*, 8, 7–20.

Phillips, P. W. B. (1990) *Wheat, Europe and the GATT: a Political Economy Analysis*. London: Pinter Publishers.

Pick, D.H. and Park, T.A. (1991) 'The competitive structure of U.S. agricultural exports', *American Journal of Agricultural Economics*, 73(1), 133–41.

Piel, G. (1992) 'Globalopolies', *The Nation*, May, 18, 652–3.

Raghavan, C. (1990) *Recolonization: GATT, the Uruguay Round and the Third World*. Penang, Malaysia: Third World Press.

Ramsamooj, D. (1991) 'Japan in Mexico: taking the long view', *Business Mexico*, May, 14–18.

Rayner, A. J., Ingersent, K.A. and Hine, R.C. (1990) 'Agriculture in the Uruguay Round: prospects for long-term trade reform', *Oxford Agrarian Studies*, 18(1), 3–21.

Raynolds, L., Myhre, D., McMichael, P., Carro-Figueroa, V. and Buttel, F. H. (1992) 'The new internationalization of agriculture: a reformulation', unpublished ms. Cornell University: Field of Development Sociology.

Revel, A. and Riboud, C. (1986) *American Green Power*. Baltimore: The Johns Hopkins Press.

Riethmuller, P. (1992) 'Japanese direct foreign investment in agricultural industries: a review of some recent developments', *Agribusiness*, 8(1), 23–33.

Ritchie, M. (1990) 'Trading away the family farm: GATT and agriculture', *Multinational Monitor*, 11, 11, 26–8.

Rosson, C.P., Curtis, C.E., Auburn, G.W. and Carriker, G.L. (1989) 'The international soybean situation: can Southern soybeans compete?', *Journal of Agribusiness*, 7(1), 49–55.

Ruggie, J.G. (1982) 'International regimes, transactions, and change: embedded liberalism in the post-war order', *International Organisation*, 36(2), 379–415.

Sato, K. (1991) 'Japan's resource imports', *The Annals of the American Academy of Political and Social Science*, 513, 76–89.

Schaeffer, R. (1990) 'Trading away the planet', *Greenpeace*, 11(10), 13–16.

Schott, J. J. (1990) 'The Uruguay Round: what can be achieved?', 1–50, in J. Schott (ed.) *Completing the Uruguay Round: A Results-Oriented Approach to the GATT Trade Negotiations*. Washington, DC: Institute for International Economics.

Shwedel, S. and Haley, K. (1992) 'Foreign investment in the Mexican food system', *Business Mexico*, special edition, 48–55.

Stanley, K. (forthcoming) 'Industrial change and the transformation of rural labor markets in the U.S. meatpacking industry', in P. McMichael (ed.) *Agro-Food System Restructuring in the Late Twentieth Century*. Ithaca: Cornell University Press.

Tubiana, L. (1989) 'World trade in agricultural products: from global regulation to market fragmentation', 23–45, in D. Goodman and M. Redclift (eds) *The International Farm Crisis*. New York: St. Martin's Press.

Ufkes, F. (1993) 'Trade liberalization, agro-food politics, and rural restructuring', *Political Geography*.

UNCTAD (1990) *Agricultural Trade Liberalisation in the Uruguay Round: Implications for Developing Countries*. New York: United Nations.

US Congress (1989) *Agricultural Progress in the Third World and its Effect on U.S. Farm Exports*. Washington, DC: Congressional Budget Office.

Vollrath, T. and Scott, L. (1991) 'Developing countries as a source of U.S. export growth', 16–26, in *Developing Economies Agriculture and Trade Report*. Washington, DC: USDA–ERS.

Watkins, K. (1991) 'Agricultural and food security in the GATT Uruguay Round', *Review of African Political Economy*, 50, 38–50.

Watts, M. (1990) 'Peasants under contract: agro-food complexes in the Third World', 149–62, in H. Bernstein, B. Crow, M. Mackintosh and C. Martin (eds) *The Food Question: Profits versus People*? New York: Monthly Review Press.

Wessel, R. (1983) *Trading the Future. Farm Exports and the Concentration of Economic Power in our Food System*. San Francisco: Institute for Food and Development Policy.

Winters, L. A. (1990) 'The road to Uruguay', *Economic Journal*, 100(403) 1288–303.

Wysham, D. (1990) 'Big business hijacks GATT', *The Nation*, December, 17, 770–3.

For Product Safety Concerns and Information please contact our EU representative GPSR@taylorandfrancis.com
Taylor & Francis Verlag GmbH, Kaufingerstraße 24, 80331 München, Germany

www.ingramcontent.com/pod-product-compliance
Lightning Source LLC
LaVergne TN
LVHW020638300926
849161LV00004B/744

* 9 7 8 1 0 3 2 4 9 7 0 6 8 *